Polic
draw
argu
polic
of la
the i
to th
sum
insig
topic
time
and i
persp

ANN
Read
and p

The Law in Context Series

Editors: William Twining (University College London),
Christopher McCrudden (Lincoln College, Oxford) and
Bronwen Morgan (University of Bristol).

Since 1970 the Law in Context series has been in the forefront of the movement to broaden the study of law. It has been a vehicle for the publication of innovative scholarly books that treat law and legal phenomena critically in their social, political and economic contexts from a variety of perspectives. The series particularly aims to publish scholarly legal writing that brings fresh perspectives to bear on new and existing areas of law taught in universities. A contextual approach involves treating legal subjects broadly, using materials from other social sciences, and from any other discipline that helps to explain the operation in practice of the subject under discussion. It is hoped that this orientation is at once more stimulating and more realistic than the bare exposition of legal rules. The series includes original books that have a different emphasis from traditional legal textbooks, while maintaining the same high standards of scholarship. They are written primarily for undergraduate and graduate students of law and of other disciplines, but most also appeal to a wider readership. In the past, most books in the series have focused on English law, but recent publications include books on European law, globalisation, transnational legal processes and comparative law.

Books in the Series

Anderson, Schum & Twining: *Analysis of Evidence*
Ashworth: *Sentencing and Criminal Justice*
Barton & Douglas: *Law and Parenthood*
Beecher-Monas: *Evaluating Scientific Evidence: An Interdisciplinary Framework for Intellectual Due Process*
Bell: *French Legal Cultures*
Bercusson: *European Labour Law*
Birkinshaw: *European Public Law*
Birkinshaw: *Freedom of Information: The Law, the Practice and the Ideal*
Cane: *Atiyah's Accidents, Compensation and the Law*
Clarke & Kohler: *Property Law: Commentary and Materials*
Collins: *The Law of Contract*
Cranston: *Legal Foundations of the Welfare State*
Davies: *Perspectives on Labour Law*
Dembour: *Who Believes in Human Rights? The European Convention in Question*
de Sousa Santos: *Toward a New Legal Common Sense*
Diduck: *Law's Families*
Elworthy & Holder: *Environmental Protection: Text and Materials*
Fortin: *Children's Rights and the Developing Law*
Glover-Thomas: *Reconstructing Mental Health Law and Policy*
Gobert & Punch: *Rethinking Corporate Crime*
Goldman: *Globalisation and the Western Legal Tradition: Recurring Patterns of Law and Authority*
Harlow & Rawlings: *Law and Administration*
Harris: *An Introduction to Law*
Harris, Campbell & Halson: *Remedies in Contract and Tort*

Harvey: *Seeking Asylum in the UK: Problems and Prospects*
Hervey & McHale: *Health Law and the European Union*
Holder and Lee: *Environmental Protection, Law and Policy*
Kostakopoulou: *The Future Governance of Citizenship*
Lacey, Wells & Quick: *Reconstructing Criminal Law*
Lewis: *Choice and the Legal Order: Rising above Politics*
Likosky: *Law, Infrastructure and Human Rights*
Likosky: *Transnational Legal Processes*
Maughan & Webb: *Lawyering Skills and the Legal Process*
McGlynn: *Families and the European Union: Law, Politics and Pluralism*
Moffat: *Trusts Law: Text and Materials*
Monti: *EC Competition Law*
Morgan & Yeung: *An Introduction to Law and Regulation: Text and Materials*
Norrie: *Crime, Reason and History*
O'Dair: *Legal Ethics*
Oliver: *Common Values and the Public–Private Divide*
Oliver & Drewry: *The Law and Parliament*
Picciotto: *International Business Taxation*
Reed: *Internet Law: Text and Materials*
Richardson: *Law, Process and Custody*
Roberts & Palmer: *Dispute Processes: ADR and the Primary Forms of Decision-Making*
Scott & Black: *Cranston's Consumers and the Law*
Seneviratne: *Ombudsmen: Public Services and Administrative Justice*
Stapleton: *Product Liability*
Tamanaha: *The Struggle for Law as a Means to an End*
Turpin & Tomkins: *British Government and the Constitution: Text and Materials*
Twining: *General Jurisprudence: Understanding Law from a Global Perspective*
Twining: *Globalisation and Legal Theory*
Twining: *Rethinking Evidence*
Twining & Miers: *How to Do Things with Rules*
Ward: *A Critical Introduction to European Law*
Ward: *Law, Text, Terror*
Ward: *Shakespeare and Legal Imagination*
Zander: *Cases and Materials on the English Legal System*
Zander: *The Law-Making Process*

Perspectives on
Labour Law

A. C. L. Davies

Fellow and Tutor in Law, Brasenose College
Reader in Public Law, University of Oxford

CAMBRIDGE
UNIVERSITY PRESS

CAMBRIDGE UNIVERSITY PRESS
Cambridge, New York, Melbourne, Madrid, Cape Town, Singapore, São Paulo, Delhi

Cambridge University Press
The Edinburgh Building, Cambridge CB2 8RU, UK

Published in the United States of America by Cambridge University Press, New York

www.cambridge.org
Information on this title: www.cambridge.org/9780521722346

First published 2004
Second edition 2009

Printed in the United Kingdom at the University Press, Cambridge

A catalogue record for this publication is available from the British Library

Library of Congress Cataloguing in Publication data
Davies, A. C. L. (Anne C. L.)
  Perspectives on labour law / A.C.L. Davies. – 2nd ed.
    p.   cm.
  Includes index.
  ISBN 978-0-521-89757-0 (hardback)   1. Labor laws and legislation–Great Britain.
  2. Employee rights–Great Britain.   I. Title.
  KD3009.D375   2009
  344.4101–dc22   2009008467

ISBN 978-0-521-89757-0 hardback
ISBN 978-0-521-72234-6 paperback

For my parents

Contents

Preface

For many students, the first few weeks of a course in labour law can seem rather daunting. Many of the subject's main principles are derived from statute, rather than case law, so there is less room for the kind of detailed case analysis familiar from core subjects like contract and tort. Policy discussions also play a much greater role in labour law than they do in, say, land law or trusts. When writing about anti-discrimination law, for example, labour lawyers think about whether positive discrimination should be permitted, or whether employers should be allowed to say that 'market forces' led them to pay men more than they pay women doing equal work.

The subject's emphasis on legislation and on policy arguments is confusing enough. But life gets even more difficult when we look at the way in which labour lawyers construct their policy arguments. In what Hugh Collins has termed the 'productive disintegration' of labour law, writers now draw on a wide range of other disciplines and approaches in order to make sense of the law.[1] As Chapter 1 will show, labour lawyers have traditionally used industrial relations, a branch of sociology, as a frame of reference. But this discipline has been joined by various kinds of economic analysis, arguments from social justice and the discourse of fundamental human rights.

This array of perspectives on labour law is what gives the subject its fascination. But for newcomers it can seem bewildering. Each perspective has its own methodology and its own set of internal problems. To understand a piece of labour law writing which draws on economic arguments, it is necessary to understand how economists think: the methods they use and the assumptions they make. To understand a piece of labour law writing which draws on human rights arguments, it is helpful to understand some of the more theoretical debates about what it means to say that someone has a 'right'. And all this must be done while students are trying to absorb the basic rules and principles of a large and highly complex body of law.

This book is here to help. Its aim is to introduce two of the main perspectives used in the analysis of labour law today – human rights and economics – and to

---

1 H. Collins, 'The productive disintegration of labour law' (1997) 26 *ILJ* 295.

show how they play out in some of the key areas of the law. It will not be argued that either perspective is 'correct' or preferable to the other. Each perspective offers different insights. If we work from a single perspective, there is a danger that we will blind ourselves to initiatives that do not fit with our view of the world. Collins argues that this is what happened to many labour lawyers in the 1960s and 1970s who continued to analyse the law using an outdated sociological model.[2] Equally, however, it is important to remember that the perspectives themselves are far from being one-dimensional. There are different schools of thought in economics and in the literature on human rights. There is no single 'economists' view' on the national minimum wage, for example. So we need to develop a nuanced understanding of the perspectives themselves.

Part I of this book introduces the two perspectives. Chapter 1 offers a brief history of labour law from 1945 to the present, showing how labour lawyers' arguments have changed over time. At first, the subject was dominated by sociological analysis. But as government policies changed, particularly from the 1970s onwards, rights and economics became increasingly relevant to labour lawyers' thinking. Indeed, since 1997, the government has explicitly sought to strike a balance between workers' rights and business efficiency. Chapter 2 introduces the economics perspective. It explains economists' methodology and identifies two competing schools of thought: neoclassical economics, which tends to be hostile to labour law, and new institutional economics, which suggests that legal regulation can be beneficial. Chapter 3 introduces the rights perspective. It explains the historical development of international human rights law and discusses some of the complex issues that arise when we try to interpret rights and to apply them to particular situations. Chapter 4 looks at the way in which labour law is created and applied: at the layers of international, regional and domestic regulation that make up the subject. This is essential because labour law cannot be understood as a purely 'domestic' subject. The rights and economics arguments play out in different ways at the different levels, often leading to conflicts between them. Part II of the book applies the insights of rights theorists and economists to a selection of topics in labour law. The aim is to provide an accessible introduction to each topic, and to demonstrate the interplay between the rights and economics perspectives.

This book is intended to be read at least twice. The first time you read it, use it as an introduction to the basic principles of labour law and to the policy arguments surrounding the subject. Once you have studied labour law in detail and looked at the cases and statutes for yourself, I hope you will return to this book, perhaps as part of your revision. The second time you read it, try to use it to develop your own perspective on labour law, and to think about how you might defend that perspective against the arguments of others. Each chapter concludes with suggestions for further reading, and questions to consider while you do the

---

2 Ibid.

reading. Part of the point of the further reading is to give you more detail about the law, and a more in-depth account of the perspectives, than can be provided in a relatively short introductory book. But do not be surprised if some of the reading challenges the arguments described in the relevant chapter. One writer might argue that one of the perspectives used does not offer any valid insights into the law. Another writer might argue that two of the perspectives need to be combined in order to understand the law properly. Yet another writer might argue that the law is best explained and developed using an entirely different approach, not considered in this book at all. This might seem a bit unsettling at first. But if you persevere, you will find that the further reading gives you a much richer understanding of labour law.

This edition incorporates developments up to the end of September 2008, though I am grateful to the publisher for allowing me to incorporate references to the Employment Act 2008 during the production process.

Anne Davies
Oxford
October 2008

Acknowledgements

Like its predecessor, this book owes a great deal to my experience of teaching labour law at the University of Oxford. I would like to thank my fellow labour lawyers in Oxford, both past and present, for their support and intellectual companionship, and successive generations of Oxford students, who have been the unwitting guinea pigs for both editions, for their sharpness and enthusiasm. Amir Fuchs provided excellent research assistance during the preparation of the first edition. I am grateful to Brasenose College for financial support, and to my colleagues (current and former – you know who you are), particularly Bill Swadling, for moral support.

The series editors for Law in Context, Chris McCrudden and William Twining, provided wise advice during the development of the initial proposal and helpful comments on drafts of both editions. The second edition would not have been possible without their encouragement and enthusiasm. I am indebted to the editorial staff of Cambridge University Press for their professionalism and efficiency in seeing the book through to publication.

And finally, my biggest debt of gratitude is, as always, to my parents, to whom this book is dedicated, for their unstinting love and support, and for keeping my prose under control.

Table of statutes

Table of statutory instruments

Table of EU legislation

Table of international instruments

Table of cases

Abbreviations

Statutes and statutory instruments

DDA 1995	Disability Discrimination Act 1995
EA 2002	Employment Act 2002
EE(A)R 2006	Employment Equality (Age) Regulations 2006
EE(RB)R 2003	Employment Equality (Religion or Belief) Regulations 2003
EE(SO)R 2003	Employment Equality (Sexual Orientation) Regulations 2003
EqPA 1970	Equal Pay Act 1970
ERA 1996	Employment Rights Act 1996
ERA 1999	Employment Relations Act 1999
FWER 2002	Flexible Working (Eligibility, Complaints and Remedies) Regulations 2002
HRA 1998	Human Rights Act 1998
ICER 2004	Information and Consultation of Employees Regulations 2004
MPLR 1999	Maternity and Parental Leave etc. Regulations 1999
NMWA 1998	National Minimum Wage Act 1998
NMWR 1999	National Minimum Wage Regulations 1999
PALR 2002	Paternity and Adoption Leave Regulations 2002
PTWR 2000	Part-Time Workers (Prevention of Less Favourable Treatment) Regulations 2000
RRA 1976	Race Relations Act 1976
SDA 1975	Sex Discrimination Act 1975
SSCBA 1992	Social Security Contributions and Benefits Act 1992
TULRCA 1992	Trade Union and Labour Relations (Consolidation) Act 1992
WTR 1998	Working Time Regulations 1998

Law reports and periodicals

BJIR	British Journal of Industrial Relations
ECR	European Court Reports
EHRLR	European Human Rights Law Review
EHRR	European Human Rights Reports
ICR	Industrial Cases Reports
ILJ	Industrial Law Journal
ILR	International Labour Review
IRLR	Industrial Relations Law Reports
JIEL	Journal of International Economic Law
LQR	Law Quarterly Review
MLR	Modern Law Review
OJLS	Oxford Journal of Legal Studies
PL	Public Law
UNTS	United Nations Treaty Series

Others

ACAS	Advisory, Conciliation and Arbitration Service
BERR	Department for Business, Enterprise and Regulatory Reform
CAC	Central Arbitration Committee
CEDAW	Convention on the Elimination of All Forms of Discrimination Against Women
CRC	Convention on the Rights of the Child
DTI	Department of Trade and Industry
EAT	Employment Appeal Tribunal
ECHR	European Convention on Human Rights (European Convention for the Protection of Human Rights and Fundamental Freedoms)
ECtHR	European Court of Human Rights
ECJ	European Court of Justice
ECSR	European Committee on Social Rights
EES	European Employment Strategy
EHRC	Equality and Human Rights Commission
EOC	Equal Opportunities Commission
ESC	European Social Charter
ETUC	European Trade Union Confederation
EWC	European Works Council
GATT	General Agreement on Tariffs and Trade
ICCPR	International Covenant on Civil and Political Rights
ICERD	International Convention on the Elimination of All Forms of Racial Discrimination

ICESCR	International Covenant on Economic, Social and Cultural Rights
ILO	International Labour Organization
SMP	Statutory Maternity Pay
SPP	Statutory Paternity Pay
TUC	Trades Union Congress
UDHR	United Nations Universal Declaration of Human Rights
WERS	Workplace Employee Relations Survey
WTO	World Trade Organization

Part I

1

A brief history of labour law

Labour lawyers today commonly think about their subject using ideas about workers' rights, economic efficiency for firms or for the market as a whole, or social justice for workers. These ideas are not new. But they did not play a major role in the early history of labour law. In the 1950s, labour lawyers used sociology to make sense of their subject. This chapter will explain how rights and economics – the two key perspectives to be used in this book – started to feature more commonly in labour lawyers' thinking in the 1970s, and attained the central place they have today.[1] It will also demonstrate the importance of using more than one perspective to understand the law.

Collective laissez-faire – the 1950s

The work of Otto Kahn-Freund has exercised, and continues to exercise, a considerable degree of influence over labour lawyers' thinking. Writing in the 1950s, he drew on industrial relations theory – a branch of sociology – in order to understand the law.[2] This was essential because anyone using a 'black-letter' approach – in other words, looking solely at the legal materials – would have acquired a wholly misleading knowledge of the relationship between employers and employees. For example, there were few legal controls on the circumstances in which employees could be dismissed. At common law, the contract of employment could be terminated if the employer gave notice. The courts did not inquire into whether or not the employer had a good reason for the dismissal. And there was no statutory intervention in this area until 1971. But this did not necessarily mean that, in practice, employers had an unfettered power to dismiss their employees. Where trade unions were present in a workplace, they were often able to use their collective strength to protect individual employees against arbitrary dismissal.

Drawing on sociology, Kahn-Freund developed a sophisticated theory of labour law called 'collective laissez-faire'. Kahn-Freund's insight was that in

---

1 See, generally, H. Collins, 'The productive disintegration of labour law' (1997) 26 *ILJ* 295; P. Davies and M. Freedland, *Labour Legislation and Public Policy* (1993).
2 See O. Kahn-Freund, 'Legal framework', in A. Flanders and H.A. Clegg (eds.), *The System of Industrial Relations in Great Britain: Its History, Law and Institutions* (1954).

Britain, the law played a very minor role in industrial relations, particularly in comparison with other industrialised Western nations. There were relatively few statutes obliging employers to treat individual workers in particular ways or even to promote collective bargaining between trade unions and employers. Instead, employers and trade unions were left to regulate their own affairs. It was this policy of 'non-interference' that Kahn-Freund labelled collective laissez-faire.

But collective laissez-faire did not mean that the law played no role at all. In the nineteenth and early twentieth centuries, the common law courts were hostile to the trade unions. The courts cast doubt on the legality of trade unions by declaring that their aims fell foul of the doctrine of restraint of trade.[3] And they set about developing various economic torts – conspiracy, inducing breach of contract, interfering with trade or business – which exposed strike organisers to civil liability. In the infamous *Taff Vale* case of 1901, the House of Lords held that unions could be sued in tort in their own name and held liable for the actions of their officials.[4] Collective bargaining could not easily take place under these conditions. Successive governments therefore intervened with statutes which removed the common law obstacles to collective bargaining. The Trade Union Act 1871 declared that the doctrine of restraint of trade did not apply to unions. The Trade Disputes Act 1906 protected unions from tort liability and provided that strike organisers could not be held liable for the torts of conspiracy, interference with business or inducing breach of contract. Kahn-Freund used the term 'negative law' to describe this facilitative legislation.[5]

But collective laissez-faire was more than just a description of the law. Kahn-Freund also saw it as an ideal for the law to strive towards, for three main reasons. First, he argued that legal intervention was unnecessary because collective bargaining was an effective way of protecting workers. The presence of unions successfully redressed the power imbalance between workers and employers. Second, he claimed that workers' rights were more secure if they were acquired through collective bargaining rather than through constitutional or legislative guarantees. He believed that if the government had not granted the rights in the first place, it could not take them away. Third, he thought that collective laissez-faire was more flexible than legislation because it allowed unions and employers to decide things for themselves and to respond to changing circumstances.

The demise of collective laissez-faire – the 1960s and 1970s

In the 1960s and 1970s, governments became increasingly interested in promoting workers' rights and managing the economy more actively. They also wanted to reduce the level of strike action – partly for economic reasons and partly because

---

3 *Hornby* v. *Close* [1867] LR 2 QB 153.
4 *Taff Vale Railway* v. *Amalgamated Society of Railway Servants* [1901] AC 426.
5 Kahn-Freund, 'Legal framework', p. 44.

strikes came to be seen as a problem in their own right. Collins has argued that the theory of collective laissez-faire exercised something of a stranglehold over labour law thinking through this period, though perhaps it is easier to recognise the significance of the changes with the benefit of hindsight.[6]

Promoting workers' rights

In the 1960s and 1970s, people began to question the fairness of a system which relied almost entirely on collective bargaining to protect workers. In the eyes of its critics, collective bargaining suffered from two major flaws. First, it did not cover all industries or workplaces. In 1967, it was estimated that 50 per cent of manual workers and 30 per cent of white-collar workers were union members.[7] Although these figures are much higher than their modern equivalents, they still suggest that many workers were not protected by collective bargaining. Second, collective bargaining did not necessarily promote the interests of all sectors of the workforce. In 1951, only 27 per cent of women workers were union members, compared to 56 per cent of men.[8] Unions naturally focused on protecting the majority of their members. This led them to ignore or even to attack women's claims for better treatment at work, particularly in the area of equal pay.

One major statutory response to the first of these concerns was the unfair dismissal legislation, introduced in 1971.[9] The legislation (discussed in detail in Chapter 9) sought to regulate the circumstances in which an employer could dismiss an employee. The employer had to have a reason for the dismissal and had to act reasonably in making the decision to dismiss. This was a radical departure from the common law, which did not inquire into the employer's reasons at all. Advocates of the legislation pointed to the unfairness of the common law position. Although unions did much to prevent arbitrary behaviour by employers, not all employees were protected by collective representation.

The concern that unions might not protect all sections of the workforce was addressed in the anti-discrimination legislation. The Equal Pay Act 1970 (which came into force in 1975) established the basic principle that women who were doing the same work as men should receive the same pay and other benefits under their contracts of employment. An important further step came with the enactment of the Sex Discrimination Act 1975 (SDA), which tackled the many other respects in which employers might discriminate: in recruitment, training, promotion and so on. It also attacked discrimination by unions against members and applicants for membership. Parliament's first attempt to tackle race discrimination, the Race Relations Act 1968, made little impact. Responsibility for enforcing the Act was given to a statutory body, the Race Relations Board, but its

6 Collins, 'The productive disintegration of labour law'. Cf. Lord Wedderburn, 'Collective bargaining or legal enactment: the 1999 Act and trade union recognition' (2000) 29 *ILJ* 1.
7 Davies and Freedland, *Labour Legislation*, p. 46.   8 Ibid.
9 Industrial Relations Act 1971, ss. 22–32.

powers were limited. The Act's weaknesses were addressed by the Race Relations Act 1976, which contained very similar provisions to those set out in the Sex Discrimination Act 1975. Individuals were given a right to bring proceedings under the 1976 Act, and the new statutory body, the Commission for Racial Equality, had much stronger enforcement powers than the old Board.

The anti-discrimination legislation was obviously a significant move away from collective laissez-faire: the idea that unions and employers should be left to determine employees' terms and conditions for themselves. It was argued that some rights were so fundamental that they should be protected for all employees, regardless of employers' or unions' attitudes. Indeed, the legislation challenged some established industrial relations practices – for example, it was common prior to the SDA for unions to agree that part-time workers should be dismissed before full-time workers when a firm had to make some workers redundant. In *Clarke* v. *Eley (IMI) Kynoch*,[10] this was held to be discriminatory because the majority of part-time workers are female.

The advocates of collective laissez-faire sought to modify their theory in order to incorporate the unfair dismissal and anti-discrimination legislation. They argued that the legislation created a 'floor of rights' on which collective bargaining could build. As Wedderburn explains:

> The statutory 'floor of rights' now extends into many facets of employment law … but it does not normally prevent the erection of superior conditions by way of collective bargaining. It was meant to be a floor not a ceiling.[11]

In some ways, this is a useful method of analysis. To use the example given by Wedderburn himself, unions have often been able to negotiate more generous redundancy payments for employees than those provided for in legislation. But Collins has strongly criticised the 'floor of rights' argument, claiming that labour lawyers' determination to cling on to the collective laissez-faire analysis blinded them to the true significance of the new developments.[12] There are certainly some problems with the 'floor of rights' idea. First, for those workers not protected by collective bargaining, the floor is indeed a ceiling. Second, as Davies and Freedland argue, it has not always been the case that the aims of legislation have coincided with those of collective bargaining.[13] As explained above, unions were slow to take up the anti-discrimination agenda, and some of the practices they agreed with employers had a discriminatory effect. The government's intervention could be seen as a way of regulating the unions, not just supporting their activities. We could therefore view the legislation of the late 1960s and the 1970s as the beginning of a shift away from collective laissez-faire. Either way, this period marks the emergence of workers' rights as a central concern of modern labour law.

---

10 *Clarke* v. *Eley (IMI) Kynoch* [1983] ICR 165.
11 Lord Wedderburn, *The Worker and the Law* (3rd edn., 1986), p. 6.
12 Collins, 'The productive disintegration of labour law'.
13 Davies and Freedland, *Labour Legislation*, pp. 383–4.

Managing the economy

During the 1960s and 1970s, collective laissez-faire came under attack from another direction. Successive governments began to take a more active role in managing the economy. Their main goal was to ensure that the UK had a favourable balance of trade – in other words, that the value of the products exported by the UK exceeded the value of the products imported by the UK. This was thought to be a sign of a prosperous economy. But the level of inflation was very high during this period. This meant that UK products were expensive and could not compete effectively in world markets. Since inflation was, in part, attributable to the high wage demands being made by unions, the government was bound to come under pressure to intervene more fully in industrial relations, and thus to abandon the policy of collective laissez-faire.

Economists have various ways of explaining inflation. The 'cost-push' theory links inflation most closely to the activities of workers and unions.[14] Workers always want to get paid more, and employers always want to make more profit. From time to time, workers will succeed in persuading their employer to pay them more. This will reduce the employer's profits. So the employer passes on the cost to the consumer by raising the price of its products. This restores the employer's profits to their earlier levels. But then the whole process begins again: products are more expensive, so workers start to demand further pay rises. The result is a 'price-wage spiral'. External factors can also contribute to inflation. In 1973, for example, the oil-producing countries raised the price of oil by a considerable margin. This had a knock-on effect on the price of other products and raised the cost of living generally, thus leading to further wage demands by workers.

Governments responded to spiralling inflation by trying to place limits on the wage increases unions could achieve through collective bargaining, through what were known as 'incomes policies'. One of the most extreme versions of incomes policy was that contained in Part IV of the Prices and Incomes Act 1966, which applied from August 1966 to August 1967. This allowed the government to ban an employer from paying a higher wage than that paid on 20 July 1966. It was enforced by criminal sanctions against employers, and against unions which put pressure on employers to pay more. The government used its powers to enforce a six-month pay freeze, followed by six months of 'severe restraint' in which only very limited pay increases were permitted. Compulsory incomes policies were, however, highly controversial and were used by governments as a last resort. At other times, voluntary incomes policies were pursued. In 1976–7, for example, the unions agreed to a 5 per cent limit on pay rises in order to combat spiralling inflation, which had reached 27 per cent in 1976. But voluntary incomes policies were never very stable. They were unpopular with grass-roots trade union

---

14 Two key assumptions underlie this theory: that governments increase the supply of money in response to demand, and that the prices of goods are essentially determined by what they cost.

members, who saw their standard of living decline during periods of restraint. And democratically elected trade union leaders had to respond to their members' concerns. By 1978–9, for example, the TUC was refusing to agree to another request from the government for a 5 per cent limit on pay rises.

It is fair to say that despite the incomes policies, no government in this period succeeded in getting inflation under control. But the incomes policies are highly significant for what they tell us about labour law. They show that governments' desire to manage the economy was so great that they did not have any qualms about intervening in the process of collective bargaining. At first, labour lawyers might have dismissed this as a temporary suspension of collective laissez-faire. But if the economic problems could not be resolved, it was hard to see when this 'suspension' might end.

Reducing the number of strikes

The other major problem faced by governments in the 1960s and 1970s was the high level of strike action. In 1964–6, for example, 190 working days per 1,000 employees were lost because of strikes.[15] Unions were in a relatively powerful position because unemployment was low. Employers could not afford to ignore the demands of workers who could easily move to jobs elsewhere. Strikes were a cause of concern for two reasons. First, it was thought that they were contributing to the UK's economic problems. If UK firms were hit by high levels of strike action, they might not be able to deliver their products to purchasers on time. This would give them a reputation for unreliability which would harm their chances of exporting goods abroad. The balance of trade might start to tip in the wrong direction. Second, there was a growing feeling that the level of strike action was a sign that the unions were out of control. Davies and Freedland suggest that the high levels of strike action at this time produced 'a crisis of truly constitutional proportions'.[16] Those on the right of the political spectrum in particular began to argue that the trade unions were running the country, not the government.

In 1965, the Labour government set up a Royal Commission, usually known as the Donovan Commission, to investigate the strike problem.[17] Much of the evidence given to the Donovan Commission advocated a stronger role for the law in regulating industrial relations. Nevertheless, the Commission broadly adopted the collective laissez-faire view set out by Kahn-Freund in the 1950s: that the law should intervene as little as possible. The Commission's main recommendation was that employers and unions should change the way in which they conducted collective bargaining.[18] At that time, bargaining tended to take place

---

15 See the *Report of the Royal Commission on Trade Unions and Employers' Associations* (1968) (Cmnd 3623), p. 95.
16 Davies and Freedland, *Labour Legislation*, p. 242.
17 *Report of the Royal Commission on Trade Unions and Employers' Associations.*
18 Ibid., Chapter 16.

between unions and employers' associations covering all the firms in a particular industry. But it was supplemented by informal bargaining between shop stewards (trade union representatives for small workgroups) and managers in particular workplaces. Shop stewards often called unofficial 'wildcat' strikes to protest at managers' decisions. Unions had very little control over their behaviour. The Donovan Commission attributed the strike problem to the split between the two types of bargaining. The Commission argued that bargaining should instead take place at plant or company level. This kind of bargaining would be conducted by union leaders, taking into account the needs of all the various workgroups. It was hoped that this would put an end to supplementary bargaining by shop stewards, and hence to wildcat strikes. The change was not to be brought about by law. Instead, the Commission expected employers and unions to alter their practices voluntarily. In fact, some employers and unions had already begun to bargain on this basis and the change spread rapidly.

By the time the Donovan Commission reported, in 1968, the strike problem had worsened. The Labour government accepted many of the Commission's proposals, but wanted to make greater use of the law to prevent strikes.[19] For example, it wanted to require unions to ballot their members before taking strike action. The government never managed to enact its plans – in part because of opposition from the unions. It then lost the general election in 1970 and the Conservatives came to power. They believed that the only way to reassert government control over industrial relations – and thus to achieve economic progress – was to provide a comprehensive legal framework to regulate trade unions and, most importantly, strike action. The Industrial Relations Act 1971 reflected two main policies. First, it sought to reduce or eliminate unofficial action organised by shop stewards by leaving such action exposed to the full force of the common law of tort.[20] Second, trade unions were given a strong incentive to behave 'responsibly' (as the government saw it) in their use of the strike weapon. The statute listed various 'unfair industrial practices' for which unions could be liable. This was used to ban, for example, strike action against firms not directly involved in a dispute with the union.[21] However, the government's grand scheme met with considerable resistance from the trade unions. The unions' most successful strategy was to refuse to register under the Act. Because the Act's protections were confined to registered unions, all strike action by unregistered unions was exposed to liability at common law. It might be supposed that this would have put the unions in an impossible position. But the government quickly realised that a situation in which all strike action was unprotected was unsustainable. The Act's failure was a major factor in the government's electoral defeat in 1974.

19 See the White Paper *In Place of Strife: A Policy for Industrial Relations* (1969) (Cmnd 3888).
20 This was the intended effect of s. 96.   21 Industrial Relations Act 1971, s. 98.

The Labour government elected in 1974 tried a new tactic. It did a deal with the unions, sometimes known as the 'Social Contract'. It promised to enact more favourable labour legislation if the unions would limit their wage demands and, in consequence, the incidence of strikes. The new legislation had two key features. First, it marked a return to the pre-1971 approach to regulating trade unions and strike action. It left the common law to define the wrongs committed by unions and strike organisers, but provided a set of immunities to protect them from liability.[22] Second, the legislation put in place various strategies for *supporting* collective bargaining. People sometimes describe the legislation as a return to collective laissez-faire, but this is not entirely accurate because it went far beyond Kahn-Freund's 'negative law'. For example, the Employment Protection Act 1975 included a 'recognition procedure' which could, under certain circumstances, lead to an employer being obliged to bargain with a particular union.[23] Although the unions welcomed these changes, they did not keep their side of the bargain. There was a wave of strike action in late 1978 and early 1979 which is sometimes referred to as the 'winter of discontent'. Yet again, a failure to control the strike problem contributed to the downfall of the government.

The history of industrial conflict law in the 1960s and 1970s tells us a lot about the changing shape of labour law. It shows the demise of collective laissez-faire: governments of both political persuasions were prepared to use the law much more extensively. And it reinforces the importance of the economic perspective. Although strikes were seen as a problem per se, governments were also motivated to intervene by the fact that they disrupted the national economy. But the two strategies tried during this period – comprehensive legislation and the Social Contract – were largely unsuccessful.

Individualism and deregulation – the 1980s and early 1990s

The years 1979–97 saw successive Conservative governments adopting a novel approach to labour law. The three themes we have identified so far – promoting workers' rights, tackling the strike problem and promoting economic growth – were ongoing concerns. But they were defined in new ways, and new strategies were adopted for addressing them. We will examine each of these themes in turn, and conclude by looking at the links between them.

Protecting workers' rights: individualism

One of the key ideological commitments of the Conservative Prime Minister, Margaret Thatcher, was individualism: the idea that individual rights and

---

22 Trade Union and Labour Relations Act 1974, ss. 13–17, as amended, Trade Union and Labour Relations (Amendment) Act 1976.
23 Employment Protection Act 1975, ss. 11–16.

interests should always prevail over collective concerns. This gave rise to an inevitable clash with labour law's traditional emphasis on collective solidarity in trade unions as the best mechanism for protecting the individual. The government identified two main categories of individual who, it argued, might be harmed by powerful unions: those who did not wish to join a union at all, and those union members who did not agree with their leaders' policies.

Those who did not wish to join a union at all were most likely to be harmed by the 'closed shop'. This term is used to describe a workplace in which all employees are required to be members of a particular trade union. The government gradually dismantled the legal protections of the closed shop until it was made wholly unlawful in 1988. Section 11 of the Employment Act 1988 gave individuals a right, as against the employer, not to be dismissed or subjected to detrimental treatment on the grounds that they were not trade union members. This had the effect of abolishing the closed shop because employers were no longer able to dismiss employees who refused to join the union. The closed shop is, of course, highly controversial.[24] Many trade unionists argue that although each individual worker loses his or her freedom of choice about union membership, a strong union is the best way to protect individual interests. A union with 100 per cent support in the workplace is bound to be in a good bargaining position. From a rights perspective, however, the closed shop is much harder to justify. Most theorists would see freedom of association as protecting people's choices: individuals should be able to choose which organisations to join and organisations should be allowed to choose whom to admit. The idea of an enforced association is hard to square with a right framed in these terms.

The second category of workers who, in the government's view, might be adversely affected by trade union power were those union members who disagreed with their leaders' policies. The Employment Act 1988, s. 3, gave individuals the right not to be 'unjustifiably disciplined' by their union. This prevented unions from taking any disciplinary action against members who refused to take part in a strike. The government argued that this protected the individual's freedom of choice. But trade unionists saw this right as yet another misguided attack on collective strength. It was claimed that individuals would ultimately lose out because unions would be weakened if they could not force all their members to take strike action.

The government's preferred interpretation of workers' rights was therefore very different from that advanced during the 1960s and 1970s. It sought to use workers' rights to protect individuals from the collective strength of trade unions, rather than to protect them from the power of their employers.

---

24 See Chapter 11.

Tackling strikes

Those theorists who take a more sceptical view of the government's promotion of individual rights would argue that its policies were part of a broader aim of reducing the power of the trade unions. The government adopted two main strategies to tackle the strike problem. One was to dismantle the laws of the 1970s which offered positive support for collective bargaining – for example, in 1980, the recognition procedure in the Employment Protection Act 1975 was abolished.[25] This left a union without any legal remedies where it had a high level of support in a particular workplace but the employer nevertheless refused to recognise it for collective bargaining. The second, and most important, strategy was to narrow the circumstances in which strike action would be protected from liability in tort.

Several examples could be given of this second strategy, but for reasons of space we will consider just one. The Trade Disputes Act 1906, s. 4, had granted trade unions complete immunity from liability in tort.[26] This was designed to ensure that employers could only sue strike organisers (although they too had some immunity) and would have no chance of getting at union funds in legal actions. The Employment Act 1982 took away the unions' blanket immunity and subjected them to the immunity rules governing strike organisers instead.[27] The statute did set a limit on the amount of damages that could be awarded against a union, but it was more common for employers to seek an injunction to stop the action. If the union breached the injunction it was exposed to unlimited fines for contempt of court. In 1990, s. 6 of the Employment Act broadened the range of officials for whose actions the union could be held liable. These provisions were intended by the government as an attack on the 'privileged position' of trade unions. The government portrayed the immunities as putting the unions 'above the law', and argued that an increase in liability would encourage unions to behave more responsibly.

In a Green Paper published in 1991, the government claimed that its attempt to reduce the power of the unions had succeeded.[28] The level of strike action was significantly lower and, it was suggested, the UK had become an attractive location for foreign firms. These arguments are, however, fiercely disputed. The level of unemployment rose substantially during the 1980s. This tends to reduce the incidence of strikes because workers are grateful to have a job at all. Moreover, union membership declined, in part because there were fewer jobs in manufacturing industries, the unions' traditional stronghold. These economic factors must also have played a part in reducing strike levels: indeed, some would say that they are the main explanation for the change.

---

25 Employment Act 1980, s. 19.
26 This had been repealed by the Industrial Relations Act 1971, but was re-enacted in s. 14 of the Trade Union and Labour Relations Act 1974.
27 Employment Act 1982, ss. 15–16.
28 Department of Employment, *Industrial Relations in the 1990s: Proposals for Further Reform of Industrial Relations and Trade Union Law* (1991) (Cm 1602).

Reducing burdens on business

In the late 1980s, the rhetoric of tackling the strike problem began to give way to a much broader set of ideas, sometimes labelled 'deregulation'. The government began to portray laws which regulated the conduct of firms – on matters such as health and safety, environmental protection or employment – as 'burdens on business'.[29] The government argued that, as far as possible, these burdens ought to be removed, because they imposed costs on businesses and made them less competitive. Moreover, in the late 1980s, the government became increasingly focused on the need to create jobs to combat the problem of high unemployment.[30] It was argued that employers would be more willing to take on additional workers if they could do so cheaply: in other words, without having to provide them with costly legal rights. This provided another reason for reducing the level of regulation.

There are many examples of the deregulatory trend. One strategy was to repeal existing protective statutes. In 1993, the government abolished the Wages Councils.[31] These were bodies which set a minimum wage for workers in a particular trade. Although the Wages Councils had never set particularly high rates of pay, they did provide some protection for workers in the lowest-paying industries. But the government argued that they stifled competition between firms and priced workers out of jobs.

Another strategy was to restrict access to employment rights. So, in 1979, the 'qualifying period' (the time an employee had to work before he or she could bring a claim) for unfair dismissal was raised from six months to one year,[32] and in 1985 it was raised again to two years.[33] This was presented as a measure to increase flexibility in the labour market and to create jobs. It was felt that employers would be more willing to take on new workers if they had a relatively long period in which they could dismiss those workers without fear of legal action. But this move deprived a substantial number of workers of the law's protection.

A third strategy was to ignore changes in the workplace which a more regulation-minded government might have chosen to control. For example, during this period, many employers started to arrange for their staff to have self-employed status, rather than employee status. This saved money for employers because (as we shall see in Chapter 5) self-employed workers have hardly any employment rights. Many labour lawyers see this as a form of 'cheating' which the government should have controlled. But since the government's own policy was to reduce labour costs, it was hardly going to stop employers who had found a way of doing this for themselves.

---

29 Department of Trade and Industry, *Burdens on Business: Report of a Scrutiny of Administrative and Legislative Requirements* (1985).
30 Department of Employment, *Employment for the 1990s* (1988) (Cm 540).
31 Trade Union Reform and Employment Rights Act 1993, s. 35.
32 Unfair Dismissal (Variation of Qualifying Period) Order 1979 (SI 1979/959).
33 Unfair Dismissal (Variation of Qualifying Period) Order 1985 (SI 1985/782).

Promoting workers' rights: EC law

The UK joined the EC in 1972. Although the Community began life as an economic union, its role in labour law has increased over time. During the 1980s and early 1990s, Community law was a source of new developments in workers' rights against their employers.

Sex discrimination law had an established legal basis in what was then Article 119 of the Treaty. The European Court of Justice (ECJ) developed this body of law in a series of test cases. For example, the Equal Pay Directive of 1975 confirmed that Article 119 included a principle of 'equal value': where a woman's work could be rated as of equal *value* to that done by a man (on a series of headings like effort, concentration and so on) she should receive equal pay.[34] This was more generous than the Equal Pay Act 1970, which only covered cases where the woman's work was the *same* as the man's or where the employer had voluntarily ranked the two jobs as equal.[35] After the Commission brought infringement proceedings before the ECJ,[36] the UK government was obliged to amend the law to include the equal value principle.[37]

However, at the political level, the Conservative government was able to resist many proposals for new EC legislation. In particular, the government 'opted out' of the Protocol and Agreement on Social Policy of the Maastricht Treaty, so that the UK was not subject to the employment directives enacted under it. This limited the extent to which Community law could counteract deregulation in the UK.

Conclusion

Although it is possible to identify distinctive strands of reasoning in the Conservative policies of the 1980s, they are all linked to some extent. The government's unwillingness to promote workers' rights against their employers (except when required to do so by Community law) was linked to its desire to deregulate the employment market. The government's interest in individual rights against trade unions could not be entirely separated from its attack on the unions: it was thought that trade union members were moderate and would undermine their leaders' radical policies. And the attack on collective bargaining and strike action was linked to deregulation because it provided another way of giving employers greater freedom to make decisions for themselves. All three strands were held together by the government's overall economic policy of promoting a free market. Thus, although the use made of rights and economics arguments in this period was radically different from the use made of such arguments in the 1960s and 1970s, they retained their status as essential tools of analysis for the labour lawyer.

---

34 Directive 75/117/EC, Art. 1.   35 EqPA 1970, s. 1.
36 (Case 61/81) *Commission* v. *UK* [1982] ECR 2601.
37 Equal Pay (Amendment) Regulations 1983 (SI 1983/1794).

'The third way' – 1997 to the present

The Labour government elected in 1997 brought a new approach to labour law. It remained concerned with our two familiar themes: workers' rights and a prosperous economy. But it argued – in the White Paper *Fairness at Work*, in particular – that it was not correct to view the interests of management and the interests of labour as diametrically opposed.[38] It rejected the traditional 'right' and 'left' in British politics in favour of a 'third way', which sought to reconcile the two.[39] There was an initial flurry of new legislation, followed by a quieter period in which the government continued to make minor adjustments to the law.

The traditional right-wing approach to workers' rights was, as we have seen, to present them as a burden on business. The traditional left-wing response was to argue for the promotion of workers' interests as a means of redistributing wealth from management to labour. The third way draws on an emerging school of thought in economics ('new institutional economics', discussed in more detail in Chapter 2) which identifies positive economic benefits flowing from labour rights. Put very simply, the argument is that if workers are treated with respect, both individually and collectively, they will work harder. Firms will recoup the cost of labour rights through gains in quality and productivity. Collins has given this strategy the more forward-looking label 'regulating for competitiveness'.[40]

In individual employment law, the government has introduced several new rights. For example, the national minimum wage guarantees a certain hourly rate to virtually all workers. This was justified, in part, as a means of preventing the exploitation of vulnerable workers.[41] But economic arguments also played an important role. In the global economy, UK firms cannot realistically compete solely on price. Labour costs are bound to be higher because workers would not accept the low wages paid in developing countries. The government argues that the UK should compete instead on the basis of its ability to produce high-quality, technologically advanced goods and services. The minimum wage prevents firms from competing on the basis of low costs and forces them to focus on innovation. Moreover, well-paid workers will work harder for the firm.

The government has been somewhat less hostile to European directives in labour law. Soon after coming into power, it signed the Protocol and Agreement on Social Policy of the Maastricht Treaty, which the Conservatives had refused to do. The directives agreed by the other Member States by this route – such as the Parental Leave Directive and the Part-Time Workers Directive – were extended

---

38 DTI, *Fairness at Work* (1998) (Cm 3968).
39 See, generally, A. Giddens, *The Third Way* (1998).
40 H. Collins, 'Regulating the employment relation for competitiveness' (2001) 30 *ILJ* 17, and 'Is there a third way in labour law?', in J. Conaghan *et al.* (eds.), *Labour Law in an Era of Globalization* (2002).
41 DTI, *Fairness at Work*, para. 3.2. See Chapter 8 for detail.

to the UK and implemented.[42] The EU has also been a significant source of new legislation requiring employers to consult workers on major business decisions – for example, through works councils.[43] Again, the government has drawn on third-way arguments when implementing new European measures – for example, it has argued that works councils can offer a way for firms to enhance productivity by improving communication with the workforce.[44] Indeed, 'regulating for competitiveness' is central to the EU's labour law agenda. The Commission's policy documents focus on ways of creating a flexible, highly skilled workforce and high levels of employment across the EU.[45] However, this does not mean that the UK government always agrees with EU policy on labour law. It has continued to resist new legislation in certain areas.

Collective labour law has, arguably, presented the government with the greatest difficulty in policy terms. The Labour Party is closely associated with the trade union movement and depends on it for financial support. But the third way rejects traditional left-wing ideas about the redistribution of wealth and the promotion of workers' rights for their own sake. The third-way justification for trade unionism – set out in *Fairness at Work* – is that unions can contribute to productivity within firms by improving communication with management.[46] In particular, the government has emphasised the idea of 'partnership' between management and unions, in which the two sides work together towards the common goal of making the firm more successful. To this end, the government has made some changes to collective labour law, the most obvious being the reintroduction of a statutory recognition procedure.[47] This enables a union to force an employer to recognise it for collective bargaining if it has a high level of support in the workplace. However, the government has retained most of the Conservative legislation restricting industrial action.

Although the period since 1997 has been dominated by the third way, more traditional rights and economics arguments continue to play a role. The third-way justification for labour rights depends on demonstrating that the gains in productivity that flow from labour rights outweigh their costs. Thus, the concern that labour rights impose costs on firms must still be taken into account. For example, the government has made a series of changes to unfair dismissal law with the intention (though not always the effect) of reducing the costs to firms of defending unfair dismissal claims.[48] Critics have argued that the government

---

42 Directive 96/34/EC (extended to the UK by Directive 97/75/EC) and Directive 97/81/EC (extended to the UK by Directive 98/23/EC) respectively.

43 See Chapter 10.

44 DTI, *High Performance Workplaces – Informing and Consulting Employees* (2003), para. 1.1.

45 European Commission, *Modernising Labour Law to Meet the Challenges of the 21st Century* (2006).

46 DTI, *Fairness at Work*, para. 4.12.   47 See Chapter 10.

48 For a critique of these provisions (which were repealed by the Employment Act 2008) see B. Hepple and G.S. Morris, 'The Employment Act 2002 and the crisis of individual employment rights' (2002) 31 *ILJ* 245.

is too willing to give in to employers' arguments about costs, and have, at times, questioned the government's commitment to the third way.

It is also important to note the ongoing relevance – and even strengthening – of rights arguments (framed in the traditional way, not in terms of their economic benefits) during this period. The Labour government was responsible for the enactment of the Human Rights Act 1998 (HRA), which came into force in 2000, giving effect in English law to most of the rights in the European Convention on Human Rights (ECHR). Although the domestic courts have given few significant human rights decisions in the field of labour law, the European Court of Human Rights (ECtHR) has heard some important cases on freedom of association (Article 11) in particular.[49] These decisions have forced the government to make significant changes to the relevant legislation.

The third way raises some very interesting issues for labour law because of its novel approach to the rights and economics arguments. Why should we believe the third-way economic arguments instead of the deregulation ones? Are firms which compete on the basis of productivity more successful than those which compete on the basis of low labour costs? And are there any rights which cannot, or should not, be justified in economic terms? Chapters 2 and 3 will explore these issues in greater detail.

Studying labour law today

Lawyers tend not to discuss their 'methodology' – the techniques they use to study their subject. But most lawyers use a theory of some kind to help them make sense of the legal materials.

As we have seen, the traditional approach to understanding labour law was Kahn-Freund's theory of collective laissez-faire. He thought that industrial relations should be left largely to management and unions, with limited legal intervention to support their activities. He evaluated legal developments in terms of their impact on trade unions. Today, it is no longer appropriate to think in terms of laissez-faire, given the high level of legislative intervention in both collective and individual labour law. Nevertheless, many labour lawyers continue to approach the subject from a strongly pro-union standpoint. However, although trade unions continue to play an important role, around three-quarters of the UK workforce are not union members, and in many workplaces there is no union presence at all. As a result, the trade union perspective may not be able to provide a complete 'take' on the subject.

There are many other approaches we could use to study labour law. One is social justice: many labour lawyers are concerned with the extent to which labour law succeeds in redistributing wealth from employers to the workforce and in ensuring

---

49 *Wilson* v. *UK* (2002) 35 EHRR 20; *ASLEF* v. *UK* (2007) 45 EHRR 34. See Chapter 11.

the fair treatment of those who are discriminated against or socially excluded.[50] Another is the Rule of Law in the formal sense.[51] It is often useful to consider whether or not a particular statute can readily be understood by those to whom it applies, so that they can adjust their conduct accordingly. Another is regulatory theory.[52] Regulation scholars study the best legal techniques for persuading people to behave in particular ways. Since labour law is about changing how employers behave, their insights can be very valuable. Yet another is sociology. Socio-legal scholars are concerned with the impact of law in society, and they often conduct empirical research to assess how particular policies are working in practice. Research of this kind offers a valuable perspective on all aspects of labour law. This is because policy proposals should, wherever possible, be based on an accurate understanding of what is happening in the workplace, not just on guesswork.

This book will draw on these approaches where they have useful insights to offer, but its main focus will be on theories of workers' rights and arguments from economics. These perspectives have been chosen because (as this chapter has shown) they have become increasingly significant in policy debates in recent years. Governments have taken the view that there is a link between labour law and economic prosperity, though they have differed markedly as to whether economic prosperity is best served by 'deregulating' the labour market or by adopting a 'regulating for competitiveness' approach. Governments have also become more interested in protecting individual rights, though again there have been competing interpretations: should rights be protected for their own sake, or because of their contribution to economic prosperity? Should individuals be granted rights to protect them against trade unions, or should rights be used to strengthen the trade union movement? These debates have given rise to an exciting body of literature on labour law which moves beyond the traditional intellectual confines of collective laissez-faire. The next two chapters will explore economics and rights perspectives on labour law in greater depth.

Further reading

For a detailed account of the development of labour law from the 1950s to the early 1990s, see P. Davies and M. Freedland, *Labour Legislation and Public Policy* (1993). Chapters 1 and 11 summarise the book's argument, but it is worth reading in full if you have time. Developments since the 1990s are covered in P. Davies and M. Freedland, *Towards a Flexible Labour Market* (2007). On the early history of labour law, see D. Brodie, *A History of British Labour Law* (2003).

---

50 Collins, 'The productive disintegration of labour law', p. 306.
51 J. Raz, 'The Rule of Law and its virtue' (1977) 93 *LQR* 195.
52 See, for example, R. Rogowski and T. Wilthagen, 'Reflexive labour law: an introduction', in R. Rogowski and T. Wilthagen (eds.), *Reflexive Labour Law* (1994); C. McCrudden, 'Equality legislation and reflexive regulation: a response to the Discrimination Law Review's consultative paper' (2007) 36 *ILJ* 255.

Otto Kahn-Freund's classic statement of collective laissez-faire can be found in Chapter 2 of A. Flanders and H.A. Clegg (eds.), *The System of Industrial Relations in Great Britain: Its History, Law and Institutions* (1954). The full title of the Donovan Report is the *Report of the Royal Commission on Trade Unions and Employers' Associations* (1968) (Cmnd 3623). Chapters 1–4 are particularly useful for their defence of collective laissez-faire and for the snapshot they offer of industrial relations in the late 1960s. You should think particularly carefully about the place of law in a system of collective laissez-faire. What roles did the law play? How important was the law? Did Kahn-Freund underestimate its importance? Can you trace the influence of rights arguments or economics arguments before the 1970s?

The argument that subsequent generations of labour lawyers ignored analytical approaches other than collective laissez-faire is developed in H. Collins, 'The productive disintegration of labour law' (1997) 26 *ILJ* 295, though his claims are strongly challenged by Lord Wedderburn, 'Collective bargaining or legal enactment: the 1999 Act and trade union recognition' (2000) 29 *ILJ* 1.

Because of the piecemeal nature of Conservative legislation in the 1980s, it is difficult to pinpoint a single statement of government policy for that period. But it is believed that Mrs Thatcher was inspired by the writings of F.A. Hayek. Chapter 18 of *The Constitution of Liberty* (1960) will give you a taste of his views.

The White Paper *Fairness at Work* (1998) (Cm 3968) remains the clearest statement of 'New' Labour policy on labour law. For a sophisticated theoretical account of the 'regulating for competitiveness' approach, see H. Collins, 'Regulating the employment relation for competitiveness' (2001) 30 *ILJ* 17, and 'Is there a third way in labour law?', in J. Conaghan *et al.* (eds.), *Labour Law in an Era of Globalization* (2002); and for a critique, see S. Fredman, 'The ideology of New Labour law', in C. Barnard *et al.* (eds.), *The Future of Labour Law* (2004). For a detailed analysis of legislation since 1997, see Davies and Freedland, *Towards a Flexible Labour Market*, above. In what ways does *Fairness at Work* diverge from the policies of the Conservative governments? In what ways does it continue those policies? There is a substantial critical literature on these developments from the perspective of workers' rights in particular. Much of this will be referred to in later chapters, but as an introduction it would be worth looking at S. Fredman, 'Women at work: the broken promise of flexicurity' (2004) 33 *ILJ* 299, and P. Smith and G. Morton, 'Nine years of New Labour: neoliberalism and workers' rights' (2006) 44 *BJIR* 401. Many labour lawyers remain strong advocates of collective bargaining. For an excellent overview of the issues facing the trade union movement today, see K.D. Ewing, 'The function of trade unions' (2005) 34 *ILJ* 1. What role should trade unions play nowadays? What should be the relationship between collective bargaining and statutory rights for workers?

2

Economics perspectives on labour law

As Chapter 1 explained, governments of the 1960s and 1970s became increasingly worried about the economic implications of labour law. They were concerned about the contribution unions' wage demands made to inflation, and about the impact of strikes on productivity. These concerns remained relevant in the 1980s, and a new one was added: that labour law might be contributing to high levels of unemployment. The Labour government has seen labour law in a different light: as a means of promoting productivity and competitiveness.

These developments in government policy have been paralleled by a growing interest among academic labour lawyers in the use of economics perspectives on their subject. In the 1980s, for example, the government drew heavily on the arguments of economists who favoured 'free markets', in which regulation by labour law would be kept to a minimum. Some labour lawyers responded by showing that not all economic analysis pointed in this direction: that there is also a significant school of thought which views labour law as one of the ways in which the government can help firms to become more successful. Later chapters of this book will explore the competing conclusions reached by economists on a selection of topics in labour law.

But all of this can seem rather daunting to lawyers with no background in economics. The purpose of this chapter is to demystify the subject by explaining some of the basic concepts economists use, and their application to labour issues. The first section will give a very brief account of the central core of economics: the subject's methodology and assumptions. The second section will examine microeconomics. This is the study of particular markets and of the forces of supply and demand which determine prices. The discussion will focus on the work of labour economists in studying the labour market. The impact of labour law is a matter of some controversy in economics, so in the third section of this chapter the two main schools of thought on this issue will be examined. Finally, the fourth section will consider some topics in macroeconomics – the study of national and regional economies – which are of particular relevance to labour law.

What do economists do?

As lawyers, we need to understand and respect the techniques economists use;[1] otherwise, we will not be able to make good use of – or fair criticisms of – their arguments. 'Positive' economists produce theoretical models which predict how people will behave *assuming* certain facts to be the case.[2] They then test these models against real-world empirical evidence. Normative economists use this data to produce policy recommendations. The key to understanding economic analysis is to grasp the crucial role played by assumptions.

Economists start from the premise that resources such as labour, capital, land, time and personal income are scarce. This means that everybody must make choices – for example, workers have to choose between having more leisure time and having more income from employment.[3] Economists' key assumption is that people make these choices *rationally*. They weigh up the costs and benefits of each option and select the one that will make them richer ('maximise their wealth') or make them happier ('maximise their utility') or satisfy more of their prefer-ences.[4] So, if a worker opts for more leisure time, an economist would infer that he or she values the benefits of leisure more highly than the extra income to be obtained from working longer hours. Moreover, economists commonly assume that people's basic preferences remain *stable over time*, so that if the economic environment changes, their behaviour will change too, in response. If wages rise, the leisure-loving worker might decide to reduce his or her working time even further, because the same income can be generated in fewer hours.

One of the most profound criticisms made of economics is that the key assumptions of rational and consistent behaviour are often false. Simon's famous model of 'bounded rationality' suggests that individuals do not, in practice, make decisions through a process of rational choice.[5] They often 'make do' with a satisfactory choice – even if, in theory, better options exist – and reassess their choices only occasionally, when some crisis occurs. A worker who is satisfied with his or her current wage might stay in the job even though better-paying jobs are available. He or she might only start to think about these other jobs after an argument with his or her manager. Similarly, in practice, people's preferences do change over time. For example, as workers get older, they are likely to take a much greater interest in what kind of pension scheme their employer offers.

---

1 Economists communicate through graphs and equations, as well as prose. This book avoids both techniques because they are unfamiliar to lawyers and can be rather off-putting. The further reading at the end of this chapter does, however, introduce them. Once you have under-stood them, you will see that they are able to convey complex ideas more efficiently than words. For an introduction, see R. Cooter and T. Ulen, *Law and Economics* (5th edn., 2007), Chapter 2.
2 M. Friedman, *Essays in Positive Economics* (1953), pp. 3–43.
3 For more detail, see Chapter 6.
4 These are versions of utilitarianism, discussed in Chapter 3.
5 H. Simon, 'Rationality in psychology and economics' (1986) 59 *Journal of Business* S209–S224.

Most economists would reject these criticisms. They acknowledge that their fundamental assumptions may not hold true in all circumstances, but they argue that the assumptions are essential to their methodology. They analyse real-world phenomena by building theoretical models. These models only work if they simplify the real world considerably. The assumptions are the means of simplification. Without the assumption that people behave rationally, it would be impossible to predict how people would respond to changes in economic circumstances. Without the assumption that preferences are stable over time, any change in people's behaviour could be attributed to a change in their preferences, rather than to their response to new economic conditions.[6] Friedman argues that economic models should be judged not on the validity of their assumptions, but on the accuracy of their predictions.[7] For example, rather than testing whether or not workers behave rationally, we should test whether or not some workers respond to a wage rise by opting to work fewer hours.

The best view is probably somewhere in between the extremes set out by Simon and Friedman. Economic models should usually be tested for their ability to predict how people will behave in the real world. But if a model is used *normatively*, to make policy recommendations, it would be foolish to ignore doubts about the empirical validity of its underlying assumptions. This applies not just to the core assumptions of rational and consistent behaviour, but to the multitude of other assumptions made by economists to simplify the world. It is important to look carefully at the assumptions being made whenever you read an economist's work. When two writers disagree, it is often because they are using different sets of assumptions.

Microeconomics

Microeconomists are concerned with markets.[8] Markets determine the prices of particular goods and services by bringing together buyers and sellers. The labour market determines the price of labour (wages) by bringing together employers (the buyers of labour) and workers (the sellers of labour). This section will introduce markets in general, before turning to the special issues raised by labour markets.

Markets

Markets come in two types. Product markets are those in which goods or services are bought and sold. Factor markets are those in which the factors of production – the things needed to produce goods and services, such as land, labour and machinery – are bought and sold. Economists consider two main types of market player: firms and households. Firms are sellers in product markets and

6 G. Becker, *The Economic Approach to Human Behavior* (1976), pp. 3–14.
7 Friedman, *Essays in Positive Economics*.
8 For an introduction, see Cooter and Ulen, *Law and Economics*, Chapters 1 and 2.

buyers in factor markets. Households are buyers in product markets and sellers in factor markets.

The price of any particular product or factor is determined by the forces of supply and demand in the market. Generally, economists conclude that as prices go up, demand falls and supply rises. In the market for cars, firms will be willing to supply cars in larger numbers if they can get more money for them. But households will buy fewer cars as they become more expensive. In theory, the 'invisible hand' of the market will drive firms and households to what is known as the 'equilibrium' or 'market-clearing' price. This is the price at which supply and demand are equal. Households are willing to buy a certain number of cars at this price, and firms will produce exactly that number.

What determines the forces of supply and demand? Economists start with the assumption that firms want to maximise their profits. This involves doing two things: choosing the output of products that will generate the most income from sales, and choosing the combination of inputs (labour, machinery, raw materials) that will produce this output at the least possible cost. An equation called a 'production function' can be used to express all imaginable combinations of inputs and outputs for a particular firm: the different quantities of inputs the firm could use to produce different levels of output, and the different ways in which the inputs could be combined to produce a given level of output. Each firm calculates the combination of inputs and outputs that will maximise profits on the basis of two crucial factors: the prices of the inputs it is buying and the prices it can get for the products it is selling.

Economists treat households in a similar way. They assume that households seek to maximise their pleasure, or to satisfy as many of their preferences as possible. Each household has a 'utility function', which expresses all imaginable ways in which products could be combined by the household to produce a given level of pleasure or satisfaction, and all imaginable quantities of products the household could consume in order to produce different levels of pleasure or satisfaction. How does the household decide how many products to consume, and in what combination? The household decides by looking at the prices of products and at the income it has available in order to buy them.

The best combination of inputs (for firms) or products (for households) is referred to as the 'optimal' or 'efficient' combination. The optimal combination of inputs for a firm is the one in which extra money spent on one input (another worker, for example) would yield exactly the same return as the same money spent on another input (a machine, for example). If a firm would benefit more from hiring workers than it would from buying machines, we can say that it has not reached its optimal combination of inputs. It needs to hire more workers until the return from hiring each additional worker is equal to that from buying additional machines. What stops firms from simply wanting more and more of each input is the so-called law of diminishing marginal productivity. The value of adding extra inputs (extra workers, for example) increases up to a point and then starts to decline: instead of producing more outputs, the workers are just getting in each other's way.

A similar analysis applies to households. The optimal combination of products is the one at which extra money spent on one product would yield the same satisfaction as the same money spent on another product. If a household would gain more satisfaction from additional chocolate than it would from biscuits, it is clear that the household has not reached its optimal combination. But households do not (in theory) want more and more of each product. Most products are subject to the law of diminishing marginal utility: more chocolate makes you happier up to a point, but then it starts to make you feel sick.

Labour markets

Labour economists study the concepts of supply, demand and prices in labour markets. The labour market is a factor market in which workers offer their services for sale and firms are buyers. But it has several special features. First, the supply of labour raises complex issues. Workers cannot supply their labour without supplying themselves, so they care about more than just the wage they will get for the job. They also consider matters such as job security and the safety of the working environment. Moreover, workers' decisions about how much labour to supply are closely tied up with how much money they want to have available to spend as consumers, and with the career decisions of other members of their household. Second, employers might have subjective preferences about who they employ. An employer who discriminates against women may pay them less than men, even though they are equally productive workers. Employers are unlikely to differentiate between other factors of production – machines or raw materials – in quite the same way. Third, workers often join together in trade unions to sell their labour as a group. As we shall see, the impact of unions on the labour market is a highly controversial issue.[9]

Economists find much to study in the issue of labour supply. They begin at the most basic level, with the individual's labour supply decision: whether to work at all, and if so, for how many hours. At any given wage, the worker can achieve various different combinations of income and leisure. This is called the 'budget constraint'. The worker selects a combination in the light of his or her preferences for work or leisure: some people are more workaholic, or more leisure-loving, than others. These preferences may change (if the worker wins the lottery or decides to retire, for example), but economists assume for the purposes of argument that they remain stable over time. In Chapter 6, we will see that many economists reject the idea of having any legal control over how many hours people can work because they regard it as an unwarranted interference with individuals' preferences.

Obviously, the amount of labour an individual chooses to supply is influenced by changes in the wage rate. On the one hand, if the wage rate rises, the individual

---

9 See Chapters 10–12.

can earn the same amount of money in less time, so he or she might opt to work fewer hours (the 'income effect'). On the other hand, for each hour of leisure the individual takes, he or she is sacrificing a larger chunk of income, so he or she might decide to work more hours (the 'substitution effect'). Which of these effects dominates depends on the individual's preferences. Individuals may be more or less responsive to changes in the wage rate: in technical terms, individual labour supply may be more or less 'wage-elastic'.

It is also helpful to think about the labour supply decision not just as an individual choice, but as a decision made in the context of a household.[10] Within each household, there is a need to decide how individual members should divide their time between paid work, work in the household (cooking, childcare and so on) and consumption (enjoying the goods the household has produced). The rational household will allocate family members to the tasks they are best at: those in which they have a 'comparative advantage'. If, for example, unpaid leave to care for children is available to both parents, it makes sense for the parent who earns less to take the leave. The parent who earns more has a comparative advantage in the labour market.

The demand for labour, like the demand for all the other factors of production, is *derived* from the demand for the firm's products. The firm wants employees for the contribution they make to production, rather than for their own sake. Labour is subject to the law of diminishing marginal productivity. For example, a manufacturing firm will benefit from hiring workers up to the point at which all its machines are fully operational. There is nothing to be gained by hiring any more workers because they will not contribute anything further to productivity.

Various factors may cause a firm's demand for labour to change. The most obvious is a change in the demand for the firm's products: if demand increases, the demand for labour will also increase. Another is a change in the price of the other factors of production. If the price of machinery falls, the demand for labour may be affected in one of two ways. If the machines can be used to replace workers, the demand for labour will decrease. But if the machines need workers to operate them, the demand for labour will increase.

The demand for labour may be more or less *elastic*. This means that employers may be more or less sensitive to changes in the wage rate. Elasticity depends on a variety of factors. One is the elasticity of demand for the firm's products, for the obvious reason that the demand for labour is derived from the demand for products. Another is the proportion of the firm's costs which is accounted for by labour: firms are more likely to respond to wage changes where wage costs make up a substantial proportion of their total costs. A further factor is the extent to which other inputs can be substituted for labour. If the firm could potentially replace workers with machines, a change in the wage rate might prompt it to buy new machines. Elasticity is an important concept in the analysis of labour

10 G. Becker, 'A theory of the allocation of time' (1965) 75 *Economic Journal* 493.

law because legal regulation often increases employers' costs. If demand is highly elastic, an increase in regulation is more likely to prompt employers to take action to offset the increase in their costs. If demand is inelastic, an increase in regulation is less likely to worry the employer.

The forces of supply and demand combine in the market in order to determine the wage rate. In a perfectly competitive market, the wage rate will be fixed at a level at which workers are willing to supply exactly the number of hours that employers want to buy. Individual firms in this market will simply offer the equilibrium wage: they can hire as many units of labour as they want at this price. If they offer a lower wage, no-one will be willing to work for them. It is unnecessary for them to offer a higher wage, since they can obtain all the labour they need at the equilibrium rate.

The operation of the labour market is, of course, affected to a very great extent by labour law. An obvious example is the introduction of a minimum wage. This interferes directly with the normal process of wage determination in the market by setting a floor below which wages cannot fall. It usually requires employers to pay some workers a higher wage than they would have received if the law had not intervened. Similarly, if the law allows strong trade unions to exist, they may be able to bargain with employers for higher wages than their members would otherwise have achieved by the operation of market forces. These and other examples will be considered in detail in later chapters.

Labour law: two schools of thought

So far, we have been looking at the relatively uncontroversial questions of what labour economists study and how they go about it. But just as lawyers disagree about the merits of a recent judgment or a new piece of legislation, economists disagree about the impact of different aspects of labour law on the labour market. Very broadly, we can divide economists into two camps: 'neoclassical' and 'new institutional'. They differ as to the goals they are pursuing (what their ideal labour market would look like) and the assumptions they use in their analysis. Those in the neoclassical camp tend to be hostile to legal intervention; those in the new institutional camp argue that labour law can benefit workers, firms and the economy as a whole.

To understand these two schools of thought, it is helpful to begin by looking at the context in which they are writing. The main challenge facing the UK economy today is globalisation.[11] This term can mean many things, but for our purposes it refers to the process by which goods and services can be produced on a global scale without regard for national borders. Globalisation is made possible by advances in transport, telecommunications and information technology. For example, a car sold in the UK might be made up of components manufactured

---

11 See U. Beck, *What is Globalization?* (2000), pp. 1–21.

in several different countries and assembled in Germany; the components can be ordered in an instant by email. Or a telephone call to a British bank might be answered by a call centre worker in India. Because customer records are stored on computer, there is no need for the worker to be at the customer's local branch. In developed countries like the UK, globalisation is often seen as a threat. Firms can now locate their factories or call centres anywhere in the world. And they may well decide to avoid the UK because wage levels are high compared to those in developing countries. So how can the UK stay competitive?

Neoclassical economics

Neoclassical economists respond to the problem of globalisation by extolling the virtues of the free market.[12] If employers are allowed to run their businesses as they see fit, with a minimum of outside intervention, they will be able to compete on a global scale. If firms in other countries can operate more cheaply, employers will respond by finding ways to cut their own costs. And if firms are profitable, society as a whole – and the employees of those firms in particular – will reap the benefit. On this view, legal regulation is perceived as a problem because it limits the options open to employers and imposes additional costs on them which may make them uncompetitive. Ultimately, this harms the very workers the legislation was seeking to protect.

The starting point for much economic analysis of law is the Coase theorem.[13] Coase argued that, in principle, if the law imposed a particular requirement on people in a market, it would make no difference to the outcomes of that market. If the rule led to inefficient outcomes, people would get round it by contracting with each other until an efficient outcome was reached. Imagine that the law requires employers to give employees paid holidays. This increases employers' costs by requiring them to pay workers while they are not working, and to make arrangements for other workers to do the jobs of those who are absent. The employer would not want to see its profits reduced, so it would pass the cost of this benefit on to the employees by cutting their wages. The new benefit does not change the allocation of resources in society: the employer pays the employees the same amount but it is made up of wages and paid holidays instead of just wages as before.[14] Many labour lawyers would be horrified at this outcome because it does nothing to redistribute wealth from the employer to the employees, but economists are concerned with efficiency, not redistribution.

However, a major qualification of the Coase theorem – and this is its crucial insight – is that this efficient solution can only be reached when transaction costs

---

12 For an introduction (using examples from American law) see R.A. Posner, *Economic Analysis of Law* (6th edn., 2003), Chapter 11, and (focusing on dismissal law) R.A. Epstein, 'In defense of the contract at will' (1984) 51 *University of Chicago Law Review* 947.

13 R. Coase, 'The problem of social cost' (1960), 3 *Journal of Law and Economics* 1.

14 L.H. Summers, 'Some simple economics of mandated benefits' (1989) 79 *American Economic Review* 177; J. Gruber, 'The incidence of mandated maternity benefits' (1994) 84 *American Economic Review* 622.

are zero. Transaction costs are all the costs associated with contracting out of the new legal rule: negotiating with the employees, drafting a new contract and trying to make sure that both sides keep to their bargain, for example. In the real world, transaction costs are rarely zero. Neoclassical economists draw from this the conclusion that the government should interfere as little as possible in the labour market. Each new piece of legislation requires employers to bargain with their employees for an efficient outcome, and forces them to incur transaction costs. Thus, regulation is damaging to firms.

Neoclassical economists also emphasise the harm regulation can do to the overall level of employment. Even if the employer is willing to incur the transaction costs, it may not always be able to negotiate an efficient outcome with its workers. The law might impose a minimum wage which limits the employer's ability to cut pay below a certain level. Or workers might refuse to agree to a substantial reduction in their earnings. For example, workers whose children are grown-up might not be prepared to pay for parental leave which would only benefit younger workers. In these cases, the employer must find another way to achieve an efficient outcome. One option is to keep the overall wage bill at the same level by making some employees redundant. Another option is to pass on some of the increase in costs to customers by increasing the price of its products. Globalisation makes this option particularly risky. An increase in the price of the firm's products might cause it to lose market share, particularly where its competitors are located in other countries and are not subject to the same legislative requirements. As the firm's fortunes decline, redundancies may eventually result. Both possibilities are obviously harmful to those workers who lose their jobs. They also damage the economy as a whole, because labour is not being allocated to employers who need it.

More generally, many neoclassical economists are strong advocates of the doctrine of freedom of contract.[15] This means that people should be allowed to enter into contracts with whomever they choose, on whatever terms they wish. The law should only interfere where there is evidence that a person has not given his or her genuine consent, for example, in cases of duress or undue influence. This provides another reason for rejecting detailed legal regulation of the employment relationship. Employers and employees should be allowed to agree on whatever terms they want. If an employee is willing to agree to a contract that does not provide for paid holidays, it must be because the employee does not value them. The law should not presume to tell people what is in their best interests.

This emphasis on freedom of contract is in stark contrast to much traditional labour law thinking. Most labour lawyers argue that individual workers are not well-placed to bargain with employers, because each worker usually needs his or her job much more than the employer needs that particular worker. They argue that workers' rights should be protected either by the law or by collective

15 P.S. Atiyah, *An Introduction to the Law of Contract* (5ᵗʰ edn., 1995), Chapter 1.

bargaining, because individual workers cannot bargain for protection themselves. This often leads critics to portray neoclassical economics as hostile to the interests of employees. However, its proponents would argue that their hostility is only to labour legislation, and that it stems from their concern to protect employees. This book will give serious consideration to the arguments of neoclassical economics. The claim that legal regulation may impose costs on workers themselves ought not to be ignored.

New institutional economics

Not all economists are neoclassicists. New institutional economics emerged in the 1970s in the pioneering work of Williamson, who sought to explain why the production of goods is often organised through the creation of firms rather than through a whole series of contracts in the market.[16] The new institutionalists argue that unregulated free markets often fail to achieve efficient outcomes. This is because many of the assumptions made by the neoclassicists – that everyone has perfect information, for example – do not apply in the real world. The new institutionalists suggest that markets may need to be regulated – often through law – in order to overcome these 'market failures'.

New institutional economists reject the solution to the problems of globalisation proffered by their neoclassical colleagues.[17] They argue that no amount of cost-cutting will ever enable the UK to compete with developing countries. Because of the high cost of living in the UK, workers would simply refuse to work at wage levels that would beat those of developing countries. Thus, according to the new institutionalists, the UK should give up trying to produce those goods which can be manufactured just as well and more cheaply elsewhere. Instead, the UK should attempt to compete on some other basis than price.

One of the UK's strengths is that its workers are (in global terms) relatively well-educated and well-trained. So one possible basis for competition would be to concentrate on products that require skills and expertise. This might be true of the manufacturing of particular kinds of goods, but it is more likely to be true of the provision of services. Some services are technically complex and cannot be produced by unskilled workers: legal advice is a good example of this. Others, such as software development, require continuous updating to keep pace with an ever-changing market. Skilled workers are required to suggest and develop new ideas, and to respond to customer demand.

This approach to competitiveness has important implications for the firm's relationship with its workers. If the firm is producing technically advanced services, its workers must be well-trained. The firm may have to pay for some of this

---

16 See O.E. Williamson, 'Transaction-cost economics: the governance of contractual relations' (1979) 22 *Journal of Law and Economics* 233.

17 See S. Deakin and F. Wilkinson, 'Labour law and economic theory: a reappraisal', in H. Collins *et al.* (eds.), *Legal Regulation of the Employment Relation* (2000), and Deakin and Wilkinson, *The Law of the Labour Market: Industrialization, Employment and Legal Evolution* (2005), especially Chapter 5.

training, so it will need workers who are likely to stay in its employment over the longer term; otherwise the firm will not be able to recoup its training costs. If the firm is trying to innovate, it will need to be able to communicate successfully with its workers. Their suggestions, based on their detailed knowledge of production processes and customer needs, may be an invaluable source of new developments. And if the firm is focused on the quality of its products, it needs workers who are committed to the firm and therefore willing to work to a very high standard.

New institutionalists argue that the law can help to create this kind of relationship between a firm and its workers. One of the reasons why many workers leave their jobs is that they find it impossible to combine work with family responsibilities. The law may be able to address this problem by requiring firms to allow parents to work from home or to provide them with time off work to deal with family problems. These measures would encourage parents to stay in work and would help firms to recoup their training costs. Similarly, a firm might miss out on its employees' ideas for innovations if it never talks to them. But if the law requires the firm to set up a works council or to recognise a trade union, the law might provide a forum in which the employees are able to discuss their ideas with management.[18]

An obvious response to the new institutionalists' approach is to point out that if a measure is beneficial to firms, they will adopt it anyway, without the need for the law to make it compulsory. If a firm does not adopt the measure, this must be evidence that managers have weighed up the costs and benefits and decided that the costs are greater than the benefits. But the new institutionalists reject the neoclassical view that the market always achieves the most efficient outcomes when left to its own devices. They offer a different interpretation of the Coase theorem.[19] They argue that unregulated markets suffer from various kinds of problems which mean that transaction costs *in the markets themselves* are often very high. Employers and employees may find that it is too expensive to reach an efficient outcome on their own. This suggests that there may be a role for legal regulation where it promotes efficient outcomes.

To understand this argument, it is helpful to look at some of the 'market failures' that might generate transaction costs. One problem is that the employer and employee do not have equal bargaining power.[20] In general, the employee needs the job more than the employer needs him or her, because there are plenty of other potential employees in the market. This enables the employer to behave opportunistically: ignoring longer-term goals in pursuit of short-term savings

18 See J. Rogers and W. Streeck, 'Workplace representation overseas: the works councils story', in R.B. Freeman (ed.), *Working under Different Rules* (1994).
19 See Deakin and Wilkinson, 'Labour law and economic theory', pp. 34–8.
20 Another problem is information asymmetry: see, for example, P. Aghion and B. Hermalin, 'Legal restrictions on private contracts can enhance efficiency' (1990) 6 *Journal of Law, Economics and Organization* 381.

or profits – for example, the employer might promise the employee a bonus for achieving a particular target, and then dismiss the employee shortly before the payment becomes due in order to save money. But this is bad for the employer in the longer term because other workers will be less inclined to trust the employer and will not feel motivated by promises of bonus payments. The law can help to prevent this opportunistic behaviour by providing the employee with a degree of job security: in other words, by making it unlawful for the employer to dismiss people unless certain conditions are met.[21] The examples we considered above – about training and consultation – are also situations in which the employer might decide not to pursue long-term efficiency because of the short-term costs. Thus, the law may sometimes be able to improve on the solutions generated by markets.

Even if these arguments are accepted, there is a second problem with the new institutional approach. This problem is acknowledged by many new institutionalists themselves. It is that the benefits they identify from legal regulation will not manifest themselves in every case. Our parental leave example is a good illustration of this. A firm is most likely to be worried about retaining its employees where it has to provide them with a high level of training to meet its particular needs. But if the firm's requirement is for workers with a widely available, more general skill, it will be less worried about retention. If someone leaves, the firm can hire a replacement, and he or she will be able to start work with very little training of any kind. This means that the benefits of compulsory parental leave in helping firms to retain workers will be evident in some firms and non-existent in others. Most of the time, then, the new institutionalists will be arguing that regulation should be adopted when it benefits a majority of firms, and will not be claiming that it benefits all firms.

At this point, many new institutionalists concede that economic arguments cannot provide the whole justification for legal regulation of a particular area. Imagine that it has been calculated that the provision of parental leave will benefit 70 per cent of firms but impose a cost on the remaining 30 per cent. This suggests that parental leave should be made compulsory, but it does leave a nagging doubt about the position of the minority of firms that will not benefit. If the firms have some common characteristic – that they are all small businesses, for example – it might be possible to draft an exception that would take them outside the scope of the new legislation. But if they are all quite different, this will not be possible. Therefore, it may be helpful to employ a rights argument alongside the economic analysis. As we shall see, parental leave can be viewed as an important right for working parents, and for working mothers in particular. By helping them to balance work and family life, it broadens the range of life choices that are available to them. When parental leave is viewed in these terms, there is a good reason to make it compulsory, even if it does not benefit all firms. The new

21 See, generally, C.F. Büchtemann, 'Introduction: employment security and labor markets', in C.F. Büchtemann (ed.), *Employment Security and Labor Market Behavior* (1993).

institutionalists' argument supplies the justification for imposing parental leave on the firms that do benefit; the rights argument supplies the justification for the firms that do not. The relationship between rights and economics arguments will be explored more fully in the next chapter.

Macroeconomics

As well as having an impact on particular firms operating in particular markets, labour law also has an effect on the nation's economy as a whole, and it is this which makes it interesting to macroeconomists. Indeed, when the government is contemplating changes to labour law, it is often motivated by macroeconomic considerations as well as concerns for the well-being of particular firms and employees. We will examine two topics: productivity and unemployment.

Productivity

To measure productivity, economists work out what the output of the economy is (its gross domestic product), and divide it by the inputs that have been used to generate it (raw materials, machinery and workers). Labour productivity is a measure of output divided by the number of worker hours needed to generate that output. The productivity ratio tells us how many units of output we can obtain from one unit of input (one worker hour, for example). Productivity has increased when we are able to obtain more output from the same level of input. The general trend is for productivity to increase over time.

Rising productivity is regarded by economists as a sign of a healthy economy, for two reasons. First, it is the source of improvements in everyone's standard of living. Standards of living improve when the real wage rate rises. This occurs whenever there is an increase in the demand for labour. As demand increases more rapidly than supply, employers will have to offer more money in order to attract more workers into the labour market. What prompts this increase in the demand for labour? The answer is rising productivity. Firms will employ more workers as the value of what they can produce increases relative to the cost of employing them. So output rises, income rises and the standard of living improves.

The second advantage associated with rising productivity is that it helps to combat inflation. Inflation describes the situation in which prices rise inordinately across the economy as a whole. Both product prices and the price of labour (wages) are affected, because workers expect their wages to keep pace with the cost of living. If inflation is allowed to spiral out of control, a serious economic crisis will result. There is an important debate within economics about the precise causes of inflation, but this need not concern us here. The crucial point for our purposes is that if the wage rate does rise, inflation will not occur if that rise is offset by an increase in productivity. Imagine that a worker earns £5 an hour and produces five units of output. If the wage rate increases to £6 an hour, labour costs will rise. If labour costs rise, product prices will increase, and an inflationary spiral may begin. But if the worker's productivity increases to six units of output per hour, the rise in wages to £6 per hour is offset by the productivity increase. Labour costs remain unchanged and there is no inflationary pressure as a result of the pay rise.

Since productivity increases are a good thing, it is not surprising to find that governments are keen to encourage workers and firms to improve their productivity. One strategy is through education and training. Other things being equal, a more highly trained workforce is more productive than one with less training. Thus, if the government provides a high-quality school system and subsidises vocational training courses at colleges, these measures will help to produce a trained workforce which will make firms more productive. Another strategy is to use labour law to bring about improvements in productivity. The two schools of thought in economics are usually divided about the best way of doing this. Let us take unfair dismissal law as an example. Some neoclassical economists would argue that employers should be allowed to dismiss employees 'at will' – whenever they want and for whatever reason, or for no reason at all. The constant threat of dismissal hanging over all employees will encourage them to work hard and to be productive. Most new institutional economists would argue that unfair dismissal laws, which only allow employers to dismiss employees if certain conditions are satisfied, are a better way of improving productivity. They argue that workers will be more productive if they feel secure in their jobs. Whichever of these views is correct, they are both pursuing the same goal of improved productivity, because of the economic benefits it brings.

Unemployment

Since labour law is, on the whole, concerned with those who are in work, it may seem rather odd to consider those who do not have a job. But labour law may influence the level of unemployment. Many neoclassical economists believe that labour law creates unemployment by increasing the labour costs faced by employers. Others, mainly in the new institutional camp, argue that labour law can be used to reduce or mitigate unemployment. It is therefore useful for labour lawyers to understand how unemployment is measured and how economists explain it.

In August 2008, the unemployment rate in the UK was 5.4 per cent.[22] People count as unemployed if they want to work, are available to work and are actively seeking employment.[23] This means that the unemployment count does not include all those people who do not have a job. Some people do not want to work: for example, a person might have given up his or her job in order to care for a sick relative. Some people are unavailable for work: those in prison, for example. And

22 Source: National Statistics, *Labour Force Survey* (2008).
23 The UK uses the ILO's definition of unemployment.

some are not seeking work: those 'discouraged workers' who have tried for some time to get a job but have given up because they have not had any success. These various groups of people explain the gap between the unemployment rate of 5.4 per cent and the employment rate of 74.8 per cent for people of working age. It can be argued that the official unemployment statistics underestimate the true rate of unemployment in various ways. The 'discouraged workers' should perhaps be included because they would take a job if they could get one. Economists regard some unemployment in the economy – of between 4 and 6 per cent – as a good sign.[24] If the unemployment rate is too low, inflation may result as employers increase wages in order to recruit and retain scarce workers.

A look at the various different types of unemployment identified by economists will help to explain why it occurs. One major type of unemployment is frictional unemployment. The labour market never clears: in other words, at any one point in time, employers will be trying to fill some vacancies and jobseekers will be looking for work. Some unemployment is inevitable, even if the number of job vacancies exactly matches the number of people seeking work. Search unemployment is an important kind of frictional unemployment. It occurs when individuals spend time looking around for the best job offer and employers spend time looking for the best candidate to fill a vacancy. Another type of frictional unemployment is wait unemployment, in which workers are temporarily laid off but expect to be able to resume their jobs at a later date. Agricultural workers may be unemployed at various times during the year because of the seasonal nature of their jobs.

A second major type of unemployment is structural unemployment. This occurs when there is a mismatch between those seeking work and the job vacancies that are available. One problem might be that the unemployed workers are all in the north-west while the vacancies are all in the south-east. Another problem might be that the vacancies are all in information technology firms, while the unemployed workers are trained in car manufacturing. These mismatches can be overcome if the jobseekers are willing to relocate and retrain, but it can take some time for the situation to be resolved. Structural unemployment is much longer-lived than frictional unemployment. In August 2008, of the unemployed aged 25–49 years, 13.9 per cent had been unemployed for two years or more.[25] Many of those experiencing long-term unemployment are the victims of structural change.

A final type of unemployment is demand-deficient or cyclical unemployment. This occurs when there is a downturn in the economy. As demand for their products falls, firms will need to reduce their labour costs. This could be done either by cutting the wages of all workers or by making some workers redundant. The redundancy solution – which creates unemployment – is more common in practice. Workers are often reluctant to accept cuts in wages unless the firm is facing

---

24 For discussion, see J. Stiglitz, 'Reflections on the natural rate hypothesis' (1997) 11 *Journal of Economic Perspectives* 3.
25 National Statistics, *Labour Force Survey*.

bankruptcy. It is easier to make a few workers redundant than to alienate the entire workforce.

Most governments make it their policy to keep unemployment as low as possible. Various strategies can be used to achieve this. For example, the provision of local 'job centres' helps to reduce frictional unemployment by giving employers a means of advertising vacancies and jobseekers a way of finding out what jobs are available. The provision of training programmes may help to reduce structural unemployment by enabling those who are displaced by the demise of one industry to acquire new skills in order to work in another. Some people argue that labour law may also be used to help mitigate the problem of redundancy. A legal obligation to give the workers notice of impending redundancies may help to reduce structural unemployment by giving those workers the chance to look for a new job or to take training courses. Strong anti-discrimination laws may also be needed to ensure that the burden of unemployment does not fall unduly harshly on some groups in society. This is a particular problem in the UK at the time of writing (2008). Statistics from 2007 show that the unemployment rate for ethnic minority women was around 10 per cent, compared to 5 per cent for white women.[26] However, neoclassical economists argue that too much legal intervention in the labour market may contribute to the redundancy problem. New labour laws may increase employers' costs and may lead to redundancies where the employer cannot pass those costs on to workers through wage cuts. This argument will be a common theme in later chapters.

The role of economics perspectives

Economics teaches us to examine legal regulation for the effect it has on the ability of workers and firms to maximise their wealth or utility. Like lawyers, economists disagree quite radically about the advantages and disadvantages of particular pieces of legislation. Economics should not be expected to provide us with a set of straightforward answers. Nor should we treat economic analysis as the only valid insight into the problems of labour law. Even the most hard-line neoclassical theorist would agree that public policy does sometimes need to act on considerations other than efficiency. Arguments from social justice or human rights must also be taken into account and might well outweigh such considerations. Nevertheless, economics plays a vital role in helping us to understand the costs and benefits of policy choices.

Further reading

Later chapters will cover specific topics – discrimination, trade unions and so on – in more detail, so this chapter's further reading will explore economics more generally.

---

26 Equal Opportunities Commission (EOC), *Moving On Up? The Way Forward* (2007), p. 9.

The classic statement of the methodology of economics is M. Friedman, *Essays in Positive Economics* (1953), pp. 3–43. You may also find it helpful to look at G. Becker, *The Economic Approach to Human Behavior* (1976), pp. 3–14, and J. Coleman, *Markets, Morals and the Law* (1988), pp. 95–132. M. Blaug, *The Methodology of Economics: Or, How Economists Explain* (2nd edn., 1992), pp. 112–34, gives a helpful account of the distinction between positive and normative economics. But does the standard methodology oversimplify things? H. Simon, 'Rationality in psychology and economics' (1986) 59 *Journal of Business* S209–S224, argues that individuals do not act rationally in the sense used by economists. Instead, they 'make do' with a satisfactory decision, drawing on the information that is readily available to them. Could economists adapt their methodology to incorporate Simon's insight? Or does Simon undermine the whole basis of the discipline?

But Simon is by no means the most radical critic of economics. Many theorists argue that the discipline cannot offer any valid insights into how society should be run. Kelman, writing from the perspective of critical legal studies, rejects economics on the grounds that it makes a claim to neutrality that is wholly misleading: M. Kelman, *A Guide to Critical Legal Studies* (1987), Chapters 4 and 5. But does economics have a single political agenda? Where does new institutional economics fit into Kelman's analysis? Kennedy attacks the rationality assumption even more vigorously than Simon, arguing that individuals often do not know what is best for them: D. Kennedy, 'Distributive and paternalist motives in contract and tort law' (1982) 41 *Maryland Law Review* 563. He argues for more paternalism in public policy, but does the government really know best? Finally, Dworkin argues that economics is flawed because it pays too much attention to the happiness of society as a whole and ignores the rights of individuals: R. Dworkin, 'Is wealth a value?' (1980) 9 *Journal of Legal Studies* 191. The relationship between rights and economics will be discussed further in Chapter 3.

For the purposes of explanation, this chapter divided economists into two camps: neoclassical and new institutional. For an introduction to neoclassical theories, see R.A. Posner, *Economic Analysis of Law* (6th edn., 2003), Chapter 11, and (in the context of dismissal laws) R.A. Epstein, 'In defense of the contract at will' (1984) 51 *University of Chicago Law Review* 947. For an introduction to new institutionalism, see S. Deakin and F. Wilkinson, 'Labour law and economic theory: a reappraisal', in H. Collins *et al.* (eds.), *Legal Regulation of the Employment Relation* (2000), and Deakin and Wilkinson, *The Law of the Labour Market: Industrialization, Employment and Legal Evolution* (2005), especially Chapter 5. How different do you think the two camps really are? For example, can the new institutionalists afford to ignore the costs of the laws they are advocating? For a detailed comparison, see B.E. Kaufman, 'Labor law and employment regulation: neoclassical and institutional perspectives', *Andrew Young School of Policy Studies Research Paper Series* (July 2008), Working Paper 08–27.

The conflict between neoclassical economics and the traditional ideology of labour law is not difficult to grasp. Compare Posner or Epstein, above, with (for example) K.W. Wedderburn, 'Labour law and the individual in post-industrial societies', in K.W. Wedderburn *et al.* (eds.), *Labour Law in Post-Industrial Societies* (1994). But are labour lawyers any more likely to embrace the ideas of the new institutionalists? See F. von Prondzynksi, 'Labour law as business facilitator', in Collins *et al.*, *Legal Regulation of the Employment Relation*, cited above, for discussion.

3

Human rights perspectives on labour law

As we saw in Chapter 1, human rights perspectives on labour law first gained ground in the 1970s. Commentators began to realise that collective bargaining could not provide all the protection workers needed. In the 1980s, labour rights became highly controversial. The government was keen to uphold workers' rights in some settings but not in others. It wanted to enforce individuals' rights against trade unions (arguing that unions treated individuals unfairly), but it did not want to enforce individuals' rights against firms (because it believed in keeping the labour market as free of regulation as possible). Today, rights perspectives on labour law are very common in the literature. Many commentators use rights language in order to evaluate the current law, and in doing so they draw heavily on international and regional standards. The HRA 1998 has reinforced the rights perspective by giving greater effect to some human rights in English law.

This chapter will begin with a historical introduction to the development of human rights, focusing in particular on labour rights. This will give you an overview of the international and regional human rights instruments that will be discussed throughout the book. The second section of the chapter will turn to the complex questions of interpretation surrounding human rights: who can claim a right and against whom can they bring their claim? What exactly does any given right protect? And how (if at all) can we justify interfering with a right?

A brief overview of human rights

Since much of the discussion in this book will involve detailed examination of particular human rights, it is helpful to start with an overview of international and European human rights law. We will look first at the historical development of human rights, before outlining the two main categories of rights: civil and political, and economic and social. We will also examine the important debate about the status of these two groups of rights.

Historical development

The first major attempts to identify a list of human rights came at the end of the eighteenth century in the American Bill of Rights and the French Declaration of

the Rights of Man and Citizen.[1] Responding to years of repression by tyranni-
cal rulers, the drafters of these documents sought to lay down those rights that
would protect individuals' liberty in the future. They tried to ensure that majority rule in the new democratic states they were creating would not result in the
oppression of minorities. But despite these developments at the national level, it
was many years before human rights became an accepted part of international
law. This was largely because of the emphasis placed by international law on the
sovereignty of states.[2] What went on within a state was the concern of that state's
government and no-one else. Over time, exceptions to this principle began to
develop. One of the most significant for labour law purposes is the creation, in
1919, of the International Labour Office, the predecessor of the modern ILO,
with the task of developing international labour standards.[3] Sceptics point out
that this may have been driven by the concern of some states to protect their own
industries against competition from firms established in states with lower labour
standards. Nevertheless, the idea that international law could have something to
say about the lives of individuals was established.

The main impetus for the development of modern international human rights
law was the Second World War. Hitler's rise to power demonstrated that the democratic process was not necessarily sufficient to guard against the rise of tyranny
and oppression. After the war, the international community sought to draft human
rights instruments with a view to ensuring that the horror of fascism and the
Holocaust could never happen again. The UN Charter states that one of the purposes of the UN is to uphold respect for human rights.[4] However, it did not prove
possible to include a statement of rights in the Charter because the governments
responsible for its drafting could not agree on the content of any such statement.
In 1948, the UN General Assembly adopted the Universal Declaration of Human
Rights, a non-binding statement of both civil and political, and economic and
social rights.[5] This was eventually followed by two treaties (legally binding agreements between states) which are the foundation for modern international human
rights law: the International Covenant on Civil and Political Rights (ICCPR)[6] and
the International Covenant on Economic, Social and Cultural Rights (ICESCR),[7]
both of 1966. In the field of labour law, the ILO became established after the war

---

1 Both date from 1789. The American Bill of Rights was ratified two years later, in 1791.
2 L. Henkin, 'International law: politics, values and functions' (1989) 216 *Collected Courses of Hague Academy of International Law*, pp. 208–26.
3 See, generally, H.G. Bartolomei de la Cruz, G. von Potobsky and L. Swepston, *The International Labour Organisation: The International Standards System and Basic Human Rights* (1996), Chapter 1.
4 UN Charter, Art. 1.
5 G.A. Resolution 217A (III), G.A.O.R., 3rd Sess., Part I, Resolutions, p. 71. See, generally, J. Morsink, *The Universal Declaration of Human Rights: Origins, Drafting and Intent* (1999).
6 (1967) 999 UNTS 171. See, generally, L. Henkin (ed.), *The International Bill of Rights: The Covenant on Civil and Political Rights* (1981).
7 (1967) 993 UNTS 3. See, generally, M.C.R. Craven, *The International Covenant on Economic, Social and Cultural Rights: A Perspective on its Development* (1995).

as a specialist agency of the UN, and continued its work of developing and enforcing international labour standards. Developments in human rights at the international level were paralleled by similar moves at the European level, where the concern to avoid a recurrence of the war and the events leading up to it was particularly acute. In 1950, the European Convention on Human Rights, a statement of civil and political rights, came into force.[8] This was followed in 1961 by a statement of economic and social rights in the shape of the European Social Charter (ESC).[9] Both instruments operate under the auspices of the Council of Europe, an organisation which is entirely separate from the EU.

In recent years, there has been a growing interest in revising and updating some of these traditional statements of human rights. Some rights, as originally drafted, have come to seem outdated because of changes in social attitudes. And it has been argued that there are gaps in the protection on offer: issues that were not originally addressed are now regarded as highly important. Both these factors have been particularly relevant in the case of women's rights. A concern to improve the international protection of women's rights led to the development of the Convention on the Elimination of All Forms of Discrimination Against Women (CEDAW), which entered into force in 1981.[10] In 1996, the ESC was revised.[11] The new version contains a number of changes from the original, many of which are concerned with promoting the rights of women.

Most recently, a new player has emerged on the human rights scene, in the shape of the EU. Because the EC as originally conceived was an economic union, the Treaty of Rome 1957 contained hardly any references to human rights, with the notable exception of the right of men and women to equal pay contained in Article 119. Over the years, the Community has acquired an increasingly important role in social policy and has been an important source of protection for workers' rights. The ECJ has developed a human rights jurisprudence, with a view to ensuring that the EU's activities do not infringe citizens' rights.[12] In 2000, the Member States proclaimed the EU Charter of Fundamental Rights, a document which combines civil and political rights with a comprehensive statement of economic and social rights.[13] This is not the EU's first statement of human rights, nor is it legally binding; but it is highly significant because (if agreement can be reached) it may eventually become binding as part of the EU's treaty architecture. It is also of interest as a very up-to-date statement of human rights.

---

8 See, generally, C. Ovey and R.C.A. White, *The European Convention on Human Rights* (4th edn., 2006).

9 See, generally, D.J. Harris, *The European Social Charter* (1984).

10 1249 UNTS 13. See A. Byrnes, 'Toward more effective enforcement of women's human rights through the use of international human rights law and procedures', and R.J. Cook, 'State accountability under the Convention on the Elimination of All Forms of Discrimination Against Women', in R.J. Cook (ed.), *Human Rights of Women* (1994).

11 The UK has ratified the original version but not the revised version.

12 See, generally, P. Craig and G. de Búrca, *EU Law: Text, Cases and Materials* (4th edn., 2008), Chapter 11.

13 Ibid., pp. 412–18.

Types of rights

It will be apparent from the discussion above that the international community has, from an early stage, divided rights into two categories: civil and political, and economic, social and cultural. Civil and political rights focus on the individual in his or her capacity as the citizen of a liberal democracy. They protect the individual against the state, through rights not to be tortured or subjected to an unfair trial. And they enable the individual to take part in the democratic process, through rights to freedom of expression and to vote. Economic and social rights focus on the material needs of the individual. They include rights to health care, housing, social security, a living wage, reasonable limits on working hours and so on. Some aspects of labour law do have links to citizenship: freedom to associate with others and form groups can cover both political parties and trade unions. But economic and social rights clearly have the greatest relevance to workers.

The split between civil and political rights and economic and social rights occurred largely for political reasons. In the 1960s, Communist governments argued that economic and social rights were the most important kind, whereas Western liberal democracies placed the highest value on civil and political rights. The only way to achieve agreement on rights at the international level was to separate the two types, which explains the existence of two instruments, the ICCPR and the ICESCR. Although the UN has always asserted that the two types of rights are 'indivisible' and of equal status, the debate about their relative worth continues today.

One significant difference between the two types lies in the kind of action the state must take in order to protect them.[14] Civil and political rights can, in general, be secured by legislation which prohibits their infringement. A right not to be tortured can be protected by a ban on torture. Economic and social rights usually require positive action – and expenditure – by the state. To respect the right to health care, the state must have mechanisms in place for providing medical treatment to those who cannot afford to pay for it. This distinction is usually recognised in the drafting of human rights instruments. For example, the ICCPR requires states 'to give effect to' civil and political rights, whereas the ICESCR imposes, for the most part, a weaker obligation to 'take steps … with a view to achieving progressively the full realisation of the rights' it contains.[15]

Two further distinctions between the two types of rights flow from this. The first is that the realisation of economic and social rights depends on a state's level of development, whereas (in theory at least) it should be possible for even the poorest state to uphold civil and political rights. Since one of the characteristics of human rights is that they are 'universal' – applicable to everyone regardless of

---

14 These arguments are challenged by S. Fredman, *Human Rights Transformed* (2008).
15 Where a right does not require expenditure (such as ICESCR, Art. 8), states are expected to give immediate effect to it.

circumstances – this has led many commentators to question whether economic and social rights are truly worthy of the name. Against this, it can be argued that the rights never cease to apply: it is just that their content varies according to the wealth of the state.

The second distinction between the two types of right relates to their justiciability: in other words, whether they can be applied by courts. We expect courts to apply rights because they are meant to act as a limitation on what the executive and legislative branches of government are permitted to do. Civil and political rights are suitable for adjudication in court because they raise relatively straightforward questions of compliance. Economic and social rights are more problematic because of the variability of their content. A court is not well-placed to decide whether the government should allocate its resources to housing or to health care. It does not have the expertise or the democratic legitimacy to make these decisions. However, the difficulties of adjudicating on economic and social rights can be exaggerated.[16] Courts can decide cases in which the state has the resources but has chosen not to make them available. Courts can even decide cases involving scarce resources by asking whether the state has made *reasonable* efforts to promote individuals' rights.

There are at least three competing views on these categories of rights. The most radical form of scepticism would confine the term 'right' to civil and political rights, denying this status to all economic and social rights because of their vagueness and lack of universality and justiciability. It is often argued that if individuals have civil and political rights, they will be able to secure protection for their economic and social interests through the democratic process. Thus, there is no need to complicate the picture by giving these interests the status of rights. A more moderate form of scepticism would allow that economic and social rights are genuine rights, but would claim that they are less fundamental than civil and political rights. They are something to aspire to, whereas civil and political rights must be complied with. A third school of thought – that adopted by the UN itself – argues for the 'indivisibility' of human rights: the rights in both categories are human rights and have equal status. Theorists who take this view emphasise the importance of people's material needs: a person who is homeless or starving would probably value a right to shelter or food more highly than the right to vote.

Civil and political rights

The two most important civil and political rights of relevance to labour law are freedom of association and the right not to be discriminated against. Freedom of association features in the UN Universal Declaration of Human Rights (Art.

---

16 The South African courts do adjudicate on these issues. Leading cases include *Soobramoney v. Minister of Health* [1998] (1) SA 765 (CC); *Republic of South Africa v. Grootboom* [2001] (1) SA 46 (CC); and *Minister of Health v. TAC* [2002] (5) SA 721 (CC). For discussion, see Fredman, *Human Rights Transformed*, pp. 113–23.

23(4)), the ICCPR (Art. 22) and the ECHR (Art. 11). The ECHR definition is typical: 'Everyone has the right to freedom of peaceful assembly and to freedom of
association with others, including the right to form and to join trade unions for
the protection of his interests'. There are two important features to note about
the civil and political right to freedom of association. First, it tends to include a
right to refuse to be a member of an association alongside the right to be a member. This has been an important feature of the case law of the European Court
of Human Rights (ECtHR).[17] Second, the civil and political rights formulation
(unlike that in economic and social rights documents) does not usually specify
any consequential rights, such as a right to engage in collective bargaining or a
right to strike. Applicants to the ECtHR have sought to argue that the phrase 'for
the protection of his interests' implicitly includes these consequential rights, but
despite early indications that this interpretation would be supported, later cases
have been relatively cautious.[18]

The right not to be discriminated against features in almost every human
rights document, whether civil and political or economic and social. Article 26
of the ICCPR contains a strong anti-discrimination right:

> All persons are equal before the law and are entitled without any discrimina-
> tion to the equal protection of the law. In this respect, the law shall prohibit any
> discrimination and guarantee to all persons equal and effective protection against
> discrimination on any ground such as race, colour, sex, language, religion, political
> or other opinion, national or social origin, property, birth or other status.

This is much more clearly drafted than its equivalent in the Universal Declaration,
Article 7. Older human rights documents tend not to cover all the grounds of
discrimination that are regarded as unacceptable in modern society. Article 21(1)
of the EU Charter of Fundamental Rights is a good illustration of how the right
might be updated:

> Any discrimination based on any ground such as sex, race, colour, ethnic or social
> origin, genetic features, language, religion or belief, political or any other opinion,
> membership of a national minority, property, birth, disability, age or sexual orienta-
> tion shall be prohibited.

Some instruments contain a right not to be discriminated against which applies
only to the human rights contained in the instrument itself. This is true of
Article 2(2) of the ICESCR and Article 14 of the ECHR, so it cuts across the
divide between civil and political rights and economic and social rights. Under
this formulation, the victim of discrimination cannot complain unless one of his
or her other rights has been violated in a discriminatory manner. For example,
a person dismissed from employment as a result of discrimination would have
no grounds of complaint under Article 14 ECHR because there is no right in the

---

17 *Sorensen v. Denmark* (2008) 46 EHRR 29.   18 See Chapters 10 and 12.

Convention covering dismissal. Protocol 12 to the ECHR, which came into force in 2005, protects a free-standing right not to be discriminated against, but this has not been ratified by the UK.

Civil and political rights instruments do contain some other rights of relevance to labour law. These include freedom of religion,[19] freedom of expression[20] and freedom of assembly.[21]

Economic and social rights

For ease of exposition, economic and social rights will be considered in two groups: 'traditional' and 'modern'. The modern category will include those rights found only in the most recent instruments, such as the EU Charter of Fundamental Rights and the revised ESC 1996. We will look first at those traditional rights found in the older economic and social rights instruments, such as the ICESCR and the ESC 1961, as well as the recent instruments.

Like civil and political rights instruments, economic and social rights instruments protect freedom of association. But they usually specify in some detail what this means. Article 8 of the ICESCR protects the right to form and join trade unions. Article 8(1)(b) protects the 'right of trade unions to establish national federations or confederations', and, most significantly, Article 8(1)(d) protects 'the right to strike, provided that it is exercised in conformity with the laws of the particular country'. The ESC 1961 addresses similar issues in Articles 5 and 6, both of which have been accepted by the UK and have remained unchanged in the revised ESC 1996. Article 5 protects 'the freedom of workers and employers to form local, national or international organisations for the protection of their economic and social interests and to join those organisations'. Article 6 addresses collective bargaining in some detail. It requires governments to promote both consultation and collective bargaining, and to provide a mechanism for conciliation and voluntary arbitration to settle disputes. It also requires governments to respect 'the right of workers and employers to collective action in cases of conflicts of interest, including the right to strike, subject to obligations that might arise out of collective agreements previously entered into'. For many labour lawyers, these rights are more significant than those in civil and political rights instruments. They clearly acknowledge that effective trade union action requires more than just a right to be a member.

Economic and social rights instruments usually contain a right to work. This is true of the UN Universal Declaration (Art. 23(1)), the ICESCR (Art. 6) and the ESC 1961 (Art. 1). Although this may sound like the most important labour law right there could possibly be, it is in fact directed at the government's economic and education policies rather than at employers. Thus, Article 1 of the ESC 1961

---

19 See, for example, Art. 18 ICCPR; Art. 9 ECHR.
20 See, for example, Art. 19 ICCPR; Art. 10 ECHR.
21 See, for example, Art. 21 ICCPR; Art. 11 ECHR.

requires signatories to promote full employment and to provide vocational guidance and training.

More significant are the rights concerning wages and working conditions. Article 23(3) of the UN Universal Declaration states that 'everyone who works has the right to just and favourable remuneration ensuring for himself and his family an existence worthy of human dignity, and supplemented, if necessary, by other means of social protection'. This is echoed in Article 7 of the ICESCR and Article 4 of the ESC 1961 (which remains unchanged in the 1996 revision). Article 23(2) of the Universal Declaration states that 'everyone, without any discrimination, has the right to equal pay for equal work'. This too is repeated in the ICESCR (Art. 7) and the ESC 1961 (Art. 4(3)). The UK did not accept the latter obligation because UK law did not conform to it when the ESC was ratified in 1962.

Traditional economic and social rights instruments usually afford workers some rights in relation to working conditions. Article 2 of the ESC 1961 addresses the right to 'just conditions of work', focusing in particular on the provision of paid holidays (accepted by the UK) and the limitation of working hours (not accepted by the UK). Article 7 of the ICESCR and Article 24 of the Universal Declaration contain similar obligations. The ICESCR (Art. 7) and the ESC 1961 (Art. 3) also give workers a right to safe and healthy working conditions.

The EU Charter of Fundamental Rights (2000) and the revised ESC 1996 contain versions of all the rights we have been considering so far, but they also add some new rights which we will label 'modern' economic and social rights. In the realm of individual employment rights, one of the most significant additions is the right not to be unfairly dismissed. Article 4(4) of the ESC 1961 contains an obligation to ensure that workers receive 'reasonable' notice if their employment is to be terminated, but Article 24 of the ESC 1996 goes much further, requiring states to protect the right of workers not to be arbitrarily dismissed and to ensure that any worker who is so dismissed can obtain compensation. Article 30 of the EU Charter states that 'every worker has the right to protection against unjustified dismissal'. Article 26 of the ESC 1996 protects the right to dignity at work, and applies both to sexual harassment and to other forms of bullying ('recurrent reprehensible or distinctly negative and offensive actions directed against individual workers in the workplace or in relation to work'). The EU Charter contains a general reference to working conditions which protect a worker's dignity (Art. 31). This might be interpreted to cover bullying, but it does not spell out a detailed right not to be harassed.

Both instruments contain equality rights which are much broader than the traditional right to equal pay. Article 23 of the EU Charter states that 'equality between men and women must be ensured in all areas, including employment, work and pay'. The Article also allows positive action to improve the position of the under-represented sex in any particular situation. Article 20 of the ESC 1996 also contains a general right to equal treatment without discrimination on grounds of sex in all aspects of the employment relationship. These generous equality rights are coupled with significant new rights for working parents, both male and female. Article 33(2) of the EU Charter provides:

> To reconcile family and professional life, everyone shall have the right to protection from dismissal for a reason connected with maternity and the right to paid maternity leave and to parental leave following the birth or adoption of a child.

The ESC 1961 was unique among traditional instruments in providing a right to maternity leave (Art. 8). This was substantially amended in 1996 so that it focuses solely on protecting pregnant women and nursing mothers. Outdated references to protecting all women engaged in night work or dangerous work have been removed. Article 27 of the ESC 1996 promotes equal treatment between men and women workers with family responsibilities and those without. Signatory states are obliged to promote the provision of childcare facilities, to ensure that parental leave is available, and to ensure that workers cannot be dismissed solely on the ground of their childcare responsibilities.

Finally, the modern economic and social rights instruments include rights for workers to be informed and consulted within the firm. As Chapter 10 will explain, some European countries have a long tradition of 'works councils', groups of employee representatives who meet regularly with the employer to discuss a range of workplace issues. There is no equivalent tradition in the UK because of the policy of collective laissez-faire outlined in Chapter 1. The most general right in the ESC 1996 is Article 21, which requires states to ensure that consultation takes place regularly on the financial position of the undertaking, and, when necessary, on important business decisions that might affect workers' interests. Article 29 offers a more specific right to consultation in the event of collective redundancies. Article 28 addresses the rights of workers' representatives, requiring that they should have the facilities they need to carry out their role and that they should be protected from discriminatory treatment. Finally, Article 22 requires states to protect the right of workers to take part in the determination and improvement of their working conditions and working environment, including health and safety issues and social facilities. The EU Charter (Art. 27) contains a general right to information and consultation to be elaborated in accordance with relevant Community and national law.

International human rights instruments and domestic law

Chapter 4 will demonstrate that there is an important relationship between these various international and regional instruments and domestic law. The development of new standards at the international level may lead to changes in English law, as the government makes a commitment on the international level to bring domestic law into compliance. Or the development of new standards in English law may lead the government to put pressure on other countries to adopt the same standards so that UK firms do not suffer a competitive disadvantage in comparison to their foreign counterparts. More generally, and perhaps most importantly for our purposes, international human rights standards are often used by commentators as a set of benchmarks against which to measure domestic law. Those that have been agreed in Europe carry weight because they show what countries with similar economic and social contexts consider to be appropriate protection for workers. Those that have been agreed internationally are, arguably, even more powerful because they reflect the consensus of countries facing different economic circumstances and cultural norms. However, despite the strong rhetorical force which the label 'right' instantly grants, we must scrutinise rights arguments – whether made by governments or by commentators – with care. This is because any given right is open to a variety of different interpretations.

Interpreting rights

Our discussion of the interpretation of rights will be divided into four topics. The first two relate to the people involved: who can claim a right and against whom can the right be claimed? The second two relate to the content of the right in question: what exactly does the right protect and what weight does it carry in argument? It is impossible to provide definitive answers to these questions: the answers depend on the right we are considering and the context in which it is being applied. The identity of the right-holder might be quite different for the right not to be discriminated against and the right to strike, and the content of the right to strike might vary as between the ILO jurisprudence and the decisions of the House of Lords. But it is important to understand that these questions exist and that they need to be asked in any rights debate. This will help you to make critical use of the rights literature.

Right-holders

Most of the time, it is obvious who can claim a right. If a woman is refused a job because of her sex, she can claim that her individual right not to be discriminated against has been violated. The position is more complicated where the right is one that could belong to an individual or to a group. The right to strike is a good example. Does it belong to a group, such as a trade union, or to each worker as an individual?

The answer depends in part on the underlying basis of the right to strike: why do we give people a right to strike in the first place?[22] One view is that the right to strike is essential to support collective bargaining by trade unions. When union leaders go to the employer with their pay demands, they need to have some kind of threat in order to persuade the employer to listen to them. Strike action constitutes that threat. On this basis, strike action is a right for trade unions: for groups of workers, not individuals. On another view, however, the right to strike is an individual right to stop work in order to protest at the employer's actions.

---

22 See Chapter 10.

It might be based on one of a number of rights traditionally held by individuals, such as freedom of expression. On this view, every individual would have the right to strike, regardless of whether or not a union was involved.

The identity of the right-holder is particularly important in the situation in which a union has organised a strike but some members do not want to take part.[23] If the right belongs to individuals, they have a choice about whether or not to exercise it. It would be wrong for anyone to compel them to exercise their right to strike when they have expressed a preference for going to work. If the right belongs to the union, however, the position can be interpreted differently. In order to exercise its right to strike, the union can only act through its members. It can be argued that the strike will not be effective unless all the members take part. Therefore, the union should be permitted to discipline its members if they refuse to strike.

It is fair to say that group rights are a relatively new development in international law. Traditionally, theorists have assumed that rights would be held by individuals. This helps to explain why many labour lawyers are sceptical about human rights approaches to their subject.[24] They fear that a human rights argument will involve giving more power to individuals at the expense of trade unions. They argue that although this may seem beneficial to individuals, it harms them over the longer term. This is because groups of workers in trade unions can balance out the employer's superior economic strength; individuals cannot do so, however many rights the law gives them.

Rights against whom?

The international and regional instruments we considered earlier impose obligations on the state to protect and promote the rights they contain. To comply with these obligations, the state may need to impose duties on private individuals. For example, the right not to be discriminated against requires legislation to ensure that employers, landlords, retailers and other private individuals do not discriminate. It is not enough for the state itself to refrain from discriminating. But there is a broader debate about whether human rights themselves should be regarded as rights against everyone (with 'horizontal' effect) or as rights against the state (with 'vertical' effect only). This debate has important practical ramifications when a state enacts a set of human rights guarantees.

The emphasis on rights as claims against the state reflects, in large measure, the historical development of human rights. Civil and political rights were a response to the emergence of national governments with real power to intervene in their citizens' actions. The state was seen as the most likely candidate to interfere with individuals' freedom of speech or to take away their right to vote. Economic and social rights are also focused on the state. The concern here was

23 See Chapter 11.
24 See, for example, K.D. Ewing, 'The Human Rights Act and labour law' (1998) 27 *ILJ* 275.

that the state might provide citizenship rights to individuals while leaving them in poverty and ignorance. The rights set out a model of how the state should use its wealth.

The idea that rights should in themselves be enforceable against private individuals has its origins in the modern concern with power in all its guises. Today, it is widely acknowledged that governments are not the only powerful institutions in society.[25] Indeed, other institutions – large multinational corporations, for example – may wield more power than some governments. Human rights activists have therefore sought to impose the responsibility for respecting human rights on anyone who might violate them. From an employee's point of view, it does not matter whether he or she is forbidden to join a trade union by a government decree outlawing collective action or by a threat from the employer that all union members will be dismissed. Both actions violate the right to freedom of association.

Against this, it can be argued that it is unfair to subject private individuals to the obligation to comply with human rights guarantees when they are broadly framed and difficult to interpret. It is a breach of the Rule of Law requirement that individuals should be able to understand the law and use it to plan their lives.[26] The government should take responsibility for interpreting human rights and ensuring that they are given effect in the ordinary law. Individuals should be able to comply with human rights simply by acting lawfully. Any breaches of human rights by private parties should be remedied by the government.

This debate is of particular relevance to labour law because workers' rights are likely to be violated by employers, most of whom are private individuals or firms. When looking at particular human rights guarantees, particularly in domestic law, it is important to ask whether or not they can be enforced against private parties. In Chapter 4, we will consider this issue in relation to the HRA 1998.

Scope

Perhaps the most important issue of interpretation in human rights is scope: what exactly does each human right protect? Does the right to strike protect all strikes, whatever their motivation? Does the right not to be unfairly dismissed apply when the employee has been at fault? Does the right not to be discriminated against apply to discrimination on the grounds of a person's genetic features? All these questions will be discussed in later chapters. For now, we will examine some general points about interpreting rights. The important message is that there are no simple answers.

A first point to note is that most international human rights instruments have a mechanism for interpretation. Often, this takes the form of a court or commission which can hear complaints from groups or individuals within signatory

25 For discussion, see D. Oliver, *Common Values and the Public–Private Divide* (1999), pp. 31–7.
26 J. Raz, 'The Rule of Law and its virtue' (1977) 93 *LQR* 195.

states who feel that their rights have been violated. The court or commission's role is to interpret the human right in question and to apply it to the case. These interpretations have considerable authority as 'official' statements of the meaning of a right in a particular instrument. For example, the European Committee of Social Rights interprets the ESC. It assesses whether states' regular reports show that they are in compliance, and hears complaints from bodies such as trade unions under the collective complaints procedure. The ECtHR has power to adjudicate individual claims that signatory states have violated Convention rights, and to award compensation. The various interpretative bodies do not exist in a vacuum: they often refer to each other's interpretations. For example, the ECtHR sometimes refers to ESC jurisprudence when deciding cases on trade union rights.[27]

With many international instruments, it is possible to gain access to the *travaux préparatoires* – documents which explain the process of drafting and the intentions of the drafters. The *travaux* may be of use when a word or phrase is ambiguous, by giving an indication of what the drafters had in mind.[28] However, there are problems. One is that international instruments are often deliberately ambiguous because the many signatories cannot agree on a definite interpretation. The *travaux* may just show that there was a dispute about the meaning of a particular provision. Another is that when older instruments are applied to modern problems, the *travaux* may not offer any guidance. The question whether an older guarantee against discrimination should cover discrimination on the grounds of a person's genetic features is unlikely to have been dealt with in the *travaux*. Human rights instruments are usually treated as 'living' documents which can be adapted to new circumstances and are not confined to the meanings originally intended by the drafters.[29]

When interpreting a human rights guarantee, it is particularly important to have regard to the purpose being served by the right: what are we using it to protect? It is impossible to interpret human rights texts without getting into a discussion of their underlying values. Differences of opinion between those interpreting human rights – whether officially or as commentators – often stem from differences in identifying and understanding those underlying values. One basis commonly advanced for human rights is that they preserve individuals' liberty or autonomy.[30] Individuals should be able to make choices about their lives with the minimum of interference from other people, and should be able to make plans in a relatively stable and well-ordered society. Rights to freedom of expression and religion give individuals a private sphere within which they can decide, without interference, what to say and what to believe. Another possible basis for

27 See, for example, *ASLEF* v. *UK* (2007) 45 EHRR 34.
28 See the Vienna Convention on the Law of Treaties (1969) 1155 UNTS 331, Arts. 31 and 32.
29 See, for example, *Tyrer* v. *UK* (1979–80) 2 EHRR 1, p. 10.
30 H.L.A. Hart, 'Bentham on legal rights', in A.W.B. Simpson (ed.), *Oxford Essays in Jurisprudence: Second Series* (1973).

human rights is that they protect individuals' dignity.[31] Human rights are needed to ensure that each individual is treated with equal concern and respect by society. The right not to be discriminated against is an obvious example of this. It prevents us from treating individuals differently on the basis of characteristics that do not make them any less worthy of our respect.

Our particular concern in this book will be with labour rights. Many labour rights are human rights applied in a labour relations setting. As a result, they have the same underlying justification. The right not to be discriminated against by an employer is not very different from the right not to be discriminated against by government officials. But there are some rights which only apply in labour law. Some of the economic and social rights, like the right to a fair wage or to paid holidays, are examples of this. These rights can be justified either in a labour-specific way or in a more general way. For example, it could be argued that the right to a fair wage stems from the inequality of bargaining power that usually exists between worker and employer. The worker cannot bargain for a fair wage and therefore needs the protection of the law to prevent exploitation by the employer. That would be a labour-specific justification. A more general justification would appeal to a broader value such as dignity. Here, the argument would be that we can put a minimum value on labour. Any worker who is made to work for less is being treated as if he or she is less worthy of concern and respect than other people. His or her dignity is violated. We shall see in later chapters that our choice of justification for labour rights can have important consequences for their interpretation. In general, the choice of a broader justification enables labour lawyers to bolster their arguments with powerful ideals that have widespread support. But sometimes a labour-specific justification is preferable because ideals drawn from other spheres of activity may have unintended consequences in labour law.

The interpretation of human rights is a complex and challenging task which provokes controversy among and between human rights bodies, governments and commentators. When looking at competing interpretations it is important to examine the underlying justification being offered for the right in question. This is also relevant when assessing whether or not an interference with the right can be justified, and it is to this that we will now turn.

Weight

Rights carry special weight in political argument. If they had the same status as any other consideration, there would be no point in attaching the label 'right'. They could easily be overridden by other arguments. At the same time, however, it is clear that rights are not absolute. A right cannot be exercised without any regard to the costs it might be imposing on others. For each right, we need to decide to what extent interferences or exceptions can be permitted.

---

31 R.M. Dworkin, *A Matter of Principle* (1985), Chapter 17.

Let us begin by examining the role of rights in political argument. To do this, we need a general theory of how political decisions are made. Utilitarianism is a useful starting point. Utilitarianism focuses on the consequences of actions. The early utilitarians evaluated actions in terms of how much pleasure and pain they would give.[32] Thus, they argued that a particular action should be taken where it maximised pleasure and minimised pain in society. More modern versions usually rephrase this in terms of the satisfaction of people's preferences: a particular action should be taken when it will satisfy the largest number of preferences. Utilitarians are often classified as 'act-utilitarians' or 'rule-utilitarians'. Act-utilitarians weigh up the consequences of each proposed action taken on its own.[33] Rule-utilitarians examine each proposed action in the light of general rules which have been found in the past to maximise pleasure and minimise pain.[34] Rule-utilitarianism is often regarded as more practical than act-utilitarianism because less effort needs to be put into each individual decision.[35] But it is not entirely convincing. If a rule-utilitarian insists on keeping to a rule even if it will lead to pain in a particular case, he or she is no longer a true utilitarian examining the consequences of his or her actions. If the rule-utilitarian disregards the rule, his or her approach is no different to that of an act-utilitarian who would decide each case on its merits, taking into account the general benefit to society that arises if people usually comply with rules.

A common criticism of utilitarianism is that it allows substantial harm to be caused to a few individuals, provided that the general welfare is improved. Is the happiness of the many sufficient to outweigh the misery of the few? To use a classic example, imagine that a terrorist has planted a bomb somewhere in a busy city centre, and will only reveal its exact location if tortured. The torture will cause profound misery for the terrorist and for his or her torturers. Nevertheless, an act-utilitarian would probably carry out the torture, on the basis that the pain caused to the terrorist and the torturers would be outweighed by the pleasure given to those who were evacuated before the bomb went off. A rule-utilitarian might manage to avoid this solution. He or she could argue that there was a general rule that torture by the state was unacceptable, which should be upheld regardless of the circumstances. But this falls into the trap, noted above, of abandoning utilitarianism's basic focus on the consequences of actions. In any event, the critics of utilitarianism feel that there is something missing from

---

32 J. Bentham, *An Introduction to the Principles of Morals and Legislation* (1876; ed. J.H. Burns, H.L.A. Hart and F. Rosen, 1996), Chapter 1; J.S. Mill, *Utilitarianism* (1863; ed. R. Crisp, 1998), Chapter 2.

33 Bentham and Mill are usually regarded as act-utilitarians, though for a rule-utilitarian interpretation of Mill, see J.O. Urmston, 'The interpretation of the moral philosophy of J.S. Mill' (1953) 3 *Philosophical Quarterly* 33.

34 See, generally, B. Hooker, 'Rule-consequentialism, incoherence, fairness' (1995) 95 *Proceedings of the Aristotelian Society* 19.

35 R.M. Hare, 'Ethical Theory and Utilitarianism', in H.D. Lewis (ed.), *Contemporary British Philosophy* (4th series, 1976).

this argument. They argue that utilitarianism should be qualified by respect for people's *rights*.

There are two main theories about the role that rights should play. On the first theory, rights should have special weight in the utilitarian calculation in that they should count for more than other kinds of interests. However, a right could be outweighed by a large number of ordinary interests. On the second theory, rights should have priority over other kinds of interests and could not be outweighed by them, however many of them there were. Dworkin is the most famous exponent of the second view:

> Individual rights are political trumps[36] held by individuals. Individuals have rights when, for some reason, a collective goal is not a sufficient justification for denying them what they wish, as individuals, to have or to do, or not a sufficient justification for imposing some loss or injury upon them.[37]

These 'rights as trumps' almost always outweigh ordinary interests, save in exceptional cases when it is necessary to 'prevent a catastrophe'.[38]

However, the difference between the two theories may not be so great as it seems. Dworkin only accords 'trumps' status to fundamental rights. He accepts that other, lesser rights can be limited 'to obtain a clear and major public benefit'.[39] Thus, his approach to non-fundamental rights is exactly the same as that adopted by theorists who take the first view. So both camps accept that rights can be outweighed by ordinary interests. The only difference between them is that those who take the second view, like Dworkin, argue that there is a small category of fundamental rights to which this basic rule does not apply.

Whichever theory we adopt, we need to attribute some value or weight to the right under consideration. This is because we need to decide how many ordinary interests are needed on the other side of the scales in order to outweigh it. And if we are adopting Dworkin's view, we also need to know whether the right is in the 'fundamental' category, so that it cannot be outweighed at all. But how do we decide how important a particular right is? One factor to take into account is the underlying rationale of the right. If the right is protecting a person against a very serious form of harm – being tortured, for example – we might consider it to be more important (or more likely to be 'fundamental') than a right that is protecting a person against a lesser form of harm, such as being made to work long hours. Another factor to look at is whether any theorists or human rights organisations have come up with a helpful classification. For example, some attempt

---

36 This metaphor is from card games. A trump card is one that beats cards from other suits even though its numerical value is lower. So if hearts are trumps, the two of hearts will beat a high-value card like the king of spades.
37 R. Dworkin, *Taking Rights Seriously* (2ⁿᵈ impression with appendix, 1978), p. xi.
38 Ibid., p. 191.
39 Ibid.

has been made by the ILO to identify fundamental labour rights.[40] It has chosen, among others, the right not to be discriminated against and the right to freedom of association. It has argued that these rights represent part of the bare minimum that should be upheld by all states, regardless of their circumstances. But all such classifications can be contested. We could argue, for example, that the right to a minimum wage is just as important because it safeguards workers' dignity and protects them from exploitation. In short, according weight to a particular right always involves a highly controversial value judgement.

On the other side of the scales (unless we have a Dworkinian fundamental right to uphold) there are 'ordinary interests'. What are these ordinary interests? In labour law, they are often made up of arguments about the economic impact of a particular right on the employer and on the economy. Let us take the right to equal pay as an example. This right allows a woman to claim that she is doing the same job as a man and should be paid the same wage. If her claim is success-ful, the employer's wage bill will rise because it will be obliged to pay her more. The employer will have to increase the price of its products and may lose market share. The crucial question is whether the woman's right to equal treatment is sufficient to outweigh the potential harm to the employer. Labour lawyers are sometimes tempted to be very dismissive of employers' claims, but some caution is required because a downturn in the employer's business may affect the pay and prospects of workers as well as the employer's profits. In this case, it seems likely that the right to equal pay would prevail, because it is of considerable importance in combating discriminatory treatment. Courts and commentators struggle with these issues all the time.

The need to weigh rights against ordinary interests helps to demonstrate why labour lawyers have been so interested in the work of those economists who iden-tify positive benefits to firms in complying with labour rights. Their arguments often suggest that a new labour right will not impose costs on employers. This means that the right can simply be enforced without weighing it against ordinary interests. However, as we saw in Chapter 2, these economic arguments are con-troversial and may not always be able to demonstrate that a right will benefit *all* firms. It is rare to find a situation in which there are no arguments at all against a particular right. Labour lawyers may still need to be able to justify rights for their own sake and to demonstrate that they outweigh cost considerations.

Sometimes, we find that there are rights on *both* sides of the weighing scales. An obvious example is where one person's right to freedom of expression might infringe another person's right to respect for his or her privacy. Theorists in both camps agree that in this situation, one right must give way to the other. There is no other option. We simply have to make a choice about which right to pro-tect. The utilitarian calculus is helpful here because it encourages us to make the choice that will cause the lesser amount of suffering. In labour law, there are

40 ILO Declaration on Fundamental Principles and Rights at Work 1998.

many examples of conflicts between workers' rights and those of others. Imagine a group of police officers who wish to exercise the right to strike. Perhaps they have a powerful claim: staffing shortages are forcing them to patrol dangerous areas on their own, thus putting their lives at risk. But if the police officers are permitted to go on strike, law and order would quickly break down. Criminals would soon realise that they could act with impunity. The rights and freedoms of ordinary citizens would inevitably be violated. For this reason, it is usually regarded as legitimate for a government to ban police officers and others who provide 'essential services' from striking.[41]

Further reading

For an overview of international human rights law, see H.J. Steiner *et al.*, *International Human Rights in Context* (3rd edn., 2008), Chapters 1–4, or C. Tomuschat, *Human Rights: Between Idealism and Realism* (2nd edn., 2008). For an introduction to the jurisprudential issues surrounding rights, see J. Waldron, *Theories of Rights* (1984), or F.M. Kamm, 'Rights', in J.L. Coleman and S. Shapiro (eds.), *The Oxford Handbook of Jurisprudence and Philosophy of Law* (2002).

Rights theories are not without their critics. M.A. Glendon, *Rights Talk: The Impoverishment of Political Discourse* (1991), attacks rights on the grounds that they oversimplify complex debates and draw attention away from more important notions of duty and responsibility. D. Kennedy, *A Critique of Adjudication* (1997), Chapters 12 and 13, argues that rights are indeterminate: they purport to offer solutions to problems, but in practice they are too vague and contradictory to do so. For a summary of the critiques and a response, see C. Sunstein, 'Rights and their critics' (1995) 70 *Notre Dame Law Review* 727. What is the relationship between rights and duties? What role should rights play in political and legal discourse? And what conception of rights does Sunstein defend? Do you agree with the concessions he makes to the critics?

Many labour lawyers have come to regard rights analysis as a means of defending labour law in the face of globalisation. We will see many examples of this in later chapters, but for a useful overview try P. Macklem, 'The right to bargain collectively in international law: workers' right, human right, international right?', in P. Alston (ed.), *Labour Rights as Human Rights* (2005). Economic and social rights are of particular relevance to labour law: see K.D. Ewing, 'The Human Rights Act and labour law' (1998) 27 *ILJ* 275, and 'Social rights and constitutional law' (1999) *PL* 104. You should therefore familiarise yourself with the debate about the status and enforceability of economic and social rights. Compare A. Neier, 'Social and economic rights: a critique' (2006) 13 *Human Rights Brief* 1, with S. Fredman, *Human Rights Transformed* (2008), especially Chapter 3. Are economic and social rights capable of being fundamental, universal and clearly

41 For discussion, see G.S. Morris, *Strikes in Essential Services* (1986).

specifiable? Can they be enforced by the courts? Economic and social rights require the government to interfere with markets. What does this tell us about the likely attitude of neoclassical economists to economic and social rights? Why might they be more enthusiastic about civil and political rights? Revisit the readings on neoclassical economics in Chapter 2 for some ideas.

Most human rights discourse in the labour law context focuses on workers' rights, not employers' rights. Employers' rights are usually treated as important interests that may justify an interference with, or limitation of, workers' rights. Why do you think this is? Would it be helpful to think about employers' rights too? If so, what rights would employers have? This is an important issue in EU law, because employers do have rights under the free movement provisions of the Treaty. For recent developments on this, see A.C.L. Davies, 'One step forward, two steps back? The *Viking* and *Laval* cases in the ECJ' (2008) 37 *ILJ* 126.

4

Modes of regulation

In this chapter, we will focus on the various modes of regulation in labour law: in other words, on the different ways in which labour law is created and applied. You might think that this topic is too straightforward to merit a chapter to itself. Surely labour law is created by Parliament and applied by the courts? But matters are not so simple. It can no longer be argued that labour law is solely a matter for national governments. As we saw in the last chapter, some rights in the ECHR are relevant to labour law. These can now be enforced in the UK courts using the Human Rights Act 1998. Even more significantly, EU law (which takes priority over inconsistent national law) covers many aspects of employment, such as equal pay between men and women, collective consultation and the protection of atypical workers. Finally, the UK is bound in international law by ILO conventions on important areas such as freedom of association and collective bargaining.

These various layers of regulation may come into conflict with each other. For example, the EU might propose legislation designed to promote workers' rights in a particular area – collective consultation, for example – but a UK government that is keen to reduce the regulatory burdens on businesses might be hostile to such legislation. Our discussion of rights and economics perspectives on labour law is highly relevant here: when two layers of regulation come into conflict, it is usually because they are striking a different balance between rights arguments and economics arguments. The eventual outcome will depend on matters of practical enforceability: the UK may be able to resist new EU legislation at the negotiating stage, but once it has been passed, the government must implement it or face sanctions of various kinds.

The difficulties, however, are not confined to the relationship between national law and regional or international norms. Within national law, the interaction between Parliament and the courts has long been controversial and warrants study in itself. The courts have tended to draw heavily on common law doctrines when interpreting labour law statutes, prompting critics to argue that Parliament's aims are not always implemented to the full. The second part of this chapter will consider modes of regulation *within* national law.

International and regional regulation

International and regional regulation of labour law takes place against the background of a globalising world economy.[1] Globalisation pits national governments against each other as they try to attract multinational firms to invest in their countries. Many writers believe that this will lead to a 'race to the bottom': governments will reduce their labour standards to the lowest possible level in the belief that multinationals want to locate where labour is cheap. As we saw in Chapter 2, there is considerable controversy surrounding the merits of this approach. Writers who believe in preventing the race to the bottom advocate the setting of minimum labour standards at the international or regional level.[2] This would mean that labour standards were no longer an area for competition between states. However, regulation at this level can be difficult to achieve. By resisting agreement, states may feel that they are able to keep a competitive advantage for themselves. Writers who are less concerned about the race to the bottom may be suspicious of international or regional organisations. They argue that such organisations are dominated by powerful countries which already have high labour standards. These countries use the rhetoric of human rights to impose their own standards on the rest of the world. But their real motivation is 'protectionist': a desire to take away the legitimate competitive advantage of countries with lower labour standards in order to protect their own industries.

The International Labour Organization

The International Labour Organization (ILO) was established in 1919 as part of the international community's response to the First World War. In the wake of the Second World War, its role was reaffirmed and expanded, and it became one of the UN's specialised agencies, with the remit of promoting social justice and labour rights.[3] The ILO has a unique tripartite structure in which each member state is represented by trade union and employer delegates, as well as government officials. The UK is one of its 182 member states. We will look first at the work of the ILO, before turning to an examination of the ILO's relationship with UK governments.

The ILO's main method of operation is to agree detailed conventions on different aspects of labour law. There are over 150 'live' conventions, on topics ranging from health and safety to discrimination to working time. Member states may choose whether or not to ratify each convention. Once a state has ratified,

---

1 This chapter will focus on the ILO, ESC, ECHR and EU. Space precludes discussion of other parts of the international human rights regime, such as the ICCPR/ICESCR.
2 For an introduction, see E. Lee, 'Globalization and labour standards: a review of issues' (1997) 136 *ILR* 173.
3 For detail, see H.G. Bartolomei de la Cruz, G. von Potobsky and L. Swepston, *The International Labour Organisation: The International Standards System and Basic Human Rights* (1996); and for a critique, see B. Creighton, 'The future of labour law: is there a role for international labour standards?', in C. Barnard *et al.* (eds.), *The Future of Labour Law* (2004).

it is bound in international law to comply with the obligations contained in the convention.

However, one of the common criticisms of the ILO is that it is good at setting standards, but in a weak position to enforce them. Under Article 22 of the Constitution, member states must submit an annual report which explains how they are implementing the conventions they have ratified. If a state is failing to comply, another state or a trade union may bring a complaint. There are various procedures for investigating complaints and publishing reports.[4] These reports are a useful source of detailed guidance on the interpretation of ILO conventions. The ILO tries to use the threat of bad publicity to persuade governments to comply with the conventions they have ratified. Phrases like 'moral suasion' or 'the mobilisation of shame' are commonly used to describe the ILO's approach. Sometimes this is effective, but if it does not work, the ILO does not have any real sanctions to invoke.[5] A truly recalcitrant government could simply ignore the ILO's views. And since states are under no obligation to ratify ILO conventions in the first place, they could simply withdraw ratification if they were in breach.

Globalisation is often regarded as having created an 'identity crisis' for the ILO.[6] Its emphasis on detailed labour standards began to seem irrelevant in a climate of competition between states to attract multinational firms. And its inability to enforce its conventions became an embarrassment when new international organisations concerned with trade, particularly the World Trade Organization, were shown to have a much greater degree of effectiveness. The ILO responded in 1998 with the Declaration on Fundamental Principles and Rights at Work. This provides that all ILO member states, regardless of which conventions they have ratified, are bound to uphold four fundamental rights: freedom of association and collective bargaining, freedom from forced labour, freedom from child labour and the right not to be discriminated against. The Declaration gave a new impetus to the ILO's activities by encouraging it to focus on a limited group of rights, instead of trying to promote many detailed conventions. On the one hand, the Declaration can be regarded as enhancing the 'rights' orientation of the ILO. Whereas before, the ILO was clearly focused on workers' rights, the Declaration emphasises the overlap between workers' rights and fundamental human rights. The ILO has gained legitimacy by emphasising (relatively) uncontroversial rights and by tapping into the powerful rhetoric of human rights. On the other hand, some elements of the Declaration

---

4 ILO Constitution, Arts. 24–29. For detail, see F. Maupain, 'The settlement of disputes within the International Labour Office' (2000) 2 *JIEL* 273.

5 Under ILO Constitution, Art. 33, the 'Governing Body may recommend to the Conference such action as it may deem wise and expedient to secure compliance' with the recommendations of a Commission of Inquiry. This has been used only once, in 2000, to address the problem of forced labour in Burma/Myanmar.

6 See B.A. Langille, 'The ILO and the New Economy: recent developments' (1999) 15 *International Journal of Comparative Labour Law and Industrial Relations* 229.

reflect the view that international organisations like the ILO may be used to protect powerful countries from legitimate competition. Thus, the Declaration provides that:

> labour standards should not be used for protectionist trade purposes, and that nothing in this Declaration and its follow-up shall be invoked or otherwise used for such purposes; in addition, the comparative advantage of any country should in no way be called into question by this Declaration and its follow-up. [7]

This limits the ILO's ability to pursue the rights in the Declaration where they might impose costs on a country and make it less attractive as a location for multinationals. Many rights commentators have been highly critical of the way in which free trade economics arguments have been allowed to intrude into the Declaration.[8] But perhaps it would not have been possible to reach agreement on the Declaration without acknowledging those arguments.

Although the UK played an important role in the creation of the ILO, the UK government has had a difficult relationship with the Organization in recent years. The UK has ratified all the so-called 'fundamental' conventions – those which relate to the rights in the Declaration – and many others besides, but does not always comply with them in full. Perhaps the best illustration of this is in the area of freedom of association.[9] The ILO has long held the view that freedom of association is a fundamental right, and in 1950 a special Freedom of Association Committee was established to investigate alleged violations.[10] The UK has ratified both Convention 87 on Freedom of Association and Protection of the Right to Organise (1948) and Convention 98 on the Right to Organise and Collective Bargaining (1949), but it has been the subject of over eighty complaints to the Freedom of Association Committee and remains in breach of some aspects of the two conventions.

ILO conventions cannot be enforced in the domestic courts because English law takes a 'dualist' approach to international law.[11] International law and domestic law are viewed as two separate spheres. International law governs the relations between states, whereas domestic law governs the relationship between states and citizens. A citizen may not bring an action in domestic law to challenge a breach of international law.[12] This means that the only sanctions available against

---

7 ILO Declaration on Fundamental Principles and Rights at Work 1998, para. 5.
8 See, for example, Langille, 'The ILO and the New Economy'.
9 See, generally, T. Novitz, 'International promise and domestic pragmatism: to what extent will the Employment Relations Act 1999 implement international labour standards relating to freedom of association?' (2000) 63 *MLR* 379.
10 See L. Swepston, 'Human rights law and freedom of association: development through ILO supervision' (1998) 137 *ILR* 169.
11 I. Brownlie, *Principles of Public International Law* (7th edn., 2008), Chapter 2.
12 Where a statute is ambiguous, a court may refer to international obligations in order to resolve the ambiguity, applying the presumption that Parliament does not intend to legislate in breach of such obligations: *Salomon* v. *Commissioners of Customs and Excise* [1967] 2 QB 116, pp. 143–4 (per Diplock LJ).

the UK government for a breach of an ILO convention are those imposed by the ILO itself.

Thus, although the ILO 'layer' of regulation is largely rights-based, its success in pushing English law in this direction is limited. ILO standards probably have some indirect influence because they are widely used by commentators, trade unions and others in criticising the law and suggesting new policy developments, but the extent of this influence is difficult to measure.

The European Social Charter

At the regional level, the ESC might appear to be the obvious starting point for a discussion of labour rights. As a statement of economic and social rights, the rights it contains are of particular relevance to the subject. However, like ILO standards, the ESC's practical impact in English law is limited.

As Chapter 3 explained, the UK has ratified the ESC 1961. States must report regularly on their efforts to implement the rights in the Charter.[13] Their reports are reviewed by the European Committee on Social Rights (ECSR), which issues conclusions and recommendations to the signatory states. There is also a collective complaints procedure which allows trade unions and NGOs to report violations of the ESC for investigation by the ECSR. However, this procedure does not apply to the UK.

The ECSR has identified a number of areas in which English law falls short of the ESC's requirements, but its comments have limited impact on government policy.[14] Like ILO conventions, the Charter is binding in international law but has no direct effect in domestic law. However, the Charter does have some indirect influence. Because it is the 'companion' instrument to the ECHR, it is often cited by the ECtHR in cases – for example, those on trade union rights – where there is an overlap between the civil and political rights contained in the Convention and the economic and social rights contained in the Charter.[15] The jurisprudence of the ECtHR plays an important role in English law, as the next section will explain.

The European Convention on Human Rights

The ECHR was adopted in 1950. Until recently, it had similar status to ILO legislation and the ESC – it bound the government in international law but had limited consequences in domestic law – though successive governments have had a fairly good record of complying with judgments of the ECtHR. The HRA 1998, which came into force in October 2000, empowered the UK courts to decide various types of cases involving Convention rights. Thus, it is now possible for the Convention to impact on English law in two ways: through changes to

---

13 ESC 1961, Art. 21.
14 See K.D. Ewing, 'The Council of Europe's Social Charter of 18 October 1961: Britain and the 15th cycle of supervision' (2001) 30 *ILJ* 409.
15 See, for example, *ASLEF* v. *UK* (2007) 45 EHRR 34.

legislation to deal with adverse judgments of the ECtHR, and through litigation on Convention rights in the domestic courts.

The ECHR is a statement of civil and political rights, not economic and social rights, so it does not provide a complete framework for labour rights in English law. However, a number of Convention rights are applicable in labour law. The most obvious is Article 11, which protects the right to form and join trade unions. Other relevant rights include Article 8 (right to respect for private and family life), Article 9 (freedom of religion) and Article 10 (freedom of expression).

Convention rights rarely trump other considerations. Most of the rights which are relevant to labour law are *qualified*: states may justify interferences with the rights on certain grounds. Article 9(2) is typical:

> Freedom to manifest one's religion or beliefs shall be subject only to such limita-
> tions as are prescribed by law and are necessary in a democratic society in the inter-
> ests of public safety, for the protection of public order, health or morals, or for the
> protection of the rights and freedoms of others.

In the employment sphere, the reference to 'the rights and freedoms of others' could be used to bring in the employer's contractual and property interests as reasons for limiting workers' religious freedoms. The phrase 'necessary in a democratic society' has been interpreted by the ECtHR as requiring the use of a proportionality test, in which the harm to the individual is weighed against the government's reason for limiting the individual's rights.[16] This suggests that the ECtHR will scrutinise the government's arguments quite strictly. However, the level of scrutiny can vary: sometimes the judges will decide that the government is better placed to decide how to weigh up the competing factors.[17]

We saw in Chapter 3 that human rights are usually thought of as rights against the state: they apply 'vertically' rather than 'horizontally' between private parties. This is reflected in the HRA 1998, which creates in s. 6(1) a cause of action for the violation of Convention rights which is only available against public bod-
ies. A public sector worker can go to court and argue directly that the employer has violated his or her Convention rights. Section 6(1) is not available to the vast majority of people because they work for private sector employers. However, the Act does have some horizontal effect. The key provision is s. 6(3)(a), which extends the definition of 'public authority' to include courts or tribunals. This means that the courts themselves are obliged to act compatibly with Convention rights. The cases can be divided into two groups: those which fall to be decided at common law, and those which fall to be decided by the application of statutory provisions.

In common law cases involving private parties, the courts have held that they are under a duty to develop the common law in the light of the Convention.

---

16 See, for example, *Olsson* v. *Sweden* (1989) 11 EHRR 259, p. 285.
17 See *Handyside* v. *UK* (1979–80) 1 EHRR 737, pp. 753–4, and in English law, *Huang* v. *Secretary of State for the Home Department* [2007] UKHL 11; [2007] 2 AC 167.

However, this does not allow them to create a new cause of action where none existed before, because this would amount to extending s. 6(1) to private parties. Dame Elizabeth Butler-Sloss P put the point clearly in *Venables* v. *NGN*:

> That obligation on the court does not seem to me to encompass the creation of a free-standing cause of action based directly upon the articles of the convention … The duty on the court, in my view, is to act compatibly with convention rights in adjudicating upon existing common law causes of action, and that includes a positive as well as a negative obligation.[18]

Thus, in common law cases, the HRA 1998 has some horizontal effect, at least where the law can be developed incrementally to accommodate it.

The second group of cases involves statutory interpretation. This group has particular significance for labour law because most cases involve statute law rather than common law. Section 3(1) of the HRA 1998 governs statutory interpretation: 'So far as it is possible to do so, primary legislation and subordinate legislation must be read and given effect in a way which is compatible with the Convention rights'. Significantly, this section does not contain any language confining it to cases involving public authorities. The view that it should be employed in 'horizontal' cases is reinforced by the s. 6(3)(a) obligation on the courts to act compatibly with the Convention. Thus, all labour law statutes are subject to s. 3 (and, if s. 3 interpretation fails, a declaration of incompatibility under s. 4), even in a case between an employee and a private employer.

So far, the courts have shown some willingness to consider human rights issues in labour law, but this has not made much difference to the outcomes of cases. For example, in unfair dismissal claims, the task of the Employment Tribunal is to decide whether the employer has acted reasonably in dismissing the employee.[19] Broadly speaking, the courts have accepted that the reasonableness test should be informed by Convention rights where relevant.[20] So, if the employer's action infringes a right and cannot be justified, the dismissal would be unfair. In the *Copsey* case, the employer adopted a new shift system which meant that employees would have to work on Sundays.[21] The claimant refused, arguing that it infringed his religious duty as a Christian to treat Sunday as a day of rest. The employer dismissed him and he argued that the dismissal was unfair. The Court of Appeal was divided on how to approach the case, but the majority view was that the employer had not acted unfairly because it had good business reasons for changing shift patterns and because it had tried to negotiate a compromise with the claimant. The Convention jurisprudence also supports the idea that it is not the employer's job to accommodate employees' religious

---

18 *Venables* v. *NGN* [2001] Fam. 430, p. 446.   19 ERA 1996, s. 98(4).
20 *X* v. *Y* [2003] ICR 1138, paras. 15–17.
21 *Copsey* v. *WWB Devon Clays Ltd* [2005] EWCA Civ 932; [2005] ICR 1789. See H. Collins, 'The protection of civil liberties in the workplace' (2006) 69 *MLR* 619.

beliefs in organising working time.[22] The *Copsey* case shows how the HRA 1998 gives the courts a greater role in resolving clashes between rights and economics considerations in labour law cases. So far, the courts have approached this task quite cautiously.

The impact of the HRA 1998 has, arguably, been greater in the area of legislative reform than in litigation. Workers have won a number of important cases before the ECtHR, and these have prompted the government to amend the relevant legislation. The government's international law obligation to comply with the ECtHR's decisions is reinforced by the knowledge that those decisions can be 'taken into account' by the domestic courts under s. 2 HRA 1998. Article 11, on freedom of association, has been particularly important in this regard. The case of *Wilson* v. *UK* concerned an employer who offered pay rises to individual workers who agreed not to be represented by a trade union for the purposes of collective bargaining.[23] The ECtHR found that this amounted to discrimination against the trade union members who wanted to keep collective bargaining and therefore did not get the pay rise. It held that the UK government was in breach of Article 11 because English law did not provide the affected trade unionists with a remedy. The case of *ASLEF* v. *UK* concerned a trade union which wanted to exclude an individual from membership because he was a member of a far-right political party.[24] English law did not permit this. Again, the ECtHR found a breach of Article 11, stating that unions should have control over their own membership rules, provided certain conditions were met. The government has responded to both cases by amending the relevant legislation, though (as always) there is room for debate about what exactly the ECtHR's judgments require.[25] Moreover, the judgments have ongoing relevance because the domestic courts would have to consider them if called upon to interpret the amendments (and the legislation on trade unions more generally) in the future.

Like the ILO and the ESC, the ECHR is a rights-focused layer of regulation. Unlike the ILO and the ESC, it has a direct impact in English law through the HRA 1998. Decisions of the ECtHR have prompted the government to change legislation, and the domestic courts have accepted, in principle, the relevance of Convention rights to their decisions in labour law. However, much will depend on how the relevant rights, and their limitations, are construed and applied in practice, both in the ECtHR and domestically. This is likely to be a 'hot topic' in labour law for some time to come.

The European Union

The European Union is a fascinating case-study of the interplay between rights and economics. As the early nomenclature indicates, the European Economic Community was an organisation with economic aims. Over time, the social

---

22 See, for example, *Stedman* v. *UK* (1997) 23 EHRR CD 168.
23 *Wilson* v. *UK* (2002) 35 EHRR 20.   24 *ASLEF* v. *UK* (2007) 45 EHRR 34.
25 See Chapter 11.

policy agenda has become increasingly important and EU law has begun to protect a wider range of workers' rights.[26] In recent years, some EU policy documents have begun to emphasise new institutionalist economics arguments about the role of workers' rights in enhancing business competitiveness. Nevertheless, the EU still comes in for criticism from an economics perspective, for imposing rigid and inflexible labour laws, and from a rights perspective, for being too ready to sacrifice workers' rights to economic concerns.

When the Treaty of Rome was signed in 1957, the only significant labour law provision it contained was Article 119 (now 141), giving a right to equal pay between men and women. The French government had pressed for the inclusion of this provision because France already had equal pay laws. It was feared that French products would be undercut by cheaper products from other Member States in which women were paid less than men.[27] Thus, the rationale for the EEC's initial foray into social policy was an economic one. Over time, the EU's competence to legislate in the field of labour law has expanded considerably to include equality more generally,[28] health and safety, working conditions, termination of employment, information and consultation, and collective representation,[29] though pay, freedom of association and the right to strike are specifically excluded.[30]

The EU's traditional approach to labour law has been to legislate by means of directives. Article 249 EC states that 'a directive shall be binding, as to the result to be achieved, upon each Member State to which it is addressed, but shall leave to the national authorities the choice of form and methods'. Directives must be implemented in national law by each Member State. Most directives are agreed after a complex procedure in which they are proposed by the Commission and must be agreed by the Council (made up of representatives of the Member States) and the European Parliament.[31] But in the labour law field, directives can also be enacted through a process called 'social dialogue'. Before the legislative process begins, the Commission must consult the representatives of management and labour, often referred to as the 'social partners'.[32] If the social partners so desire, they may decide to regulate the area themselves by reaching an agreement under Article 139 EC. This agreement may be enacted as a directive by the Council,[33] or implemented by further agreements between trade unions and employers' associations within each Member State.[34] The social dialogue can be regarded as a

26 For history, see C. Barnard, 'EC social policy', in P.P. Craig and G. de Búrca (eds.), *The Evolution of EU Law* (1999); and S. Fredman, 'Social law in the European Union', in P.P. Craig and C. Harlow (eds.), *Lawmaking in the European Union* (1998).
27 Barnard, 'EC social policy', p. 481.   28 Arts. 13, 137 and 141 EC.   29 Art. 137 EC.
30 Art. 137(5) EC.   31 See Arts. 137 and 251 EC.
32 Art. 138 EC. The social partners are (on the labour side) the European Trade Union Confederation (ETUC), and (on the management side) the Confederation of European Business, CEEP and UEAPME (European Association of Craft, Small and Medium-Sized Enterprises).
33 Examples include Directive 99/70/EC on Fixed-Term Work and Directive 97/81/EC on Part-Time Work.
34 See, for example, the Framework Agreement on Telework, 16 July 2002.

novel way of promoting grass-roots participation in the legislative process, and of ensuring that new legislation is responsive to the needs of those who will have to implement it.[35] But it has been criticised as undemocratic, particularly because it bypasses the European Parliament.

Although directives are often thought of as a flexible legislative instrument – leaving discretion to the Member States to implement them in national law and to make them fit with pre-existing provisions – many directives are in practice quite detailed, and this has led to the criticism that EU labour law is trying to impose a 'one size fits all' on vastly differing circumstances. While directives remain an important tool for the EU, recent years have seen a greater emphasis on non-legislative mechanisms for developing and enforcing labour law policy.[36] The 'open method of co-ordination' sets targets for the Member States to achieve in areas such as combating unemployment and improving the skills of the work-force. The Member States must report their progress to the Commission. The thinking is that Member States will be able to learn from each other by trying out different strategies and comparing their performance. Some people see this 'soft law' approach as a smart regulatory strategy; others as a dangerous sign that the EU is downplaying legislation as a means of protecting workers' rights.

The ECJ has also played an important role in the development of Community labour law, particularly in the area of discrimination law. The Court has made creative use of Article 141 in order to develop an elaborate jurisprudence on equal pay for women and men.[37] The Article 234 procedure, by which national courts can refer questions of Community law to the ECJ for determination, has been the main route for these developments.

The EU's social policy agenda is difficult to pinpoint with precision because of the range of actors involved: the Commission, the Member States (with divergent political outlooks) and the Court, among others. Traditionally, the justification for labour law directives has been to prevent a 'race to the bottom'. The EU is designed to create an internal market in which there are no barriers to trade between the Member States. One consequence of this is that firms can set up business anywhere in the EU. States wanting to attract firms might choose (on neoclassical economics principles) to make their labour costs as low as possible by reducing labour standards. This might create a race to the bottom in which states compete to have the lowest labour standards. Labour law directives prevent this by setting minimum standards applicable in all Member States.

In recent years, the EU has begun to look outwards and to consider its competitive relationship with other states around the world. In these terms, the EU is a relatively high-cost location for firms. Rather like the UK government, as we saw in Chapter 1, the EU has been drawn to new institutional economics arguments

---

35 For discussion, see B. Bercusson, 'Democratic legitimacy and European labour law' (1999) 28 *ILJ* 153.
36 See, generally, C. Barnard, *EC Employment Law* (3rd edn., 2006), Chapter 3.
37 For an overview, see Barnard, 'EC social policy', Chapter 7.

which emphasise the role of labour standards in promoting a highly productive and innovative economy. The aim is to show that expensive EU workers are, in fact, good value for money because they are highly skilled. Particular emphasis has been placed on 'flexicurity' in EU labour markets: the idea that workers should be able to move between firms and jobs (flexibility), but with the reassurance that the state will protect them – for example, through unemployment benefits (security) – if need be.[38]

The EU also has a more traditional rights agenda. Some Member States were concerned that the rights protected in their constitutions could be overridden by Community law because of the doctrine of supremacy (that EU law takes priority over national law, even national constitutional law) espoused by the ECJ.[39] The ECJ developed a doctrine of fundamental rights in response to these concerns.[40] This includes various labour rights, such as the right to strike.[41] The EU's political institutions have also been active in the field of human rights. The EU Charter of Fundamental Rights, agreed by the Member States in 2000, is the main statement of human rights in the EU. The Charter is not at present legally enforceable, although it is expected that it will be incorporated into the Treaties at some point in the future. As we saw in Chapter 3, the Charter is a comprehensive statement of human rights, with a strong emphasis on labour rights.[42]

However, many rights theorists argue that the EU remains primarily an economic institution. It makes concessions to workers' rights only when they are unlikely to impose substantial costs on businesses. One area in which this argument is often made is in relation to Article 141, on equal pay.[43] An employer can argue that differences between the pay of men and women are down to market forces, rather than discrimination – for example, if the employer's workforce is mostly female, and it offers a higher wage to a new recruit, who is male, to persuade him to take the job, this creates a pay inequality between the women and the man, but will probably be defensible on market forces grounds.[44] Firms would argue that this approach makes good economic sense, but critics are concerned that it does nothing to tackle underlying problems of discrimination within markets, such as why women are prepared to work for a wage that no

---

38 European Commission, *Towards Common Principles of Flexicurity: More and Better Jobs through Flexibility and Security* (2007).

39 (Case 6/64) *Costa* v. *ENEL* [1964] ECR 585. See, generally, P. Craig and G. de Búrca, *EU Law: Text, Cases and Materials* (4th edn., 2008), Chapter 10.

40 (Case 11/70) *Internationale Handelsgesellschaft* [1970] ECR 1125. See Craig and de Búrca, *EU Law*, Chapter 11.

41 (Case C-438/05) *International Transport Workers' Federation* v. *Viking Line* [2008] All ER (EC) 127.

42 See, generally, B. Hepple, 'The EU Charter of Fundamental Rights' (2001) 30 *ILJ* 225.

43 See, for example, S. Fredman, 'European Community discrimination law: a critique' (1992) 21 *ILJ* 119, pp. 130–2.

44 See *Rainey* v. *Greater Glasgow Health Board* [1987] AC 224; (C-127/92) *Enderby* v. *Frenchay HA* [1993] ECR I-5535.

man will accept.[45] More recently, the clash between rights and economics in the EU has become more stark after a series of decisions on the relationship between labour rights and employers' free movement rights under the Treaty. In *Viking*, for example, the ECJ held that a union could not lawfully organise a strike where this would prevent a firm from exercising its freedom of establishment rights by relocating to another Member State.[46] If the strike deterred the firm from relocating, the union would have to show that it was acting proportionately: in other words, the courts would have to weigh the aims of the strike against the harm to the employer. Again, there is economic logic to these decisions: the point of the EU is to create an internal market in which firms can move to more profitable locations. But trade unionists have argued that more weight should be given to the right to strike as a fundamental right, and to the need to prevent a race to the bottom in their members' terms and conditions of employment.

Successive UK governments have had a difficult relationship with the EU in the employment field, tending to argue that EU law is overly protective of workers' rights and takes insufficient account of the needs of businesses. The Conservative governments of 1979–97 expressed open hostility to new EU legislation.[47] They vetoed measures which required the unanimous approval of the Member States, and refused to be bound by the Social Chapter signed by the other Member States in Maastricht in 1992, which extended the EC's competence in the field of social policy.

Since 1997, the Labour government has adopted a more conciliatory tone and has signed up to the Social Chapter.[48] But the government remains sceptical about the value of some new EU measures, despite its commitment to economic arguments which promote labour rights. For example, the government opposed the Framework Directive on Informing and Consulting Employees,[49] arguing that it would impose an unnecessary burden on businesses.[50] When opposition failed, the government sought to limit the obligations the Directive would impose. For example, as Bercusson explains, the original draft stated that an employer's decision could not take effect until after it had consulted its employees.[51] This provided a strong sanction for a failure to consult. The UK government successfully argued that this provision should be struck out in favour of a discretion on the part of Member States to prescribe an appropriate penalty for failure to consult.[52]

Once a directive has been agreed, the government must implement it within the specified time period or face sanctions of various kinds. These include enforcement proceedings brought by the Commission before the ECJ, or actions for damages under the *Francovich* principle by individuals who are harmed by

45 Fredman, 'European Community discrimination law'.
46 *International Transport Workers' Federation* v. *Viking Line*; and see A.C.L. Davies, 'One step forward, two steps back? The *Viking* and *Laval* cases in the ECJ' (2008) 37 *ILJ* 126.
47 See P. Davies and M. Freedland, *Labour Legislation and Public Policy* (1993), pp. 576–99.
48 DTI, *Fairness at Work* (1998) (Cm 3968), p. 9.   49 Directive 2002/14/EC.
50 DTI, *Fairness at Work*, p. 22.
51 B. Bercusson, 'The European social model comes to Britain' (2002) 31 *ILJ* 209, pp. 239–40.
52 Directive 2002/14/EC, Art. 8.

the failure to implement.[53] Individuals may also be able to invoke Community law directly in the national courts under the doctrine of direct effect. Nevertheless, the government may have further opportunities to limit the impact of a directive where the directive itself allows the government to choose between different implementation options. For example, the Directive on Fixed-Term Work gives Member States various options for preventing the abuse of successive fixed-term contracts.[54] One is to limit the duration of successive fixed-term contracts. The UK has placed a maximum limit of four years on such contracts, which contrasts with, for example, two years in Germany.[55] This is permitted by the Directive but gives UK employers greater flexibility than their German counterparts.

What role for national law?

It seems appropriate to conclude our discussion of modes of regulation by considering whether there are any issues on which the UK government can enact what it pleases, unconstrained by the ILO, the ESC, the ECHR or the EU.[56] In fact, there are two main areas of discretion. The first is pay. The EU has no competence on this matter[57] and the ECHR contains no relevant provisions. ILO Convention 26 on Minimum Wage-Fixing Machinery 1928 was initially ratified by the UK but was denounced in 1985. The UK has never ratified ILO Convention 131 on Minimum Wage Fixing 1970. The ESC protects the right to 'fair remuneration' in Article 4, and the ECSR regards the national minimum wage as inadequate in various respects to fulfil this right, but the UK government seems content to ignore its views.[58] The second area of discretion is the law regarding termination of employment. Although the EU has competence in this area, it has not yet exercised its powers.[59] The ECHR may have some indirect relevance – where the dismissal constitutes a violation of freedom of religion, for example[60] – but it would not apply in the vast majority of dismissal cases. The UK has not ratified ILO Convention 158 on Termination of Employment 1982, and Article 4 of the ESC only contains a limited right to notice of termination.

Purely national regulation of workers' rights is still possible in these areas. But large chunks of labour law are shared with international or regional regimes – for example, freedom of association with the ECHR, and sex and race discrimination with the EU. The aim of this discussion is not to make a point about sovereignty. Rather, it is to emphasise that the law is often the result of a compromise struck between the government and an international or regional regime. Compromises are necessary because a different interpretation of rights and

---

53 (Cases C-6 & 9/90) *Francovich and Bonifaci v. Italy* [1991] ECR I-5357.
54 Directive 99/70/EC, cl. 5.
55 M. Weiss, 'The Framework Agreement on Fixed-Term Work: a German point of view' (1999) 15 *International Journal of Comparative Labour Law and Industrial Relations* 97.
56 Of course, it is not inconceivable that the government could withdraw from these institutions, but this remote possibility will be disregarded for the purposes of the present discussion.
57 Art. 137(5) EC.   58 See ECSR, *Conclusions XVIII-2 (United Kingdom)* (2007).
59 Art. 137(1)(d) EC.   60 *Copsey* v. *WWB Devon Clays Ltd*.

economics arguments is likely to hold sway at each level of regulation. The shape of those compromises will depend on the relative power of the government and the other levels of regulation. A rounded understanding of labour law must be alive to the conflicts and tensions inherent in multi-layered regulation.

Modes of regulation within national law

At the national level, labour law is made up of statutes and statutory instruments proposed by the government and approved by Parliament, case law developed by the courts, and, in some instances, by negotiations between employers and workers. These institutions may come into conflict because of the different ways in which they strike a balance between rights arguments and economics arguments. The balance struck by governments depends on their political complexion and on the social and economic circumstances they face. The changing shape of labour law over the last century and into the present day was considered in Chapter 1. The outcome of negotiations between employers and workers depends heavily on their relative bargaining positions. The role of such negotiations will be considered in later chapters. Our focus here will be on the courts. Labour law only fully acquired the status of a subject in its own right in the second half of the twentieth century. It is made up, in part, of elements of tort, contract and public law. Not surprisingly, the courts have drawn heavily on techniques from these more familiar subjects in employment cases. This approach has been criticised by many labour lawyers. They argue that the courts favour employers against employees, and employers or individual union members against trade unions. In other words, the courts favour neoclassical economics arguments over workers' rights.

Parliament has delegated to the courts the task of defining 'employee' – one of the central organising concepts of labour law.[61] Since an employee is a person who works under a contract of employment, the courts have gone about this task using familiar methods from the law of contract. For example, in *Express and Echo Publications* v. *Tanton*, the court found that a term entitling Mr Tanton to use a substitute instead of performing the work himself was inherently inconsistent with the existence of a contract of employment.[62] This meant that Mr Tanton was an independent contractor, beyond the scope of employment protection laws. The court stressed that the correct approach was to focus on the contract document:

> Of course, it is important that the industrial tribunal should be alert in this area of the law to look at the reality of any obligations. If the obligation is a sham, it will want to say so. But to concentrate on what actually occurred may not elucidate the

---

61 ERA 1996, s. 230(1).
62 If the power to substitute is limited, it will not have this effect: *MacFarlane* v. *Glasgow CC* [2001] IRLR 7.

full terms of the contract. If a term is not enforced, that does not justify a conclusion that such a term is not part of the agreement.[63]

As a matter of contract law, this is entirely correct. The 'parol evidence rule' states that where the parties have put their contract in writing, the document should, on the whole, be treated as the sole source of the terms of the contract.[64] But labour lawyers have argued that the decision works to the disadvantage of employees. Contracts of employment are usually drafted by employers or their legal advisers and offered to employees on a 'take it or leave it' basis. Employers may be tempted to insert terms that are inconsistent with a contract of employment in order to ensure that individuals do not acquire employee status and all the employment rights this would bring. The narrow notion of a 'sham' term in *Tanton* does not offer much protection to employees in this situation.

The courts have also drawn on the techniques of public law in employment cases.[65] In unfair dismissal, the Employment Tribunal must decide whether the employer acted 'reasonably' in dismissing the employee.[66] This test was interpreted by the EAT in *Iceland Frozen Foods* v. *Jones* to require an assessment of whether the conduct of the employer was within a 'band of reasonable responses' to the situation.[67] The notion of a 'band of reasonable responses' emphasises the fact that more than one course of action might be reasonable and indicates that tribunals should only interfere in extreme cases. It is similar to the *Wednesbury* formula in public law, which allows courts to review the decisions of public authorities only where they are 'so unreasonable that no reasonable [authority]' would have made them.[68] In public law, this approach was justified by the argument that judges were not well-placed to second-guess the decisions of politicians and skilled administrators. Whatever the merits of this argument in public law, labour lawyers have argued that it is indefensible in the employment sphere. Employment tribunals consist of two lay members (one with union experience and one with employer experience) and a legally qualified chairman. It is claimed that tribunals do have the experience that would be required for a more searching review of the employer's conduct.

The courts' use of public law techniques has had radically different results in cases brought by individuals against trade unions.[69] The courts have taken the view that the individual is in a vulnerable position when faced with the collective strength of the union. They have therefore used public law principles designed

---

63 *Express and Echo Publications* v. *Tanton* [1999] ICR 693, p. 697 (per Peter Gibson LJ).
64 *Jacobs* v. *Batavia & General Plantations Trust Ltd* [1924] 1 Ch 287. For the many exceptions to the rule, see E. Peel, *The Law of Contract* (12th edn., 2007), pp. 213–23.
65 For discussion, see P.L. Davies and M.R. Freedland, 'The impact of public law on labour law 1972–1997' (1997) 26 *ILJ* 311.
66 ERA 1996, s. 98(4).
67 *Iceland Frozen Foods* v. *Jones* [1983] ICR 17, pp. 24–5 (per Browne-Wilkinson J).
68 *Associated Provincial Picture Houses* v. *Wednesbury Corporation* [1948] 1 KB 223, pp. 228–30 (per Lord Greene MR).
69 There is now extensive statutory regulation of this area. See Chapter 11 for detail.

to prevent the abuse of power when interpreting the contract of membership between the union and the individual. For example, in *Esterman* v. *NALGO*, the union instructed its members not to volunteer to help with local government elections as part of a dispute with local authority employers.[70] The claimant disobeyed the instruction and was threatened with disciplinary proceedings. The court took the unusual step of granting an injunction to prevent the union from hearing the disciplinary proceedings, on the grounds that no reasonable union acting in good faith could have found that the complainant was unfit to be a member of the union. Instead of asking whether the union was in breach of contract, the court asked the public law question of whether the union had acted rationally. Decisions like *Esterman* have the merit of protecting individual union members against unfairness. Such protection was particularly import-ant when closed shops were lawful, because individuals working in closed shops who were expelled from their unions would also lose their jobs.[71] But labour law-yers have criticised the courts for denying unions the autonomy to set and apply their own rules. The courts may need to revise their approach in the light of the ECtHR's decision in *ASLEF* v. *UK*, discussed above, in which trade union auton-omy was found to be a central principle within Article 11 of the Convention.[72]

There is much debate as to the motivation behind these decisions. On one view, they are simply technical applications of rules from other areas of law which happen not to fit very well with the underlying themes of labour law. On another view, it can be argued that the courts are (consciously or unconsciously) inclined to favour employers.[73] A belief in the liberty of the individual makes the courts unsympathetic towards the collective power of trade unions. And a belief in free-dom of contract makes the courts unsympathetic towards attempts to regulate the contract of employment by granting statutory rights to workers. These tra-ditional concerns of the common law are closely related to those of neoclassical economics, discussed in Chapter 2.

If the courts do have a tendency to favour employers over unions and employees, this is likely to bring them into conflict with other layers of regula-tion – for example, they may be reluctant to use ILO standards in their deci-sions, or they may construe the rights in the ECHR narrowly. They may also come into conflict with the government when it passes legislation based on rights or new institutional economics arguments. Later chapters will consider a number of important judicial decisions in labour law. As you examine these decisions, you need to decide whether or not labour lawyers' criticisms of the courts are valid.

---

70 *Esterman* v. *NALGO* [1974] ICR 625.   71 See Chapter 11.
72 *ASLEF* v. *UK* (2007) 45 EHRR 34. See also ILO Convention 87 on Freedom of Association and Protection of the Right to Organise 1948, Art. 3.
73 See, for example, J.A.G. Griffith, *The Politics of the Judiciary* (5th edn., 1997), especially Chapter 3.

Further reading

S. Deakin and G.S. Morris, *Labour Law* (4th edn., 2005), Chapter 2, or H. Collins, K.D. Ewing and A. McColgan, *Labour Law: Text and Materials* (2nd edn., 2005), Chapter 1, give an account of the sources and institutions of labour law. For introductory accounts of the roles of the ILO, ECHR and EU, see, respectively: H.G. Bartolomei de la Cruz, G. von Potobsky and L. Swepston, *The International Labour Organisation: The International Standards System and Basic Human Rights* (1996); C. Ovey and R.C.A. White, *The European Convention on Human Rights* (4th edn., 2006); and C. Barnard, *EC Employment Law* (3rd edn., 2006), Chapters 1–3.

What factors influence whether or not English law is brought into compliance with international human rights obligations? Consider (among others): the legal status of international human rights instruments; the moral legitimacy of particular instruments; the extent to which they take account of concerns about costs; government policy; the role of complaints mechanisms; and the role of trade unions and other campaigning organisations. For discussion in relation to the ILO, see T. Novitz, 'International promise and domestic pragmatism: to what extent will the Employment Relations Act 1999 implement international labour standards relating to freedom of association?' (2000) 63 *MLR* 379. On the ECHR see, for example, A.L. Bogg, 'Employment Relations Act 2004: another false dawn for collectivism?' (2005) 34 *ILJ* 72, pp. 72–5, and H. Collins, 'The protection of civil liberties in the workplace' (2006) 69 *MLR* 619. On EU law see, for example, M. Hall, 'Assessing the Information and Consultation of Employees Regulations' (2005) 34 *ILJ* 103, and A. McColgan, 'The Fixed-Term Employees (Prevention of Less Favourable Treatment) Regulations 2002: fiddling while Rome burns?' (2003) 32 *ILJ* 194.

Some modes of regulation were excluded from the discussion in this chapter for reasons of space, but you should also think about what influence they might have. Have a look at H.J. Steiner *et al.*, *International Human Rights in Context* (3rd edn., 2008), Chapters 3, 4 and 10, for more detail on the ICCPR and ICESCR. On the former, see also D. Fottrell, 'Reinforcing the Human Rights Act – the role of the International Covenant on Civil and Political Rights' (2002) *PL* 485.

Within domestic law, you should think about the role of the courts in interpreting labour legislation. For general discussion of this topic, see P.L. Davies and M.R. Freedland, 'The impact of public law on labour law 1972–1997' (1997) 26 *ILJ* 311, and S. Anderman, 'The interpretation of protective employment statutes and contracts of employment' (2000) 29 *ILJ* 223. Why do the courts approach labour law cases in the way that they do? Is it due to political bias, or are there other plausible explanations? What strategies can the legislature adopt to ensure that the courts give full effect to provisions that are intended to protect workers?

Part II

5

Who is protected by employment law?

This chapter will be an important testing-ground for your views on the various theoretical positions we have explored so far. Its topic is: who is protected by employment law? You might expect that the whole workforce would be protected, but in fact this is not the case. The law divides people up into three groups – employees, workers and the self-employed – and offers them different levels of protection. Employees are the traditional subjects of employment law, so they get all the available rights. Self-employed people are thought to be capable of looking after themselves, so with a few exceptions they are not given any rights at all. This twofold classification has come to seem problematic in recent years because of the rising number of so-called 'atypical workers': people who do not fit within the law's definition of an employee but do not seem to be genuinely self-employed either. Since 1997, some legislation has used a third concept – 'worker' – to include these people. Workers do not have as many rights as employees, but they are better protected than the self-employed.

From a neoclassical economics perspective, labour rights are viewed as a burden on business. If an employer is obliged by the law to confer rights on workers, it will compensate for this increase in its costs either by cutting those workers' wages or by making some of them redundant. The employer will also be reluctant to create new jobs. But if the law allows the existence of different categories of people in the workforce, some of whom have fewer rights, employers are provided with a welcome opportunity to reduce their costs. New institutional economists take a very different view. They argue that labour rights help to make workers more productive by making them feel secure in their jobs and valued by the firm. Although rights are costly, they also bring compensating economic benefits. On this view, rights should be available to everyone.

Most rights theorists would also argue that rights should be granted to all. Rights are usually formulated in universal terms: 'Everyone has the right to …' Technical distinctions between different categories of people in employment should not be used to deny protection to certain groups. However, there are some possible exceptions to this general rule. One is that certain groups may not need the protection of the law because they are able to secure protection through their own bargaining power. A more controversial exception is to suggest that because some rights are often considered to be less fundamental than others, these less significant rights need not be granted to everyone. However, it is difficult to identify a fair way to decide who should be in this privileged subset.

Typical and atypical workers

Most writers approach this topic by drawing a distinction between typical and atypical workers. This terminology is not entirely helpful. It implies that atypical workers are the exception rather than the rule, and while this is probably true today, they may one day come to outnumber typical employees. And it implies that atypical workers are a single group with the same characteristics, whereas in fact workers may be atypical in a variety of different ways. But we need to begin by identifying the typical worker. He or she works:

– for a single employer
– on an indefinite contract (i.e. one with no end date)
– at the employer's premises
– regularly for that employer whether or not the firm is busy.[1]

The atypical worker is a person whose employment diverges from this norm in *one or more* respects. It is unusual to find a worker who is atypical in every respect. Let us examine some of the different types of atypical worker and the issues they face.

One type is the agency worker. The typical worker works for one employer that makes use of his or her services. The agency worker works for an employment agency, which hires out his or her services to a 'principal' or 'user'. So who employs the agency worker? In general, it is unlikely to be the user.[2] The user just has a commercial contract with the agency. It is more likely to be the agency, but often the agency will arrange things so that the worker is self-employed.[3] If the worker cannot identify an employer, he or she will not be able to claim any employment rights, except in the rare cases in which statutes make explicit provision for agency workers.[4] Also, agency workers may find that they do not get the same terms and conditions of employment (rates of pay, for example) as the user's permanent staff.

Another type of atypical worker is the fixed-term worker. The typical employee usually has an indefinite contract, with no fixed end point. This contract can be terminated by the employer, but in doing so, the employer must comply with the requirements of unfair dismissal law.[5] The fixed-term worker is employed for a

---

1 Many people would add that typical workers work full-time, making part-time work a form of atypical work. We will consider working hours in Chapter 6.
2 *James* v. *Greenwich LBC* [2008] EWCA Civ 35; [2008] ICR 545.   3 Ibid.
4 These include a duty not to discriminate (for example, RRA 1976, s. 7, and see *Harrods* v. *Remick* [1998] 1 All ER 52) and a duty to pay the minimum wage (NMWA 1998, s. 34).
5 See Chapter 9.

specified period of time. This may seem attractive, because at least the worker knows when he or she must look for a new job. However, in practice, fixed-term workers may be in an uncertain position. Often, the employer will leave open the possibility that the fixed-term contract might be renewed: for example, if the firm remains busy or if a woman on maternity leave decides not to return to work. But the individual is always vulnerable to losing his or her job whenever the fixed-term contract comes to an end.

A third group of atypical workers consists of those who work at home, in contrast to typical workers who work at the employer's premises. 'Traditional' homework is a relatively low-paid and predominantly female occupation, common in industries such as garment manufacturing. Women take in sewing to do at home and are paid for each garment they complete. More recently, improvements in communications technology have made it possible for many office workers to work from home, using email and the internet to keep in touch with their employer. This form of working – sometimes known as teleworking – is often popular with parents who wish to have more flexibility in combining their work with family life. One problem faced by homeworkers is that the employer may not give them equal terms and conditions with those doing similar work on the employer's premises.[6] It may be difficult for homeworkers even to discover this because they do not meet other employees. This leads to the further problem that homeworkers may not be involved in collective activities in the workplace – for example, they are unlikely to be members of trade unions.

Perhaps the commonest group of atypical workers consists of those who work on an 'as required' basis. Typical employees expect to turn up for work regardless of whether or not the firm is busy enough to need their services. The employer takes the risk that employees may sometimes be idle during quiet periods. But those who work on an 'as required' basis must bear the risk of a shortage of work themselves. This group covers a multitude of different contractual arrangements. One subset consists of zero-hours workers, who are under contract to the employer but who are not guaranteed any particular number of hours per week. Another consists of casual or temporary or freelance workers, who are hired when they are needed. They may work for several different employers or regularly for one employer. These various kinds of workers cannot predict how much they will earn each week.

Researchers have tried to determine what proportion of the UK workforce is atypical, but this is quite difficult to do. Burchell *et al.* conducted a survey in which they asked individuals what their employment status was. They estimated that 86 per cent of the British workforce were typical employees.[7] However, one obvious problem with the survey method is that people may not classify

6 See DTI, *Telework Guidance* (2003), implementing EU (2002) Framework Agreement on Telework.
7 B. Burchell, S. Deakin and S. Honey, *The Employment Status of Individuals in Non-Standard Employment* (1999).

themselves accurately. Burchell *et al.* interviewed some of their respondents to find out how they were classifying themselves, and after these interviews they were only able to say with certainty that 64 per cent were employees. Another 30 per cent might or might not have been employees. Indeed, the tests applied by the courts to decide who is a typical employee and who is not are so ambiguous that researchers may not be able to classify people with any certainty even when presented with all the details of their employment relationship.

The Workplace Employee Relations Survey (WERS) approaches the question of employment status from a different perspective.[8] Instead of asking what proportion of the workforce are typical employees, it focuses on what proportion of workplaces use atypical workers. In 2004, 30 per cent of workplaces were employing some people on fixed-term contracts. In many cases, fixed-term contracts were being used where indefinite contracts had been used in the past.[9] Around 16 per cent of workplaces were using agency workers and around 6 per cent were using homeworkers.[10] Zero-hours contracts were found in 5 per cent of workplaces.[11]

Economics perspectives

Writers in the neoclassical tradition identify two main benefits to employers from using atypical workers.[12] One is that the employer is able to shift the risk of a downturn in business to the workers, instead of having to shoulder the risk itself. The other is that atypical workers do not qualify for many statutory employment rights, making them cheaper to hire than employees. New institutional economists question the wisdom of both these strategies. They argue that individuals will be more productive if they have secure jobs and if their rights are respected by their employer.

Employees in 'typical' jobs expect to turn up for work each day, and to get paid, regardless of whether or not the firm is busy. The employer takes the risk that the employees may not always have work to do. But some kinds of atypical work involve passing this risk on to the worker. For example, casual workers are called in by the employer *only* when the firm is busy. The employer makes a saving because it does not have to pay these workers when they are not needed. In practice, most firms cannot manage without some 'typical' employees. If the employer runs a shop, it would not make sense to send all the staff home when the shop was quiet, since customers would quickly lose patience with a shop that did not keep to its advertised opening hours. But it would make sense for the employer to have a 'core' workforce of full-time employees, and then to

---

8 B. Kersley *et al.*, *Inside the Workplace* (2006).   9 Ibid., pp. 80–2.   10 Ibid., pp. 103–5.
11 Ibid., pp. 79–80.
12 The classic study is J. Atkinson, *Flexibility, Uncertainty and Manpower Management* (1984).
    See also H. Collins, 'Independent contractors and the challenge of vertical disintegration to
    employment protection laws' (1990) 10 *OJLS* 353, pp. 356–62.

supplement them with a 'periphery' of casual workers who could be brought in during busy periods.[13] This is often referred to in the literature as 'numerical flexibility', and it can generate considerable cost savings for some employers.[14]

Atypical workers are cheaper to employ not just because they work only when they are needed, but also because they do not qualify for all of the employment rights granted to employees. This links to the first advantage and is also a benefit to employers in itself. The fact that atypical workers do not qualify for unfair dismissal protection or redundancy payments allows employers to hire and fire them at will, in pursuit of numerical flexibility. And their lack of rights also saves employers money. As we saw in Chapter 2, neoclassical economists regard employment rights as a burden on business. The employer's labour costs are made up of the wages it must pay and the cost of providing employment rights. The employer's aim is to keep these costs as low as possible, so whenever a new employment right is introduced, the employer will either reduce the employees' pay or reduce the number of people it employs. Atypical workers are cheaper to employ because they are entitled to fewer costly rights on top of their wages. Thus, the employer can save money by converting existing employees into atypical workers. And when new labour rights are introduced by the government, it is less likely that atypical workers will qualify for them and therefore less likely that the employer will need to cut wages or make people redundant in order to absorb them.

Many writers in the neoclassical tradition would claim that the existence of atypical work is beneficial to workers as well as to employers, even though workers do not get so much legal protection. They point to two main advantages. First, they argue that an atypical job is better than no job at all.[15] Employers are more likely to create new jobs if they can do so cheaply and without making a long-term commitment. Second, they argue that not everyone wants a 'typical' job. Students or parents with childcare responsibilities might be glad of some extra income occasionally, without having to take on a permanent job. However, not all forms of atypical work are convenient for workers. A parent needs to know when he or she is likely to be called in to work so that childcare can be arranged, but the firm might want workers who can be called in at very short notice.

New institutional economists take a very different view on the availability of employment rights. They argue that employment rights can make a positive contribution to the profitability of firms.[16] They would therefore wish to see rights afforded to the entire workforce – to atypical workers as well as to typical employees – unless it can be shown that a particular right would not enhance competitiveness. As we saw in Chapter 2, their perception of employment rights stems from their desire to see firms competing not just on the price of their products, but on their quality and innovation.

---

13 Atkinson, *Flexibility*, Chapter 5.   14 Ibid., para. 4.4.   15 Ibid., para. 3.15.
16 See, generally, S. Deakin and F. Wilkinson, 'Rights vs efficiency? The economic case for transnational labour standards' (1994) 23 *ILJ* 289.

Economists in this tradition are particularly concerned that atypical workers are unlikely to receive very much training from their employer or employers. The rational employer decides whether to offer training by comparing the costs of the training with the benefits it will secure from having a more skilled person in the workforce. These benefits can be calculated by looking at how much that person's productivity will increase and how long he or she will stay with the firm. This last consideration helps to explain why it does not make sense to train atypical workers. A permanent employee might stay with the firm until retirement. A flexible worker is less predictable: he or she might leave if a permanent job became available at another firm, for example.

The natural reluctance of employers to train atypical workers has a number of harmful economic consequences. It is generally thought that there is a close relationship between a firm's productivity and the skills of its workforce. Highly trained staff will take care over their work and will respond quickly to new situations as they arise. Moreover, they may be able to perform a variety of different tasks within the firm. This 'functional flexibility' enables the firm to remain productive when one part of the business is quiet, because employees can be redeployed on other duties.[17] This addresses the same problem as 'numerical flexibility', discussed above, but in a very different way. Thus, firms will be less productive if they do not offer training to staff. More generally, the UK is more likely to attract investment if it can offer a highly skilled and productive workforce, but this broader goal will not be met if a significant section of the workforce – the atypical workers – cannot access training. For those workers, the danger is that they will become trapped in a series of atypical jobs because they can never obtain the training they need in order to secure a more attractive 'typical' job.

Of course, one response to these arguments might be to say that they cannot be correct, because if they were, firms would not use atypical work. They would employ and train typical workers and recoup the costs through gains in productivity. The fact that firms continue to use atypical workers must mean that the benefits of training and productivity are not sufficient to outweigh the costs of typical employment, at least for some firms and some jobs. However, writers in the new institutional tradition have a number of alternative explanations of why firms might continue to use atypical workers. First, firms may be more focused on short-term gains than on longer-term performance. The advantages of typical employment may take some time to manifest themselves, whereas the advantages of atypical employment, particularly the cost savings, are immediately apparent. Second, even if firms realise the importance of focusing on long-term survival and perceive the advantages of typical work, they may find it difficult to stop using atypical work because of the fear that they will be outdone by their competitors in the short term. On this view, the government should encourage firms

17 Atkinson, *Flexibility*, para. 4.3.

to create 'typical' jobs by regulating atypical work so that it is no longer regarded as a cheap alternative.

Thus, these competing theories have important implications for the shape of labour law. From the new institutional perspective, the law should, in general, discourage the use of atypical workers because they are unlikely to be as productive as typical employees. An obvious way to do this would be to extend employee rights to atypical workers. From the neoclassical perspective, the law should not try to regulate atypical work. This would increase employers' costs and stifle job creation. But before we see how English law has responded to these arguments, we need to examine some rights perspectives.

Rights perspectives

Perhaps the best way to introduce rights perspectives on the scope of employment law is to look at the approach writers in this tradition take to the *history* of atypical work.[18] We will then examine two different ways in which rights arguments could be used: to support the granting of rights to all members of the workforce, and to support a two-tier system in which only the most fundamental rights would be guaranteed to everyone.

The strategy of protecting the workforce through minimum rights enshrined in legislation became popular in the 1970s, due to a growing realisation that not everyone was protected by collective bargaining.[19] This legislation (with the exception of the SDA 1975 and RRA 1976) granted rights to employees only. But at this stage, the choice of 'employee' as the organising concept of employment law was not particularly problematic, since atypical workers made up a tiny minority of the workforce. In the 1980s, employers began to make more use of atypical work. Since the economy was in recession, it was not surprising that employers sought ways of saving money; but atypical work involved saving money by evading the law. Employers designed contracts deliberately so that individuals would be workers without rights rather than employees with rights. The evasion was at its most blatant when employers dismissed their employees and re-engaged them on an atypical basis.[20] Moreover, as Fredman has argued, the development of atypical work had a disproportionate impact on individuals who tended to be disadvantaged in the labour market in other respects, such as the low-paid and women with childcare responsibilities.[21] From a rights perspective, it seems obvious that the government should have reacted to these developments by expanding the scope of employment law so that all members of the workforce were protected, thus restoring the law to the position it adopted at the

18 See, for example, S. Fredman, 'Labour law in flux: the changing composition of the workforce' (1997) 26 *ILJ* 337.
19 See Chapter 1.
20 For example, *Ready Mixed Concrete* v. *Minister of Pensions* [1968] 2 QB 497, discussed below.
21 S. Fredman, 'Women at work: the broken promise of flexicurity' (2004) 33 *ILJ* 299.

beginning of the 1970s. As we shall see, however, no government has yet adopted this strategy.

The argument that all rights should be afforded to all workers starts from the premise that working people face the same or broadly similar set of issues in the workplace, regardless of whether the law classifies them as typical or as atypical.[22] For example, if a person is called to a disciplinary hearing by the employer, he or she might find this situation highly intimidating and might value the presence of a union representative or other companion. And if a person's child is taken ill at school during the working day, he or she might need a reasonable amount of time off work to go and make arrangements for the care of that child. At the moment, the former right is available to workers as well as employees,[23] whereas the latter is available only to employees.[24] It is hard to see why the status of someone's contract should make this much difference.

Many commentators explain the fundamental similarity between typical and atypical workers by pointing out that both groups are (in general) *economically dependent* on the employer.[25] One manifestation of this is that both employees and workers usually rely on their main job as their source of income and could not easily manage without it if they were dismissed. But this does not fully capture the meaning of economic dependence in this context. The real question is whether these groups of people are able to negotiate with their employer – about their rate of pay or hours of work, for example. Of course, a highly skilled employee may be able to name his or her price. But for most people, jobs are offered on a 'take it or leave it' basis. This extends to employment status: it is the employer who decides whether a new recruit will be an employee or a worker. Individuals do not usually understand the significance of employee status, and even if they do, they are unlikely to have a chance to bargain about it. The only people who are not economically dependent on the employer are those who are genuinely self-employed: who run their own business and hire themselves out to a variety of customers. These are people who decide what their price is and offer it to the potential customer, and who are able to negotiate their own terms and conditions, such as the hours they will work. The implications of this for employment law are obvious. Its protection should be granted to everyone in the economically dependent group.[26] This excludes the self-employed, but includes *both* employees and workers.

However, adopting a rights perspective does not necessarily involve taking this radical view. As we saw in Chapter 3, it is common to find that some rights

---

22 See, for example, B. Hepple, 'Restructuring employment rights' (1986) 15 *ILJ* 69; Collins, 'Independent contractors'; Fredman, 'Labour law in flux'.

23 ERA 1999, s. 10.   24 ERA 1996, s. 57A.

25 For discussion and critique, see P. Davies and M. Freedland, 'Employees, workers, and the autonomy of labour law', in H. Collins *et al.* (eds.), *Legal Regulation of the Employment Relation* (2000).

26 See ILO Recommendation 198 on the Employment Relationship 2006.

are treated as more fundamental than others. It could therefore be argued that the most fundamental rights should be available to all workers, while less fundamental rights could be granted only to the smaller category of employees. Again, self-employed people would, in general, be expected to negotiate for their own protection.

But why would we want to draw these distinctions? Perhaps the most obvious reason is to respond to the neoclassical economists' argument that labour rights impose costs on employers. Some rights are clearly costly: the right to a minimum wage may require the employer to pay its workers more than it would otherwise have chosen to do. Other rights impose costs indirectly: if workers have a right to be consulted, managers must spend time preparing for, and taking part in, meetings with worker representatives. Moreover, for all rights, firms must devote resources to finding out what the law requires and to ensuring that they have procedures for complying. Thus, the decision to limit the number of people who qualify for certain rights offers a way of controlling the costs to be borne by firms.

The most direct way to implement this would be to divide rights into those which are costly and those which are less so. Firms could then be required to grant the less costly rights to all workers and the more costly ones only to employees. This sometimes happens at an international level when attempts are made to get developing countries to grant minimum rights to workers in their legislation. Emphasis is placed on 'low-cost' rights so that developing countries cannot rely on the argument that they cannot afford to comply. Two of the ILO's core rights are freedom of association and the right not to be discriminated against.[27] It is arguable that these rights can be achieved (in a basic sense, at least) without much expenditure.[28] For example, the government could simply ban discrimination on grounds of race, sex and so on, repeal any laws prohibiting trade unionism and prohibit detrimental treatment of trade union members.

But there are two major problems with this approach. The first is that it is too simplistic to equate 'cheap' rights with fundamental rights. Some rights might be considered so fundamental for the protection of workers that they should be granted to all, *even though* they will impose some costs on employers. The minimum wage might be an example of this. Basic considerations of dignity suggest that employers should not be able to get the benefit of labour without paying a reasonable price for it. But even if a more sophisticated distinction between fundamental and non-fundamental rights is developed, a second problem remains. Why is it that individuals should have more rights, just because they fall into the legal category of employee? Individuals do not, in general, choose their employment status. Employers tend to decide whether someone should be a worker or

27 ILO Declaration on Fundamental Principles and Rights at Work 1998.
28 See C. McCrudden and A.C.L. Davies, 'A perspective on trade and labor rights' (2000) 3 *JIEL* 43, pp. 49–52.

an employee, subject to the possibility that a court might see things differently. In short, an individual's status is a matter of luck. This is not a good basis on which to allocate rights.

The scope of employment law

In the 1980s, the government adopted the neoclassical economics perspective towards the scope of employment law. It allowed employers to develop new forms of atypical work and did not step in to close the legal loopholes they were exploiting. The government's policy was to reduce the burden of labour rights on businesses, so it was hardly going to interfere with employers who found ways to do this for themselves. Since 1997, the government has developed the concept of 'worker' to extend employment rights to those atypical workers who are unable to qualify for rights as employees. This has been paralleled by developments in EC law which have sought to tackle some of the specific problems faced by particular types of atypical worker. These developments suggest that the new institutional economics arguments and rights arguments have begun to have more influence. However, as we shall see, although workers are better protected than the self-employed, they do not get all the rights currently granted to employees. This suggests that neoclassical arguments about the cost of rights are still playing an important role.

Employees

According to s. 230(1) of the Employment Rights Act (ERA) 1996, an employee is 'an individual who has entered into or works under … a contract of employment'. The contract of employment is a common law concept. A person seeking to show that he or she is an employee must fulfil three criteria:

1. there must be 'mutuality of obligation' between the parties to the contract
2. there must be a relationship of employer and employee
3. the contract must not contain any terms inconsistent with the relationship of employer and employee.

At the most basic level, a contract exists when an individual does some work and the employer pays him or her for it. However, according to Freedland, the contract of employment consists of two 'levels'.[29] One level is the basic wage–work bargain just described. The other level is a promise by the employer to provide future work, and a promise by the employee to accept that work, often referred to as a requirement that there be 'mutuality of obligation'. This level is sometimes referred to as the 'global contract' because it links the separate wage–work bargains into an ongoing contract.

---

29 M. Freedland, *The Personal Employment Contract* (2003), pp. 88–92. The author makes clear that this analysis is also applicable to other types of contract, such as workers' contracts.

The mutuality of obligation requirement makes it difficult for casual workers to attain the status of employees. From the employer's point of view, the benefit of using casual workers is that they can be brought in when the firm is busy and laid off when it is not. This does not, in general, involve a promise by the employer to provide future work. Some casual workers may approach the job on a similar footing: that they are under no obligation to accept the work offered by the firm. However, other casual workers may feel that they have made a promise to accept future work. This may be because they cannot afford to live without the work, or because the employer will not contact them again if they refuse. When this occurs, the firm gains the benefit of dependent labour without having to take on the full obligations of an employer, simply by refusing to promise future work.

The point is illustrated by *O'Kelly* v. *Trusthouse Forte*.[30] The employer had a list of casual waiters who could be called in to work when needed. The waiters generally accepted the employer's offers of work, but the court found that they did this for economic reasons, not because they were legally obliged to do so. The employer made no promise to offer them work. Thus, there was no mutuality of obligation and the waiters were not employees.

Sometimes, a creative court can find a way round the mutuality requirement. In *Nethermere* v. *Taverna*, the court used the contractual device of a 'course of dealing' in order to create a global contract.[31] It held that because the employer had, in practice, provided work and the employees had accepted it over a long period of time, this had 'hardened into' a contract of employment. But the modern case law generally follows the *O'Kelly* approach.

Once claimants have proved that there is 'mutuality of obligation', they must then demonstrate the existence of an employee–employer relationship. Over the years, the courts have developed a number of tests for this. In the *Ready Mixed Concrete* case, the court held that a person was an employee if the employer *controlled* his or her work.[32] It was said that: 'control includes the power of deciding the thing to be done, the means to be employed in doing it, the time when and the place where it shall be done'.[33] In practice, however, many people who are usually thought of as employees have a substantial degree of discretion over these issues. For example, a doctor might be an employee of a hospital, but managers would not be able to tell the doctor how to treat the patients. In *Stevenson, Jordan & Harrison Ltd*, the court held that an employee was someone whose work was 'integral' to the employer's business.[34] But this is also difficult to apply. The engineer who fixes the machinery in the employer's factory may seem 'integral' when the machines have broken down, but in law he or she may well be an independent contractor or even the employee of another firm.

---

30 *O'Kelly* v. *Trusthouse Forte* [1984] QB 90. See also *Clark* v. *Oxfordshire Health Authority* [1998] IRLR 125, and *Carmichael* v. *National Power* [1999] 1 WLR 2042.

31 *Nethermere* v. *Taverna* [1984] ICR 612.   32 *Ready Mixed Concrete* v. *Minister of Pensions*.

33 Ibid., p. 515.

34 *Stevenson, Jordan & Harrison Ltd* v. *MacDonald and Evans* [1952] 1 TLR 101.

The most modern test is the 'risk' test, set out in the case of *Market Investigations* v. *Minister of Social Security*.[35] The court held that the question to ask was: who took the risk of profit and loss? If the employer bore the risk, the claimant would count as an employee. But if the claimant bore the risk, he or she would not count as an employee. This fits with the popular perception of the employer as the risk-taking entrepreneur and the employee as someone who simply works for a reliable wage. However, even this test may not work in all circumstances. Through employee share ownership or performance-related pay schemes, employers are increasingly encouraging employees to take a share of the risks associated with the business. These schemes may blur the apparently clear boundary between employer as risk-taker, and employee.

The final hurdle for the potential employee is to show that there are no terms in the contract that are inconsistent with an employment relationship. For example, the courts have stressed that an employee is someone who performs work personally for the employer. If an employee does not feel like going to work, he or she cannot simply send someone else instead. This would be a breach of contract. The courts have inferred from this that if a person does have the contractual right to send a substitute, then he or she cannot be an employee: *Express and Echo Publications* v. *Tanton*.[36] This decision has been much criticised by commentators because it provides employers with an easy way of avoiding the obligations of the employment relationship. Since employers usually draft contracts, they can simply insert a substitution clause. However, the position has been mitigated somewhat by *MacFarlane* v. *Glasgow CC*.[37] Here, the employees were able to provide a substitute, but only from a list of names approved by the employer and only when they were unable to work for some valid reason, such as illness. The court held that this more limited substitution clause was not inconsistent with a contract of employment.

Rights theorists have been highly critical of the courts' approach to the definition of 'employee'.[38] Their argument is that the courts should acknowledge the employer's role in drafting the contract and should therefore construe it purposively to protect the employee. The problem for the courts is that they are constrained by the ordinary rules of contract law when they approach the contract of employment. When a contract is in writing, the courts tend to treat the document as the source of the parties' agreement. They are reluctant to admit other evidence – for example, that the employer included a term in the document but never applied it in practice. Moreover, although the law allows the courts to question 'sham' transactions, the sham doctrine is narrowly defined and requires that both parties share an intention to deceive others as to the nature of their

---

35 *Market Investigations* v. *Minister of Social Security* [1969] 2 QB 173.
36 *Express and Echo Publications* v. *Tanton* [1999] ICR 693.
37 *MacFarlane* v. *Glasgow CC* [2001] IRLR 7.
38 See, for example, Fredman, 'Labour law in flux' and 'Women at work'.

dealings.[39] This doctrine does not apply where the employer drafts an unrealistic contract and imposes it on the individual. Some commentators have gone so far as to say that the employment relationship should be redefined as a 'status' rather than a contract in order to avoid these problems.[40]

Workers

'Worker' is a middle category between employee and self-employed. Labour law in fact contains two different definitions of 'worker', which we will label 'the worker definition' and 'the broad worker definition'. The broad worker definition (to be discussed in the next section) includes some self-employed people, whereas the worker definition does not.

The worker definition in s. 230(3) of ERA 1996 is:

> ... an individual who has entered into or works under ...
>
> a) a contract of employment, or
> b) any other contract, whether express or implied and (if it is express) whether oral or in writing, whereby the individual undertakes to do or perform personally any work or services for another party to the contract whose status is not by virtue of the contract that of a client or customer of any profession or business undertaking carried on by the individual ...

The first point to note is that this definition includes employees in paragraph (a). This means that if a statute gives a right to 'workers', employees benefit from that right as well. But so do the people who fall within paragraph (b). Thus, if a right is granted to workers it will help more people than a right which is granted only to employees. To fall within (b), the claimant must fulfil three criteria:

1. There must be mutuality of obligation between the parties to the contract.
2. He or she must be under a duty to perform the work personally.
3. He or she must not be running a business.

We have already met the first two criteria in our discussion of the definition of an employee. They are highly significant because they cast doubt on whether the introduction of the 'worker' concept will help as many atypical workers as the government claims. The authority for the proposition that workers need to show mutuality of obligation is *Byrne Brothers* v. *Baird*.[41] As we have seen, mutuality is not usually present where a worker is employed on a casual basis, so most casual workers will not be protected by the new concept. The requirement that a worker performs the work personally is expressly set out in the statutory definition itself. This makes it difficult for individuals whose contract contains a substitution clause to establish that they are workers, although, as we saw above, the courts'

---

39 *Snook* v. *London and West Riding Investments Ltd* [1967] 2 QB 786.
40 The most famous statement of this view is A. Supiot, *Beyond Employment: Changes in Work and the Future of Labour Law in Europe* (2001).
41 *Byrne Brothers* v. *Baird* [2002] ICR 667.

recent decisions indicate that a limited power of substitution is not incompatible with an obligation to perform personally.[42]

The third criterion is that a worker is someone who is not a self-employed person running his or her own business. According to *Byrne Brothers* v. *Baird*, one of the first cases on this issue, the worker concept must be understood in the light of its purpose: to extend the protection of employment law to some of the people who would not fall under the definition of an employee. Purposive approaches were criticised in *Redrow Homes*, but that case was concerned with the duty to perform work personally, so *Byrne Brothers* is still good law on the dependence test.[43] In *Byrne*, the EAT said:

> The reason why employees are thought to need such protection is that they are in a subordinate and dependent position vis-à-vis their employers: the purpose of the [worker definition] is to extend protection to workers who are, substantively and economically, in the same position. Thus the essence of the intended distinction must be between, on the one hand, workers whose degree of dependence is essentially the same as that of employees and, on the other, contractors who have a sufficiently arm's-length and independent position to be treated as being able to look after themselves in the relevant respects.[44]

The worker concept would be deprived of all its meaning if the distinction between worker and self-employed was drawn in exactly the same way as the distinction between employee and self-employed. Equally, however, the approach cannot be entirely different, since similar issues of dependence and independence arise in both situations. The EAT's solution is to use the same test for worker/self-employed as is used for employee/self-employed – whether or not the person is economically dependent on the alleged employer[45] – 'but with the boundary pushed further in the putative worker's favour'.[46]

Thus, according to *Byrne*, when the legal concept at issue in a case is 'worker', it will be harder to persuade the court that the claimant is self-employed than it would be if the legal concept at issue was 'employee'. Even so, many claimants will still be defeated by the requirements, discussed above, to show personal service and mutuality of obligation. This has led some commentators to question the practical utility of the worker definition.[47]

Self-employed people

By now, it should be reasonably clear who counts as self-employed. A self-employed person runs his or her own business and takes the risk of profit and

---

42 *MacFarlane* v. *Glasgow CC.*
43 *Redrow Homes (Yorkshire) Ltd* v. *Wright* [2004] EWCA Civ 469; [2004] 3 All ER 98.
44 *Byrne Brothers* v. *Baird*, para. 17.
45 The test derived from the *Market Investigations* v. *Minister of Social Security* case.
46 *Byrne Brothers* v. *Baird*, para. 17.
47 See G. Davidov, 'Who is a worker?' (2005) 34 *ILJ* 57, and D. Brodie, 'Employees, workers and the self-employed' (2005) 34 *ILJ* 253.

loss. He or she does not count as an employee or as a worker under the definitions we have considered so far. Indeed, he or she may be the employer of others. Self-employed people only have the chance of legislative protection when the 'broad worker definition' is used.

The 'broad worker definition'[48] is encapsulated in the following quotation:

'Employment' means employment under a contract of service or of apprenticeship or a contract personally to execute any work or labour.[49]

This definition includes employees because they are employed under a 'contract of service'. The requirements of mutuality of obligation and of a duty to perform the work personally both still apply. But, significantly, there is no exclusion for people running their own business. This means that self-employed people can fall within the broad worker definition, *but only* where they perform the work personally.[50] So a self-employed plumber who did repairs him- or herself would be a worker on this definition, but the owner of a plumbing firm who employed staff to carry out repairs would not be. This definition gives employment law its widest possible scope.

Why does it matter?

These three definitions are very important because they represent three different levels of protection in employment law. The self-employed get almost no protection, workers get some protection, and employees get all the protection the law has to offer. Litigation in this area is common as individuals strive to get into a more protected category and employers seek to avoid the legal obligations that would follow from this.

Self-employed people are, in general, outside the scope of employment law. On a practical level, it would be unfair to impose the obligations of an employer on everyone who hires a self-employed person. If I hire an electrician to fix something in my house, I do not expect to have to ensure that the electrician is observing the Working Time Regulations 1998 or being paid the minimum wage. The self-employed person is running his or her own business and should be able to negotiate for the protections he or she needs. So the minimum wage (for example) should not be an issue because the self-employed person is able to charge a rate for the job. As we saw above, this can be reconciled even with a 'rights for all' approach, because self-employed people are not being denied their rights. Instead, their rights are being enforced through their own ability to bargain for them. However, it is important to ensure that the category of self-employment is not drawn too widely to include people who are not able to protect themselves.

---

48 This label is used here because it locates the definition accurately in the employee–worker–self-employed spectrum. Confusingly, however, the legislation uses the terms 'employee' and 'employment'.
49 SDA 1975, s. 82(1).
50 This can still constitute a significant hurdle: see *Mingeley* v. *Pennock* [2004] EWCA Civ 328; [2004] ICR 727.

The only major form of protection for some self-employed persons is under the anti-discrimination legislation.[51] Statutes such as the SDA 1975 and the RRA 1976 use the 'broad worker definition', which includes those self-employed people who perform the work personally.[52] The law's policy here is to spread the protection of discrimination law – and the fundamental right to be free from discrimination – to as broad a group of people as possible. Moreover, this can be done without imposing significant obligations on others. All it means is that a householder has no right to refuse to hire a plumber on the ground that she is female, for example.

Workers get the protection of discrimination law and some additional rights as well. The term has been used in many (though importantly not all) pieces of legislation enacted since 1997. Workers benefit from:

- the national minimum wage[53]
- the working time regulations[54]
- the right to be accompanied at a disciplinary or grievance hearing[55]
- the right not to be discriminated against on the ground of working part-time[56]
- the right not to be discriminated against on grounds of trade union membership.[57]

The use of 'worker' reflects an acknowledgement on the part of the government that a growing number of people fall outside the employee definition without being genuinely self-employed, and that these people deserve some protection. Under s. 23 ERA 1999, the government took the power to extend to workers any of the rights that are currently available only to employees. This provision has not yet been invoked.

Employees are traditionally the subject of employment law and remain the best protected group. They get all the rights afforded to workers and the self-employed, and a very large number of other rights as well. These additional rights include:

- the right not to be discriminated against on the ground of having a fixed-term contract[58]
- redundancy payments[59]
- protection against unfair dismissal[60]
- maternity leave, paternity leave and parental leave[61]
- emergency leave to deal with family crises[62]
- the right to request flexible working[63]
- the right to a written statement of terms and conditions of employment.[64]

---

51 For discussion, see Davies and Freedland, 'Employees, workers, and the autonomy of labour law', pp. 278–81.
52 EqPA 1970, s. 1(6)(a); SDA 1975, s. 82(1); RRA 1976, s. 78(1); DDA 1995, s. 68(1); EE(SO)R 2003 (SI 2003/1661), reg. 2; EE(RB)R 2003 (SI 2003/1660), reg. 2; EE(A)R 2006 (SI 2006/1031), reg. 2.
53 NMWA 1998, ss. 1 and 54(3).   54 WTR 1998 (SI 1998/1833), reg. 2(1).
55 ERA 1999, s. 10.
56 Part-Time Workers (Prevention of Less Favourable Treatment) Regulations 2000 (SI 2000/1551), reg. 1(2).
57 TULRCA 1992, s. 146 (and see also s. 145A–B).
58 Fixed-Term Employees (Prevention of Less Favourable Treatment) Regulations 2002 (SI 2002/2034), reg. 1(2).
59 ERA 1996, s. 135.   60 Ibid., s. 94.
61 Ibid., ss. 71–75, 80A–E and 76–80 respectively.   62 Ibid., s. 57A.
63 Ibid., s. 80F–I.   64 Ibid., s. 1.

Some of these rights are only available after the employee has worked for the employer continuously for a specified period of time. The right to a written statement of terms and conditions is available only after one month,[65] presumably to minimise the bureaucracy which must be complied with for very short-term appointments. The right to a redundancy payment is only available to employees who have worked for one year.[66] The same is usually true of the right not to be unfairly dismissed,[67] although there are some reasons for dismissal (pregnancy, for example) which are actionable from the moment the employment starts.[68] The justification given for these qualifying periods is that they offer firms the flexibility to hire people on a short-term basis and to try them out without fear of legal action if it turns out that they are unsuitable.

The law contains provisions to help an employee to maintain a period of continuous employment even if there are gaps in his or her relationship with an employer. According to s. 212(1) ERA 1996, 'any week during the whole *or part* of which an employee's relations with his employer are governed by a contract of employment counts in computing the employee's period of employment'.[69] An unexpected effect of this is that casual workers may be able to use it in order to obtain employment rights if they have a series of contracts of employment. In *Cornwall CC* v. *Prater*, a teacher who was employed on a succession of contracts of employment was able to link them together into one continuous contract of employment for a ten-year period.[70] Importantly, the Court of Appeal held that if s. 212 applied, there was no need to show mutuality of obligation.

The different lists of rights for the self-employed, workers and employees show that the law adopts a multi-layered approach. It is clearly not the strategy of neoclassical economics; nor is it the 'rights for all' strategy suggested by many rights theorists and by some new institutional economists. There are many different ways in which we might interpret the policy underlying the law on this issue.

On one view, the government might be adopting a 'core' rights approach, in which atypical workers are given a minimum set of rights to protect their dignity at work, but do not get the full range of rights because this is thought to be too costly. This would be a 'third way' between the rights and neoclassical economics perspectives. It could be argued that the minimum wage, working time and discrimination protections constitute a 'core' of this kind. However, because the law has developed in a piecemeal way, there are some anomalies. For example, it is odd that the right not to be discriminated against on the ground of having a fixed-term contract applies only to employees. Although this may not be fundamental, it is part of a set of initiatives (to be discussed below) aimed at eliminating discrimination against atypical workers. It seems strange that it should be granted only to those who have a contract of employment.

65 Ibid., s. 198.   66 Ibid., s. 155.   67 Ibid., s. 108(1).
68 Ibid., s. 108(2).   69 Emphasis added.
70 *Cornwall CC* v. *Prater* [2006] EWCA Civ 102; [2006] 2 All ER 1013.

Another way to understand the current law might be from the new institutionalist perspective. On this view, the government may be trying to regulate atypical work so that it no longer constitutes a cheap alternative to standard employment. This would fit with the European Employment Strategy (EES), a set of EU policies designed to improve productivity and employment levels within the Member States. The EES does not advocate the abolition of atypical work, but it does suggest that it should be regulated so that the differences between typical and atypical work become less marked.[71] This is seen as a way to encourage employers to provide training for both types of workers. The overall aim is to create a labour market characterised by 'flexicurity' (a combination of flexibility and security), in which highly skilled, adaptable workers always have plenty of job opportunities (security), but can move easily from one job to another (flexibility). The key questions here are whether you think the worker definition – both in terms of its scope and the rights it affords – succeeds in making atypical work more like typical work, and whether you think employers will respond to this by providing training as the policy-makers envisage.

Perhaps more importantly, it remains to be seen how the courts will develop the worker and employee definitions. The government does not appear to intend to abolish the employee/worker distinction. It could do this by using s. 23 ERA 1999 to extend all employee rights to workers, but so far it has chosen not to do so. Logically, the three-tier approach to employment rights requires there to be a difference between each of the three tiers. At the moment, the worker definition may not be very much broader than the employee definition. Is it possible for the courts to differentiate them more sharply?

Atypical workers have other problems too

Even if atypical workers can bring themselves within the scope of some or all of mainstream employment law, by showing that they are workers or employees, this may not solve all their problems. This is because employment law is directed at the concerns of typical employees. Atypical workers may face difficulties which simply do not apply to typical employees. The EC's strategy has been to legislate separately for each group of atypical workers.[72] It has therefore been well-placed to address the unique concerns of fixed-term workers, agency workers and so on.

The Fixed-Term Employees (Prevention of Less Favourable Treatment) Regulations 2002 are intended to tackle the specific problems faced by fixed-term

---

71 European Commission, *Towards Common Principles of Flexicurity: More and Better Jobs Through Flexibility and Security* (2007).

72 Community law has not had much impact on the employee/worker debate because the scope of employment law is regarded as a matter for the Member States, though see (C256/01) *Allonby* v. *Accrington and Rossendale College* [2004] ECR I-873.

employees.[73] They implement the Fixed-Term Work Directive,[74] which was agreed by the social partners (the European employers' associations and the European Trade Union Confederation) under the social dialogue procedure.[75] The Regulations contain a basic protection against discrimination on the grounds of being a fixed-term employee.[76] This means that an individual cannot, for example, be paid less than a permanent worker simply because he or she has a fixed-term contract, unless the employer can give an objective justification for the difference in treatment. The Regulations also prevent employers from repeatedly renewing fixed-term contracts over a long period of time.[77] If a person is employed under a succession of fixed-term contracts for a period of more than four years, he or she is deemed by the Regulations to be a permanent employee. However, the employer may escape this result if it can show that there is an objective justification for continuing to employ the person on a fixed-term basis. It remains to be seen how ready the courts will be to accept employers' defences under this provision. However, the main criticism that has been made of the Regulations is that they only apply to employees. As we have seen, more people would have been protected had the term 'worker' been used instead.

The EU has recently agreed a directive on agency work. When implemented, this will provide agency workers with some protection against discrimination in their terms and conditions of employment as compared to typical workers in the user enterprise.[78] As we saw above, agency workers often face uncertainty about who, if anyone, is their employer, making it difficult for them to claim employment rights. At one point, it seemed as if the courts might develop the idea of an implied contract between the agency worker and the end user,[79] but in an important recent case they have stepped back from this idea.[80] The new directive should help because someone (the agency or the user) will have to be given responsibility for ensuring that agency workers do not suffer discrimination.

The scope of employment law – an issue to remember

The remaining chapters of this book will consider in greater detail the various employment issues we have touched on here: the minimum wage, freedom of association, unfair dismissal and so on. Each chapter will contain a brief reminder of the scope of the rights it is considering: whether they are worker rights or employee rights. As you learn about each new set of rights, you should think back to the arguments made in this chapter and consider whether you agree with the way in which the law has allocated them.

---

73 SI 2002/2034. See A. McColgan, 'The Fixed-Term Employees (Prevention of Less Favourable Treatment) Regulations 2002: fiddling while Rome burns?' (2003) 32 *ILJ* 194.
74 Directive 99/70/EC.   75 See Art. 139 EC.   76 SI 2002/2034, regs. 3–4.
77 SI 2002/2034, reg. 8.   78 European Commission press release, 10 June 2008.
79 *Dacas* v. *Brook Street Bureau* [2004] EWCA Civ 217; [2004] ICR 1437.
80 *James* v. *Greenwich LBC*.

Further reading

For a detailed textbook account of this topic, see S. Deakin and G.S. Morris, *Labour Law* (4th edn., 2005), Chapter 3, or H. Collins, K.D. Ewing and A. McColgan, *Labour Law: Text and Materials* (2nd edn., 2005), Chapter 2. M. Freedland, *The Personal Employment Contract* (2003), Chapters 1 and 2, offers a highly original and stimulating account of the issues covered in this chapter.

J. Atkinson, *Flexibility, Uncertainty and Manpower Management* (1984) is a classic statement of the advantages of atypical work from a business perspective and gives a good insight into the neoclassical arguments. Theorists in this tradition often claim that atypical work is beneficial for the worker too. What benefits might there be? Do they depend on the type of atypical work? Are some types of atypical work never beneficial? Do you agree with the view that legal regulation would stifle job creation? For some ideas, see J. Murray, 'Normalising temporary work' (1999) 28 *ILJ* 269; S. Fredman, 'Labour law in flux: the changing composition of the workforce' (1997) 26 *ILJ* 337; and D. McCann, *Regulating Flexible Work* (2008).

There is an interesting discussion of the 'flexicurity' approach in European Commission, *Towards Common Principles of Flexicurity: More and Better Jobs Through Flexibility and Security* (2007). See also DTI, *Protecting Vulnerable Workers, Supporting Good Employers* (2006). For an interesting exploration of the relationship between the government's stated 'third way' policies and their implementation in practice, see C. Kilpatrick, 'Has New Labour reconfigured employment legislation?' (2003) 23 *ILJ* 135. What does her analysis tell us about the explanatory power of the perspectives adopted in this chapter? For a critique of 'flexicurity' from a rights perspective, see S. Fredman, 'Women at work: the broken promise of flexicurity' (2004) 33 *ILJ* 299.

There is a large literature on atypical work in the rights tradition, much of which is mentioned in the footnotes to this chapter, but one of the most thought-provoking contributions is P. Davies and M. Freedland, 'Employees, workers and the autonomy of labour law', in H. Collins, P. Davies and R. Rideout (eds.), *Legal Regulation of the Employment Relation* (2000). Why should atypical workers be protected? How do these writers justify imposing additional costs on employers?

Rights theorists are strongly critical of the role of the courts in interpreting 'employee' and 'worker' in atypical work situations. You may find it helpful to revisit the discussion of the courts in Chapter 4, and S. Anderman, 'The interpretation of protective employment statutes and contracts of employment' (2000) 29 *ILJ* 223. On the 'worker' definition, see G. Davidov, 'Who is a worker?' (2005) 34 *ILJ* 57; D. Brodie, 'Employees, workers and the self-employed' (2005) 34 *ILJ* 253; and A.C.L. Davies, 'The contract for intermittent employment' (2007) 36 *ILJ* 102. If the law was reformed in line with rights arguments, what strategies could the legislature adopt to ensure that the courts gave full effect to the new provisions?

6

Working time

Working time has traditionally been regarded as a matter for collective bargaining or for managerial decision-making. Nowadays, three important aspects of working time are regulated by legislation. First, the Working Time Regulations 1998 seek to regulate the working time of all workers, by prescribing limits on the maximum number of hours that can be worked in the week and by requiring employers to give their workers daily and weekly rest breaks and annual holidays. Second, the law forbids discrimination against those who work part-time. Unless the employer can justify treating part-timers differently, it must give them the same benefits as full-timers. Third, the law provides various kinds of leave to enable employees to combine work and family life: maternity leave, paternity leave, parental leave and emergency leave. Parents may also ask for their employer's permission to work part-time or from home or in some other way that will assist them in fulfilling their family responsibilities.

In the international human rights instruments, there is a long-standing tradition of rights to reasonable limits on working hours and to paid holidays. Such rights have been framed as basic minimum standards that are necessary to ensure that all workers are treated fairly by their employers, or sometimes as an aspect of health and safety regulation. Maternity leave is also a well-established right. It reflects the dual concerns that pregnant women might suffer discrimination in the labour market and that certain types of work might pose a health hazard to pregnant women and their babies. More recent instruments have begun to include some version of the right to 'reconcile' work and family life. Some instruments base this right on the needs of working parents of both sexes; others emphasise its role in facilitating women's participation in the labour market. In general, however, the international instruments tend to contain either bare minimum standards or relatively vague aspirations, so theorists have had to elaborate on them in order to develop a detailed critique of English law.

Neoclassical economists focus on the individual's 'labour supply decision': in other words, his or her choice of how many hours to work. This approach tends to be hostile towards legal regulation of working time because it limits individuals' choices. From the new institutional economics perspective, however, controls on working time can be justified in various ways. A common argument is that the relationship between working hours and productivity is not straightforward: shorter working hours may make people more, rather than less, productive. Neoclassical writers are also critical of rights to parental leave, paternity leave and so on, because they are seen as costly for employers. But pro-labour economists argue that such rights may have compensating advantages. In particular, they make it easier for employers to recruit and retain workers, thus giving them access to a wider pool of talent.

Economics perspectives

The working week

Let us begin with a basic neoclassical account of working time.[1] This treats the number of hours worked as a choice made by each employee. Assume that the wage rate is £1 per hour and (implausibly) that the individual could work for up to twenty-four hours a day. This gives the individual a choice between twenty-four hours of leisure time and no income, or no hours of leisure time and £24 of income, or (more likely) some position in between, such as twelve hours of leisure and £12 of income. The individual's choice will be governed by a range of personal factors. For example, a parent might place a high value on leisure time because it can be spent with his or her children, whereas a student might want to work long hours in the vacation to earn more money.

If the wage rate increases, the worker's response will depend upon which of two effects is dominant: the income effect or the substitution effect.[2] The income effect in the context of a wage rate increase means that the individual's income goes up even though he or she is working the same number of hours. He or she might decide to spend this extra money on more leisure time: in other words, to reduce the number of hours worked. The substitution effect in the context of a wage rate increase means that the price of leisure (the money foregone by deciding not to work) goes up. It therefore makes sense for the worker to increase his or her working hours. Which of these effects dominates depends, again, on the individual's preferences. So in our examples above, an increase in wages might prompt the parent to enter the labour market, because in a few hours he or she can earn money to purchase additional goods for the family, and it might prompt the student to reduce his or her hours to obtain more leisure. A wage decrease has the opposite effect.

What happens if the law steps in to regulate the number of hours people can work? Let us imagine that the law states that no-one may work for more than forty-eight hours per week. This would leave some workers feeling underemployed: their preference would be to increase their income by working for more than forty-eight hours. Such sentiments are particularly likely to arise among low-paid

---

1 See, generally, P.R.G. Layard and A.A. Walters, *Microeconomic Theory* (1978), Chapter 11.
2 See L. Robbins, 'On the elasticity of demand for income in terms of effort' (1930) *Economica* 123.

workers, who may not be able to earn enough to live on if the law restricts their hours. This demonstrates that there is an important relationship between working time and the minimum wage, to be considered in Chapter 8. One option for the underemployed worker is to seek a second job to increase his or her hours and income. This defeats the law's aim of ensuring that no-one works for more than forty-eight hours. But it is difficult to prevent because the law – which regulates individual employers – cannot readily tackle the cumulative effect of several separate employment relationships.

Imagine now that the only kind of job available is one with a forty-eight-hour working week. This will leave some workers feeling over-employed. They would rather work fewer hours and have more leisure time. Instead, they are left with the difficult choice of working full-time or not working at all. If they take a full-time job, some theorists suggest that they will take more days off (such as sickness absences) because they are unhappy with the hours they are expected to work.[3] The state could intervene to help these workers by encouraging employers to provide more opportunities for part-time working. A neoclassical economist would, of course, advocate keeping the legal rights of part-time workers to a minimum, so that employers would be attracted to part-time work by its cheapness.

The new institutional economists approach the regulation of working time in a very different way.[4] They argue that controls on working time may benefit employers. At first sight, it might seem as if there is a linear relationship between hours worked and productivity: the more hours a worker works, the more productive he or she will be. But on reflection this is clearly not true. If it takes a person one hour to dig a hole of a certain depth, it is unlikely that he or she will be able to dig ten times that depth in ten hours. Even where the measure of productivity is less clear-cut, the quality of the individual's work may suffer. A shop worker may be less helpful to the customers; a doctor may administer the wrong dose of medication. A legal maximum limit on the working week would help employers to get the best out of their workers.

The obvious neoclassical response to this is to point out that no rational employer would require its workers to work long hours if this would be damaging to the firm. And a legal maximum limit would not help firms to improve safety and productivity because it would not fit their specific needs.[5] It might be unsafe for certain workers to work as many as forty-eight hours in a week, whereas others could work productively for a much larger number of hours. However, this argument assumes that employers have perfect information about safe working hours, and that they are willing to focus on considerations such as productivity

3 See, for example, S.G. Allen, 'An empirical model of work attendance' (1981) 63 *Review of Economics and Statistics* 77.
4 See, generally, S. Deakin and F. Wilkinson, 'Rights vs efficiency: the economic case for transnational labour standards' (1994) 23 *ILJ* 289.
5 A point made by C. Barnard, 'EC "social" policy', in P. Craig and G. de Búrca, *The Evolution of EU Law* (1999), p. 491, though she advocates regulation in a different form rather than no regulation at all.

and safety rather than cost. An employer might ask someone to work additional hours without realising that he or she has already reached the limit of his or her productivity. Or the employer might decide to use existing workers to do extra hours instead of incurring the expenses of recruiting and training additional staff. A legal maximum limit on the working week helps to educate employers about safe working hours, and prevents them from making decisions based solely on short-term financial concerns.

New institutional economists also argue that there are benefits for employers in the provision of part-time jobs. The reasons for this are partly macroeconomic. If the UK economy is to be as productive as possible, it must use its labour resources to the full.[6] But not all workers are able to – or want to – work full-time. Those wishing to study for new qualifications or to care for children might prefer a part-time job. From a macroeconomic viewpoint, it is better to have these people in the labour market on a part-time basis than not at all. And at the microeconomic level, firms will benefit from having access to a wider pool of talent from which to recruit their employees. However, these benefits will only arise if the part-time jobs on offer are sufficiently attractive to persuade more people to enter the labour market. Economists express this idea using the concept of the 'reservation wage'. For someone who is not currently participating in the labour market, the reservation wage is the lowest wage rate at which he or she would be willing to take a job. If part-time jobs are low-paid and have few benefits, they will fall below the reservation wage of many potential workers. But if the law steps in to ensure that part-time workers have the same pay and benefits as their full-time colleagues, and that they are entitled to the minimum wage and other legal rights, the jobs are more likely to be at or above many people's reservation wage. As usual, the rational employer facing recruitment difficulties would take these steps of its own accord, without legal intervention, but concerns about costs and being undercut by competitors might prevent this.

Leave

Neoclassical theorists argue that if the law requires employers to provide various kinds of leave for parents, they will be burdened with substantial costs. One potential cost is that of providing pay and benefits to an employee who is on leave. Of course, the law may specify that some kinds of leave should be unpaid or paid at a lower rate than the employee's usual wage. But where the leave is paid at the normal rate, the employer is receiving no work in return for its outlay. Another type of cost – which arises even if the leave is unpaid – is the cost of providing cover for the employee. This may be quite substantial. A suitable person must be recruited and trained, and there may be some loss of productivity while he or she is learning the job.

---

6 These arguments feature in many of the government's policy documents. See, for example, HM Treasury/DTI, *Full and Fulfilling Employment: Creating the Labour Market of the Future* (2002).

One way in which the employer might deal with these costs would be to pass them on to employees. The employer could calculate the overall cost of providing family-friendly working policies and deduct this from employees' wages. However, family-friendly policies present a major problem in this regard. They do not benefit all workers. While parents and those who expect to become parents may be willing to pay for the benefits, employees who do not fall into either of these categories would probably prefer to receive a higher salary instead.[7] Moreover, they may be too expensive to be offset by a pay cut. Where the employer cannot offset the costs of family-friendly policies, some redundancies may result. And the employer may be tempted to discriminate against those who are likely to use the policies when it is recruiting new workers.

New institutional economists present a very different picture of parental leave policies, arguing that they can benefit employers as well as employees. One major advantage identified in the literature is that these policies help employers to recruit and retain workers.[8] For example, a woman may be more willing to return to work after maternity leave if she is able to work flexible hours and to have time off if her child is ill. The retention of workers is particularly important for firms which have to provide a substantial amount of training before a new worker can become productive. The employer decides whether or not to provide training by comparing the costs of the training with the benefits of having a skilled individual in the workforce. But these benefits may only outweigh the costs if the worker stays with the employer for a certain number of years after receiving the training.

The real challenge facing the new institutionalists is to demonstrate that it is right for the law to require all firms to provide the various forms of family leave, even if they have low recruitment and training costs and can cope with a high turnover of workers. A number of arguments can be made.[9] One is that a reduced turnover of workers may improve productivity even if training costs are low. This is because new workers always take some time to become as productive as experienced workers. Another is that workers who feel supported by their employer in their attempts to juggle work and family life will respond by being more loyal to the firm.[10] This loyalty may make the workers more productive. Finally, workers who are happy with the way in which their work and home life are balanced will be more focused when they are at work.[11] For example, a worker

---

7 R. Drago *et al.*, 'The willingness-to-pay for work/family policies: a study of teachers' (2001) 55 *Industrial and Labor Relations Review* 22, casts doubt on this expectation. The authors found that workers who did not expect to benefit from family-friendly policies were willing to pay something towards them.

8 See, for example, DTI, *Work and Families: Choice and Flexibility* (2005).

9 DTI, *Work and Families*.

10 For example, workers who work flexibly tend to report higher job satisfaction: H. Hooker *et al.*, *The Third Work–Life Balance Employee Survey* (2007), Section 5.

11 There is empirical evidence to support this. See B. Hayward *et al.*, *The Third Work–Life Balance Employer Survey* (2007), Chapter 9, showing that 92 per cent of employers surveyed agreed with the view that 'people work best when they can balance their work and the other aspects of their lives'.

whose childcare arrangements have fallen through and who is trying to find an alternative will be distracted from his or her work. A worker who is given a day's emergency leave to resolve the problem will miss a day's work but will at least be able to concentrate when he or she returns. The new institutionalists might also strengthen their basic argument about recruitment and retention by combining it with human rights arguments, to which we will now turn.

Rights perspectives

International instruments have long been concerned with three of the issues we are considering in this chapter: limits on weekly working hours, paid annual holidays and maternity leave. Rights to reconcile work with family life are beginning to appear in more recent instruments.

Hours and holidays

Not surprisingly, hours and holidays are the exclusive preserve of economic and social rights instruments. Article 7 of the ICESCR is as follows:

> The States Parties to the present Covenant recognise the right of everyone to the enjoyment of just and favourable conditions of work which ensure, in particular ...
> (d) Rest, leisure and reasonable limitation of working hours and periodic holidays with pay, as well as remuneration for public holidays.

Article 24 of the UN Declaration is in similar terms. These rights can be seen as part of a minimum set of terms and conditions of employment from which all workers should benefit, including a fair wage and a safe working environment. They were intended to address some of the most abusive forms of work, in which low-paid workers were expected to work extremely long hours in hazardous conditions. The concern is to ensure that workers are treated fairly and with dignity.

The detail of these rights is fleshed out most fully in ILO instruments. Long working hours have been a concern of the ILO from its inception: the first convention to address working time is Convention 1 of 1919.[12] The basic ILO standards are that the working day should be limited to eight hours, the working week should be limited to forty-eight hours, and that there should be a continuous twenty-four-hour rest period in every seven days. Various exceptions are provided in the interests of business flexibility. Once a worker has completed a year's continuous service, he or she should be entitled to three weeks' paid holiday.[13] All these standards represent minimum levels of protection, so there is nothing to stop a state from introducing more favourable provisions. The UK has not ratified any of the ILO conventions concerning working time. This probably

12 ILO Convention 1 on Hours of Work (Industry) 1919. See also Convention 14 on Weekly Rest (Industry) 1921, Convention 30 on Hours of Work (Commerce and Offices) 1930 and Convention 106 on Weekly Rest (Commerce and Offices) 1957.
13 ILO Convention 132 on Holidays with Pay (Revised) 1970.

reflects the UK's tradition of collective laissez-faire: until recently, working hours were seen as a matter for unions and employers to decide through collective bargaining.[14] Legislation was only passed where workers were felt to be particularly vulnerable to exploitation.[15]

The ILO has also adopted a convention on part-time work.[16] The ILO acknowledges that part-time work is an important source of job opportunities, but argues that part-timers need protection of various kinds.[17] The Convention has not been ratified by the UK. It sets out three main principles. First, part-timers should be guaranteed the same legal rights as full-time workers in various areas, including trade union membership and activities, discrimination, maternity protection and unfair dismissal.[18] The concern here is that legislation may discriminate against part-timers even though the problems they may face in these areas are no different to those faced by full-timers. Second, part-timers should be paid the same hourly rate as full-timers.[19] This addresses the problem of discrimination by firms against their part-time employees. Third, 'where appropriate, measures shall be taken to ensure that transfer from full-time to part-time work or vice versa is voluntary in accordance with national law and practice'.[20] This encourages governments to grant individuals a right to choose the hours they work, but its wording is rather vague.

Leave

The ICESCR provides a basic right to maternity leave in Article 10(2):

> Special protection should be accorded to mothers during a reasonable period before and after childbirth. During such period working mothers should be accorded paid leave or leave with adequate social security benefits.

The ESC 1961, which has been ratified by the UK, specifies that maternity leave should be for a minimum duration of twelve weeks.[21] The revised ESC 1996[22] and the ILO Maternity Protection Convention[23] specify a minimum of fourteen weeks. The right to maternity leave itself implies a right to return to work, but CEDAW expressly states that the woman should be able to return without loss of seniority.[24] Some instruments, including the ILO Convention[25] and the ESC 1996,[26] also provide that a woman who returns to work while she is still breastfeeding should be given time off for this purpose. Several instruments state that pregnancy or the taking of maternity leave should not be permitted as grounds of dismissal.[27] Finally, it is common to find a requirement that pregnant women

---

14 See Chapter 1.
15 Examples include the Employment of Women, Young Persons and Children Act 1920 and the Coal Mines Regulation Act 1908.
16 ILO Convention 175 on Part-Time Work 1994.   17 Ibid., Preamble.
18 Ibid., Arts. 4 and 7.   19 Ibid., Art. 5.   20 Ibid., Art. 10.   21 ESC 1961, Art. 8.
22 ESC 1996, Art. 8.   23 ILO Convention 183 on Maternity Protection 2000.
24 CEDAW, Art. 11(2)(b).   25 Maternity Protection Convention, Art. 10.
26 ESC 1996, Art. 8.   27 ESC 1961, Art. 8; ESC 1996, Art. 8; CEDAW, Art. 11(2)(a).

or women who are breastfeeding should not be required to engage in hazardous work or night work.[28]

Modern human rights instruments have begun to look beyond the basic provision of maternity leave and to consider the longer-term problems of balancing work and family life faced by working parents of both sexes. Formulations of the right to reconciliation vary considerably. Perhaps the most detailed right is that contained in the ESC 1996:

> With a view to ensuring the exercise of the right to equality of opportunity and treatment for men and women workers with family responsibilities and between such workers and other workers, the Parties undertake:
>
> 1. to take appropriate measures:
>   a) to enable workers with family responsibilities to enter and remain in employment, as well as to re-enter employment after an absence due to those responsibilities, including measures in the field of vocational guidance and training;
>   b) to take account of their needs in terms of conditions of employment and social security;
>   c) to develop or promote services, public or private, in particular child daycare services and other childcare arrangements;
> 2. to provide a possibility for either parent to obtain, during a period after maternity leave, parental leave to take care of a child, the duration and conditions of which should be determined by national legislation, collective agreements or practice;
> 3. to ensure that family responsibilities shall not, as such, constitute a valid reason for termination of employment.[29]

Some of the less detailed rights place a particular emphasis on the provision of childcare facilities. This is true of CEDAW and of the Convention on the Rights of the Child.[30] The latter gives the children of working parents a right to childcare services. Others, such as the EU Charter, focus on the provision of parental leave.[31]

The international instruments also differ in the underlying basis they give to the right. The ESC right focuses on discrimination against working parents.[32] The concern is that their childcare responsibilities might make it more difficult for them to fulfil the demands made by employers, and that they might therefore need protection against unfavourable treatment. CEDAW, not surprisingly, is concerned with the elimination of discrimination against women, but so is the ILO Convention on Workers with Family Responsibilities.[33] This justification reflects the fact that although many mothers now have paid employment, and although social attitudes have changed, women still take the primary responsibility for childcare in most households. The reasons for the role of women are complex.

---

28 ESC 1961, Art. 8; ESC 1996, Art. 8; Maternity Protection Convention, Art. 3; CEDAW, Art. 11(2)(d).
29 ESC 1996, Art. 27.   30 CEDAW, Art. 11; CRC, Art. 18(3).
31 EU Charter of Fundamental Rights, Art. 33.   32 ESC 1996, Art. 27, quoted above.
33 CEDAW, Art. 11; ILO Convention 156 on Workers with Family Responsibilities 1981, Preamble.

One is that some stereotypes remain: a man who chooses to take time out from his job to care for his children may still meet with surprise. Another is labour market discrimination: since women have to interrupt their careers to give birth, and since they earn less than men on average,[34] it may be rational for them to prioritise childcare over labour market work. Yet another is the substantial proportion of lone-parent families, the vast majority of which are headed by women. These women have no choice but to take a substantial role in childcare. Taking all these factors together, many writers have concluded that since the burden of childcare falls most heavily on women, the right to reconcile work and family life should be seen as an aspect of women's right not to be discriminated against.[35]

The sex discrimination basis for the right to reconciliation has one major benefit: it links this novel right into well-established and powerful anti-discrimination norms. It becomes harder to argue against a right such as parental leave once it is made clear that discrimination against women may continue if the right is denied. However, there are two important disadvantages which will be outlined here: the temptation to stereotype women and the tendency to focus solely on childcare.[36] These difficulties are not insurmountable, but they do require careful attention when the right to reconciliation is being implemented in practice.

The stereotyping problem occurs where additional protections for working parents are available only to women or are designed in such a way as to make it likely that only women will use them. Although such protections would solve women's immediate problems of balancing work and family life, they would do nothing to promote equal parenting or to change assumptions for the future. Instead, they would serve to perpetuate the idea that the main responsibility for childcare lies with women. Interestingly, the drafters of CEDAW were alert to this concern. Article 5(a) requires states to work towards the elimination of stereotypical assumptions about men's and women's roles. It is coupled with Article 5(b), which requires states:

> To ensure that family education includes a proper understanding of maternity as a social function and the recognition of the common responsibility of men and women in the upbringing and development of their children, it being understood that the interest of the children is the primordial consideration in all cases.

This is an important statement of two principles: first, that pregnancy and maternity should be distinguished from the task of raising children, and second, that men and women both have responsibility for the latter. These two principles can be summed up in the phrase 'equal parenting'. From a rights perspective, any new development in parental leave rights must be tested for its ability to promote equal parenting.

34 See Chapter 8.
35 See, for example, C. McGlynn, 'Work, family and parenthood: the European Union agenda', in J. Conaghan and K. Rittich (eds.), *Labour Law, Work and Family: Critical and Comparative Perspectives* (2005).
36 Ibid.

A second problem with using sex discrimination as the underlying justification for the right to reconciliation is that it may lead to a focus on the raising of children as the only 'version' of family life. In practice, many workers also play a major role in caring for their elderly relatives. Some commentators would argue that this burden also falls more heavily on women, so rights to time off work to care for family members other than children could still be based on a sex discrimination rationale. In our discussion of the law, we will see that some rights do now extend beyond childcare.

The law on working time

The law on working time is quite complex, and can only be explained in outline here. The discussion will be divided into two sections. The first will consider working time rules which apply to all workers regardless of their family status, and the second will consider rules which are specifically designed to deal with the problems faced by workers with family responsibilities.

Rules applicable to all

This section will consider the Working Time Regulations 1998, which seek to regulate the working week, and the Part-Time Workers Regulations 2000, which address some of the issues faced by part-timers. It will be argued that while both sets of regulations seem to reflect rights or new institutional economics perspectives, they contain a number of provisions which respond to neoclassical concerns about the cost of rights. These provisions may serve to undermine their apparent aims.

The WTR 1998[37] implements the EC's Working Time Directive, which was enacted as a health and safety measure, designed to protect workers not only against the dangers associated with exhaustion, but also against the dangers of repetitive and monotonous work.[38] It remains to be seen whether the Regulations will make any impact on the UK's 'long-hours culture'. Although average working hours in the UK have been falling, UK full-time workers still did an average of 43 hours per week in 2007, which can be contrasted with an EU average of 41.8 hours per week.[39]

The Regulations apply to employees and workers, so their scope is broad.[40] They require the employer to give each worker 4.8 weeks' leave from work each

---

37 WTR 1998 (SI 1998/1833) (as amended). See, generally, C. Barnard, 'Recent legislation. The Working Time Regulations 1998' (1999) 28 *ILJ* 61, and 'Recent legislation. The Working Time Regulations 1999' (2000) 29 *ILJ* 167.

38 Directive 2003/88, originally Directive 93/104, enacted under then Art. 118a EC (which now forms part of Art. 137 EC). See C. Barnard, *EC Employment Law* (2006), Chapter 12. The UK government brought an unsuccessful challenge to the Directive's treaty basis: (Case 84/94) *UK* v. *Commission* [1996] ECR I-5755.

39 Source: EUROSTAT employment statistics (http://epp.eurostat.ec.europa.eu).

40 WTR 1998, reg. 2.

year.[41] This leave may be used for any purpose and must be paid at the worker's usual wage.[42] The working week is governed by two major rights. According to reg. 4, the maximum number of hours worked in a week (including overtime) should not exceed forty-eight, averaged over a seventeen-week period.[43] And under reg. 11, the worker is entitled to a continuous rest period of twenty-four hours in seven days or forty-eight hours in fourteen days, at the choice of the employer. The working day is also regulated in two main ways. Under reg. 10, the worker is entitled to a rest period of eleven consecutive hours in each twenty-four-hour period. And under reg. 12, the worker is entitled to a rest break of at least twenty minutes, to be spent away from his or her workstation, if his or her working day is longer than six hours. Some of these rights interact in important ways. In particular, although the maximum working week of forty-eight hours is only an *average* requirement, the employer's ability to demand a very long working week is limited by the obligation to provide daily and weekly rest breaks.

At first sight, the legislation appears to reflect either the rights theorists' concern with protecting the dignity of workers, or the new institutional economists' concern with promoting productivity. However, the rights are far from absolute. Some elements of the legislation balance the goal of protecting workers against employers' need for flexibility. The most significant example of this is that the individual worker can waive his or her right to the forty-eight-hour working week if he or she signs a written agreement to that effect.[44] This is not permitted under ILO standards.[45] Empirical research shows that the opt-out is widely used by UK firms because they value the flexibility it offers.[46]

Rights theorists have condemned the derogation, fearing that workers will be put under pressure by employers to waive the maximum limit.[47] Community law requires that consent be freely given.[48] Although the legislation protects workers against detriment and dismissal for asserting their rights, it may be difficult to ensure that consent is genuine in practice.[49] From a new institutional economics perspective, the possibility of waiver means that employers can, in effect, ignore the new legislation. This will prevent them from learning any lessons about how to maximise their workers' productivity.[50] But the

---

41 WTR 1998, reg. 13. This includes bank holidays and will increase to 5.6 weeks from April 2009.
42 Ibid., reg. 16.
43 The calculation of an individual's working time can be difficult, particularly when he or she is on call, but space precludes a full discussion of this issue here.
44 Directive 2003/88, Art. 22; WTR 1998, regs. 4(1) and 5.
45 ILO Convention 1; ILO Convention 14; ILO Convention 30; ILO Convention 106.
46 C. Barnard *et al.*, 'Opting out of the 48-hour week: employer necessity or individual choice?' (2003) 32 *ILJ* 223.
47 For evidence, see ibid., p. 247, though there is also evidence that workers welcome the chance to opt out.
48 (C-397/01) *Pfeiffer* v. *Deutsches Rotes Kreuz* [2004] ECR I-8835.
49 ERA 1996, ss. 45A and 101A respectively.
50 Barnard *et al.*, 'Opting out of the 48-hour week', p. 249.

waiver makes sense from a neoclassical viewpoint: it upholds individuals' right to choose how many hours they work. At the time of writing, a political agreement has been reached at European level on changes to the opt-out.[51] These include a maximum working week of sixty hours for workers who have opted out, and a ban on signing the opt-out during the first month of employment. These changes are designed to offer further protection to workers without removing the opt-out altogether.

Of course, both rights theorists and new institutionalists would support some elements of flexibility in the Regulations. For example, the rights to rest periods and rest breaks do not apply in 'special cases', such as where there is an emergency.[52] The Regulations would clearly have absurd results if they did not permit employers to ask their workers to stay late if an accident had occurred. Moreover, some of the flexible provisions only allow the employer to negotiate with trade union representatives or with the elected representatives of the workforce, rather than with workers as individuals. For example, the averaging period for the forty-eight-hour working week can be extended from seventeen weeks to any period up to fifty-two weeks, where this is for 'objective or technical reasons or reasons concerning the organisation of work', by collective or workforce agreement.[53] From a new institutional perspective, this is a valuable compromise. It offers a greater chance that the law will be beneficial to firms because it allows them to adapt it to their needs. And workers are less likely to be intimidated if they are able to negotiate as a group. From a rights perspective, the implications of this provision and others like it depend on who has the greatest bargaining power: the employer or the representatives.[54]

The other topic to be discussed in this section is the legal regulation of part-time work. There is no standard definition of part-time working – legislation defines a part-time worker as a person who does fewer hours than full-time workers in the same establishment[55] – but around 25 per cent of the workforce report that they are part-timers.[56] Part-time working is more prevalent among women than men: around 11 per cent of male workers are part-timers, whereas the figure is 42 per cent for women. Women make up around 76 per cent of the part-time workforce. For many years, the law adopted a neoclassical approach towards part-time workers. The law did not require employers to treat them in the same way as full-time workers, and indeed some differential treatment of part-timers was enshrined in legislation. The argument was that part-time work was an important source of new jobs. Employers would not create such jobs unless they were cheap. Nowadays, more emphasis is placed on a rights approach: part-timers' dignity is infringed where they are treated differently.

---

51 European Commission press release, 10 June 2008.   52 WTR 1998, reg. 21.
53 Ibid., reg. 23.
54 Barnard *et al.*, 'Opting out of the 48-hour week', found that these provisions were rarely used, due to the decline in collective bargaining.
55 PTWR 2000, reg. 2.
56 Source: National Statistics, *Labour Force Survey* (January–March 2008) (www.statistics.gov.uk).

The fact that the part-time workforce is predominantly female has played a significant role in the development of legal protection for part-timers. In the past, legislation discriminated against part-timers by making it more difficult for them to qualify for certain legal rights, such as the right not to be unfairly dismissed.[57] Those who worked for fewer than eight hours per week could not claim at all, and those who worked for fewer than sixteen hours per week could only claim after they had worked for the employer for five years, whereas the requirement for full-timers was two years' continuous service. These exclusions were challenged using sex discrimination law. In *ex p. EOC*, it was held that the requirements to work for more than eight hours per week and to work for five years for the same employer before a claim could be brought were harder for women than men to comply with because a majority of part-timers were women.[58] This amounted to indirect discrimination on grounds of sex and was unlawful.

As part of the EU's strategy of regulating various forms of 'atypical work', the social partners agreed a directive on part-time work[59] which was transposed into English law by the PTWR 2000.[60] In contrast to the sex discrimination solution, the Regulations protect men who work part-time as well as women. The main provision is reg. 5, which states that an employer may not treat a part-timer less favourably than a comparable full-timer. Importantly, however, the employer's obligation to treat part-timers in the same way as comparable full-timers is not absolute. The employer may continue to treat part-timers differently where it can offer objective justification for its actions.[61]

The main criticism of the Regulations from a rights perspective relates to the way in which a 'comparable full-timer' is defined.[62] To be comparable, the full-timer must be engaged in broadly similar work and must work under the same type of contract.[63] The first of these requirements was given a broad construction by the House of Lords in the *Matthews* case.[64] But the second requirement is quite restrictive. It means that a part-time employee can only compare him- or herself with a full-time employee, and that a part-time worker can only compare him- or herself with a full-time worker.[65] Thus, no comparison will be possible in the (not implausible) situation in which all the full-timers are employees and all the part-timers have workers' contracts. According to the government's own figures, only one-sixth of all part-time workers have a comparator within the

---

57 Employment Protection (Consolidation) Act 1978, Schedule 13.
58 *R* v. *Secretary of State for Employment, ex p. EOC* [1995] 1 AC 1.
59 Directive 97/81/EC extended to the UK by Directive 98/23/EC. See M. Jeffery, 'Not really going to work? Of the Directive on Part-Time Work, "atypical work" and attempts to regulate it' (1998) 27 *ILJ* 193.
60 SI 2000/1551.   61 PTWR 2000, reg. 5(2).
62 A. McColgan, 'Recent legislation. Missing the point?' (2000) 29 *ILJ* 260.
63 PTWR 2000, reg. 2.
64 *Matthews* v. *Kent and Medway Towns Fire Authority* [2006] UKHL 8; [2006] 2 All ER 171.
65 There is an exception which allows individuals who have changed from full-time to part-time work to compare their new terms and conditions with their old ones, regardless of contract type: PTWR 2000, regs. 3 and 4.

meaning of the Regulations.[66] As a result, the Regulations may fail properly to implement the Part-Time Work Directive. The Directive does refer to the nature of the comparator's contract as a relevant consideration, so on a narrow reading the government's transposition may be justified.[67] However, as McColgan explains, the Directive provides that where this strict comparison cannot be made, 'comparison shall be made ... in accordance with national law, collective agreements or practice'.[68] In the SDA and RRA, a hypothetical person may be used as a comparator.[69] So it could be argued that the government should have provided this as an option because it would have been 'in accordance with national law'. Thus, although the law purports to adopt a rights approach, its bold stance is undermined by the technical hurdles it places in the way of claimants. Again, it seems that concerns about the cost to firms of granting generous protection may have had some influence.

Rules applicable to workers with family responsibilities

So far, we have focused on the ways in which the law addresses the needs of full-time and part-time workers in general. We will now turn to a group of measures which are designed specifically to address the problems faced by workers with family responsibilities. Balancing work and family life is a serious issue for many workers. For example, in 2004, 54 per cent of mothers with children under 6 years of age were in work.[70]

Several of the international instruments discussed above oblige the state to take measures to ensure that workers have access to childcare facilities. However, there is a considerable shortfall of places in the UK. In 2008, there were around 1.6 million childcare places for children under the age of 8,[71] but the latest population estimates suggest that there are more than 6 million children in this age group.[72] Inevitably, the shortage of places serves to raise the price which can be charged for them, so that they are affordable only to high- or middle-income families. Access to childcare is a particular problem for lone parents, who are unable to share their responsibilities with a spouse or partner and are therefore more dependent on state- or market-provided services. However, the measures which might be taken to improve the availability of childcare are largely beyond the scope of this book. They include things like giving employers tax incentives to set up workplace crèches and providing more opportunities for people to train and qualify as childminders. We will focus instead on the obligations the law places on employers to help workers balance their jobs with family life.

---

66 Regulatory Impact Assessment (available at www.berr.gov.uk/employment/workandfamilies/part-time/ria/page19200.html).
67 Directive 97/81/EC, Annex, cl. 3.   68 McColgan, 'Recent legislation. Missing the point?'
69 See Chapter 7.   70 DTI, *Work and Families*, para. 1.7.
71 Office for National Statistics, *Social Trends* (2008), Chapter 8.
72 Source: National Statistics Population Estimates (www.statistics.gov.uk).

The law provides four types of leave.[73] The first is maternity leave.[74] All employees are entitled to fifty-two weeks' maternity leave, regardless of their length of service. A woman who has worked for the employer for twenty-six weeks ending with the fifteenth week before the expected date of childbirth, and whose earnings have reached a specified minimum amount, qualifies for Statutory Maternity Pay (SMP).[75] For the first six weeks, SMP is 90 per cent of the woman's normal weekly earnings. For the remaining thirty-three weeks, SMP is 90 per cent of the woman's normal weekly earnings, or £117.18 a week, whichever is *lower*.[76] Employers are reimbursed by the government for the SMP payments they make.[77] Women who do not qualify for SMP may be able to claim social security benefits instead. The government has undertaken to extend maternity pay to the full fifty-two weeks in the next few years.[78] If the employee opts to return to work within or at the end of the first twenty-six weeks (known as ordinary maternity leave) she is entitled to return to the same job on the same terms and conditions as if she had not been away.[79] If she takes a longer period of leave she is also entitled to return to the same job, but the employer may be able to argue that it is not reasonably practicable to permit this. In such situations the employer must offer suitable alternative work.[80]

The law also provides a limited right to paternity leave.[81] This is available to employees who have worked for twenty-six weeks ending with the fifteenth week before the expected date of childbirth.[82] They must either be the biological father of the child or the spouse or partner of the mother, and must expect to have responsibility for the child's upbringing.[83] The leave may be for one week or two consecutive weeks (at the employee's choice)[84] and must in general be taken within fifty-six days of the birth of the child.[85] Most employees are entitled to Statutory Paternity Pay (SPP), which is 90 per cent of the employee's weekly earnings or £117.18, whichever is the lower.[86] Since the leave period is relatively short,

73 See, generally, E. Caracciolo di Torella, 'New Labour, new dads – the impact of family-friendly legislation on fathers' (2007) 36 *ILJ* 318; G. James, 'The Work and Families Act 2006: legislation to improve choice and flexibility?' (2006) 35 *ILJ* 272. The rules make special provision for adoption and for disabled children. These cannot be discussed here for reasons of space.
74 The provisions on maternity leave are contained in ERA 1996, ss. 71–75 (as amended). Details are fleshed out in the Maternity and Parental Leave etc. Regulations 1999 (SI 1999/3312) (MPLR) (as amended). For their basis in EC law, see the Pregnant Workers Directive (Directive 92/85/EEC).
75 SSCBA 1992, s. 164 (as amended). Details are set out in the Statutory Maternity Pay (General) Regulations 1986 (SI 1986/1960) (as amended).
76 SSCBA 1992, s. 166.   77 Ibid., s. 167.   78 Work and Families Act 2006, s. 1.
79 MPLR 1999, reg. 18(1). Where there is a redundancy situation, reg. 10 applies.
80 Ibid., reg. 18(2).
81 ERA 1996, s. 80A–E. Detail is set out in the PALR 2002 (SI 2002/2788).
82 PALR 2002, reg. 4.   83 Ibid., reg. 4.   84 ERA 1996, s. 80A(3); PALR 2002, reg. 5.
85 ERA 1996, s. 80A(4).
86 SSCBA 1992, s. 171ZA–J; Statutory Paternity Pay and Statutory Adoption Pay (General) Regulations 2002 (SI 2002/2822).

the employee is entitled to return to the same job at the end of it.[87] The government is also proposing to introduce additional paternity leave, probably in 2009.[88] This would allow a father to take twenty-six weeks' leave where the mother chose to return to work after ordinary maternity leave. In effect, this means that the second six months of leave after a baby is born could be taken either by the mother or by the father. At present, only the mother has the legal right to take this time off as maternity leave, so this change would increase the choices open to couples.

The right to parental leave is available to parents who wish to have time off work to look after their child.[89] To qualify, the parent must be an employee who has worked for the same employer for one year.[90] The entitlement is to thirteen weeks' leave per child.[91] It must be taken before the child is 5 years old.[92] There is no obligation on the employer to pay the employee while he or she is on parental leave. The employee is entitled to return to his or her old job if he or she has taken leave of up to four weeks. If he or she has taken a longer period of leave, he or she is entitled to return to the same job unless this is not reasonably practicable, in which case a suitable alternative must be offered.[93]

The final statutory right to leave is the right to emergency leave contained in s. 57A ERA 1996.[94] This right is available only to employees, but there is no requirement to have worked for the employer for any period of time before using the right. It can be invoked when an emergency occurs concerning one of the employee's dependants: a spouse or civil partner, child, parent or other person living in the same household, such as a partner or other relative.[95] The emergencies covered include: when a dependant is ill or injured, when a dependant dies, when it is necessary to make arrangements for the care of a dependant, or when established care arrangements break down.[96] The entitlement is to take a 'reasonable' amount of time off to deal with the emergency.[97] The government's guidance, which is not legally binding, gives as an example the case of an employee whose child has chickenpox.[98] The guidance suggests that two weeks' leave to care for the child until he or she is better would not be reasonable, whereas two days' leave to take the child to the doctor and to make arrangements for his or her care would be reasonable. If the employer and employee cannot agree on the appropriate duration of the leave, the employee can complain to the Employment Tribunal and seek compensation.[99] There is no legal obligation on the employer to pay the employee during a period of emergency leave.

---

87 PALR 2002, regs. 13–14.   88 Work and Families Act 2006, s. 3.
89 ERA 1996, ss. 76–80, implementing the Parental Leave Directive (Directive 96/34/EC, extended to the UK by Directive 97/75/EC) agreed by the social partners. For detail, see MPLR 1999 (as amended).
90 MPLR 1999, reg. 13.   91 Ibid., reg. 14.   92 Ibid., reg. 15.
93 Ibid., reg. 18 and 18A. Where there is a redundancy situation, reg. 10 applies.
94 Implementing the Parental Leave Directive, MPLR 1999, reg. 13.
95 ERA 1996, s. 57A(3)–(5).   96 Ibid., s. 57A(1).   97 Ibid.
98 Department for Business, Enterprise and Regulatory Reform, *Time Off for Dependants* (2007), p. 6.
99 ERA 1996, s. 57B.

A first point to note about these various rights is that they are available only to employees, and sometimes only to employees who have satisfied a qualifying period. As we saw in Chapter 5, this is difficult to justify from a rights perspective. Atypical workers are not left wholly unprotected: they may be able to claim under the SDA 1975. The *Dekker* decision makes clear that any discrimination on grounds of pregnancy counts as direct sex discrimination.[100] Moreover, the courts assume that women have a greater role in childcare than men, so if the employer ignores a woman's childcare responsibilities it may be discriminating against her. However, this creates a considerable degree of uncertainty for workers, who may have to resort to litigation to determine their rights. From a neoclassical perspective, the fact that these rights are not granted to workers makes a major contribution to the cheapness of atypical work. Theorists in this tradition argue that employers will create more jobs as a result.

A second point to note is that much of this leave is unpaid, or paid at a rate which is much lower than most workers' usual earnings.[101] Neoclassical theorists would argue that this is essential: employers cannot be expected to pay workers while they are absent. Moreover, employers will, in any event, face the expense of hiring and training substitute workers, particularly for longer periods of leave. A new institutional critique would take a very different stance. The new institutionalists are concerned to get more workers into the labour market and to retain them even when they start a family. This goal will only be achieved if the leave provisions make a practical difference to workers' lives. For example, many workers may not be able to manage without their pay for thirteen weeks while they take parental leave. This does not necessarily mean that employers should be made to pay: subsidies could be provided by the government. The real question is whether the rights are sufficiently useful to persuade people to combine paid work with family life.

A third point relates to the concern expressed in our rights discussion that parental leave provisions might have the unfortunate side effect of stereotyping women and perpetuating the view that childcare is their responsibility alone. Theorists in this tradition find much to criticise in the law as it currently stands. For example, the availability of a year's maternity leave but only two weeks' paternity leave places very considerable emphasis on the role of the mother as the child's primary carer. The new right to additional paternity leave may redress the balance to some extent once it is brought into force, because it will allow couples to share the year's leave between them. However, the fact that leave tends to be unpaid or paid at lower rates still causes a problem, even when it is available to either parent. Empirical evidence from other European countries shows that where parental leave is unpaid, the take-up among fathers is significantly lower than where it is paid.[102] One reason for this is that due to the gender pay gap,

---

100 (Case C-177/88) *Dekker* v. *VJV-Centrum* [1990] ECR I-3941.
101 See, generally, A. McColgan, 'Family-friendly frolics: the MPLR 1999' (2000) 29 *ILJ* 125.
102 S. Fredman, *Women and the Law* (1997), pp. 219–20.

women earn less on average than men. If the father is the main breadwinner, it will be harder for the family to manage without his wage.

The rights we have considered so far give employees the possibility of taking specific periods of time off work in order to perform their family responsibilities. However, these rights do not help with the daily struggle to make sure that someone is free to collect the children from school each day or to check on an elderly relative. The choice to work part-time or flexible hours would be more helpful here. Traditionally, though, employers have tended to insist that many jobs can only be done on a standard full-time basis.

The law has tackled this in two main ways. First, some cases have held that an employer's insistence that a job can only be done full-time may be unlawful under the SDA 1975.[103] When an employer imposes a requirement of full-time working, the courts may accept that because of childcare responsibilities, the proportion of women who can comply is considerably smaller than the proportion of men who can comply. This amounts to indirect discrimination,[104] although the employer does have the opportunity of defending itself by showing that there are good business reasons for the requirement to work full-time. The SDA 1975 may also help male workers, but only where the employer allows women with childcare responsibilities to work part-time. If the employer denies this right to male workers in a similar position, the employer is engaging in direct sex discrimination.[105]

Second, the law provides a right to request flexible working which is available to both men and women independently of the SDA.[106] The right is afforded to employees (not workers) who have worked for at least twenty-six weeks for their employer.[107] They must be the parent of a child under six (sixteen from 2009) and they must be seeking to work flexibly in order to care for that child.[108] In 2007, the right was extended to employees who are seeking to work flexibly in order to care for an adult (such as a spouse, partner or family member) who is in need of care.[109] The employee may ask the employer for permission to do one of three things: to work a different number of hours, to work at different times, or to work from home.[110] For example, the employee could ask to work part-time or to work only during school hours. Detailed provision is made for the employer to hold a meeting with the employee to discuss the request and to provide written reasons for its decision.[111] Under s. 80G(1)(b), the employer may only refuse the employee's request if one of a set of listed reasons applies. They include 'additional

---

103 For example, *Home Office* v. *Holmes* [1985] 1 WLR 71. The SDA is explained in more detail in Chapter 7.

104 SDA 1975, s. 1(1)(b).   105 Ibid., s. 1(1)(a).

106 ERA 1996, s. 80F–I. See L. Anderson, 'Sound bite legislation: The Employment Act 2002 and new flexible working "rights" for parents' (2003) 32 *ILJ* 37.

107 ERA 1996, s. 80F(1); FWER 2002 (SI 2002/3236), reg. 3.

108 ERA 1996, s. 80F(1)(b)(i); FWER 2002, regs. 3 and 3A.

109 ERA 1996, s. 80F(1)(b)(ii); FWER 2002, reg. 3B.   110 ERA 1996, s. 80F(1)(a).

111 Ibid., s. 80G; Flexible Working (Procedural Requirements) Regulations 2002 (SI 2002/3207).

costs', 'inability to re-organise work among existing staff', 'inability to recruit additional staff', 'detrimental impact on performance' and so on.

The right to request flexible working has been highly controversial. From a neoclassical perspective, it interferes with the employer's ability to organise the workplace as it sees fit. For rights theorists, it is inadequate: the employee is only allowed to make a request and the employer who wants to refuse can easily identify a legitimate reason for doing so. More fundamentally, rights theorists argue that the right to reconcile work and family life should be given a bolder interpretation in English law. This would involve not only providing rights for working parents, but also reviewing traditional patterns of working time more generally. If it were made compulsory, the forty-eight-hour week could play a role in helping working parents by forcing working fathers to reduce their hours, thus giving them more time to spend with their families. And part-time work could be viewed in a wholly different light. If part-time work is seen as a vital technique for parents seeking to reconcile work and family life, the right not to be discriminated against on the grounds of working part-time does not go very far towards meeting their needs. First, it can be argued that everyone should have the right to choose part-time working (perhaps with exceptions where the employer could show a business justification for full-time working), so that they can reconcile work and family life.[112] The right to request flexible working points in this direction, but its impact is limited by the fact that the employer can easily refuse a request. Second, it could be argued that part-time workers should benefit from some protection with regard to the duration and timing of their work.[113] If the purpose of part-time work for many is to reconcile work and family life, it is very important that the work is regular and reliable.[114] A worker who needs to organise childcare is unlikely to be able to come in to work at very short notice. Some employers have designed contracts which ensure that part-timers are given notice before their hours are increased, or which limit working hours to school terms, in order to enable workers to manage their childcare arrangements.[115] For some writers, the right to reconciliation is a radical force, with implications for all aspects of working time, not just parental leave provisions. It is not difficult to imagine the neoclassical response.

Further reading

For detailed textbook accounts of this topic, see S. Deakin and G.S. Morris, *Labour Law* (4th edn., 2005), 3.90–3.91, 4.71–4.79 and 6.97–6.107, or H. Collins, K.D. Ewing and A. McColgan, *Labour Law: Text and Materials* (2nd edn., 2005),

---

112 The government considered this option before introducing the right to request flexible working, but decided that it was too strict.

113 See Jeffery, 'Not really going to work?'

114 For empirical evidence, see J. Walsh, 'Experiencing part-time work: temporal tensions, social relations and the work–family interface' (2007) 45 *BJIR* 155.

115 B. Kersley *et al.*, *Inside the Workplace* (2006), p. 250, found that 20 per cent of workplaces studied offered term-time-only contracts.

Chapter 4. On the European material, see C. Barnard, *EC Employment Law* (3rd edn., 2006), Chapters 9 and 12.

The government has tended to approach family-friendly rights from a new institutionalist perspective, arguing in particular that they will improve employers' access to skilled labour. Key policy documents include DTI, *Work and Parents: Competitiveness and Choice* (2000); HM Treasury and DTI, *Balancing Work and Family Life: Enhancing Choice and Support for Parents* (2003); and DTI, *Work and Families: Choice and Flexibility* (2005). For a detailed analysis of the empirical evidence about the costs to employers of family-friendly policies, see S. Holtermann, 'The costs and benefits to British employers of measures to promote equality of opportunity', in J. Humphries and J. Rubery (eds.), *The Economics of Equal Opportunities* (1995).

For feminist scholars, the problem with labour law is that it focuses on paid work and ignores the unpaid work women do in the home: see J. Conaghan, 'Work, family and the discipline of labour law', in J. Conaghan and K. Rittich (eds.), *Labour Law, Work and Family: Critical and Comparative Perspectives* (2005). Writers in this tradition are concerned that family-friendly policies might perpetuate stereotypes about the role of women in childcare. For critiques of domestic law from this perspective, see J. Conaghan, 'Women, work and family: a British revolution?', in J. Conaghan *et al.* (eds.), *Labour Law in an Era of Globalization* (2002); E. Caracciolo di Torella, 'New Labour, new dads – the impact of family-friendly legislation on fathers' (2007) 36 *ILJ* 318; and on EU law, see C. McGlynn, 'Work, family and parenthood: the European Union agenda', in Conaghan and Rittich, *Labour Law*. Which aspects of the current law might perpetuate stereotypes? Is the new institutionalist focus on increasing women's participation in paid work to blame for this? What are the limits of labour law in promoting equal parenting? For a broader discussion of the issues, see J. Williams, *Unbending Gender: Why Work and Family Conflict and What To Do About It* (2000). More generally, are 'family-friendly' policies in danger of perpetuating stereotypes about traditional family structures?

There is very little theoretical literature on the rights and economics aspects of working time more generally. For a detailed critique of the legislation, see C. Barnard, 'Recent legislation. The Working Time Regulations 1998' (1999) 28 *ILJ* 61, and 'Recent legislation. The Working Time Regulations 1999' (2000) 29 *ILJ* 167. To learn more about the history of the Directive and its regulatory technique, see either C. Barnard, 'EC "social" policy', in P. Craig and G. de Búrca, *The Evolution of EU Law* (1999), or B. Bercusson, *European Labour Law* (1996), Chapter 21.

The role of negotiations with trade union representatives or worker representatives in modifying the obligations set out in the WTR has attracted some interest as an example of 'smart' regulation in the new institutional tradition: see H. Collins, 'Is there a third way in labour law?', in J. Conaghan *et al.* (eds.), *Labour Law in an Era of Globalization* (2002). However, it can sit uncomfortably with a more worker-protective agenda. For discussion, see A. Bogg, 'The right to paid annual leave in the Court of Justice: the eclipse of functionalism' (2006) 31 *European LR* 892, discussing the ECJ's decision in (C131/04) *Robinson-Steele v. RD Retail Services Ltd* [2006] ECR I-2531. Should we regard labour rights as a means of protecting workers' choices or as a means of protecting their interests?

Working time rights are often cited as an example of the 'utopian' nature of economic and social rights. Do you agree? Are they more powerful if they are based on the right to safe and healthy working conditions? Is the Working Time Directive genuinely based on health and safety rights? Could working time rights be more effectively justified using the right not to be discriminated against or the right to reconcile work and family life?

7

Discrimination

Discrimination is perhaps one of the most controversial topics in labour law when it is viewed from the rights and economics perspectives. First, there is controversy between the two camps. Rights theorists are almost universally in favour of legislation to combat discrimination, whereas some (though by no means all) economists argue that governmental intervention is unnecessary. Second, there is controversy within each camp. Within the rights camp, for example, there is a fierce debate surrounding the concept of equality. Within the economics camp, there is a debate about the costs and benefits of tackling discrimination, and even a debate about whether or not discrimination exists at all.

This chapter will begin by considering economics perspectives on discrimination, since they offer a good introduction to the debate as to whether or not the law should intervene at all in this area. We will then consider the rights perspectives, which will help to explain what form legal intervention should take if it occurs. And we will conclude with a discussion of English law. The law generally adopts a rights perspective, but we need to ask which rights perspective it is and to what extent it is influenced by economic factors.

Economics perspectives

Our discussion of economic accounts of discrimination will be divided into two sections: those accounts which do not support legal intervention, and those which may be used to do so. In the former category, we find the argument that much alleged 'discrimination' may not be discrimination at all, and the argument that discrimination does exist but will ultimately be cured by the market itself. In the latter category, we find the statistical discrimination and crowding theories.

Arguments against legal intervention

Some theorists argue that what may appear to be discrimination in the labour market can be explained in other ways. This argument is most commonly made in relation to sex discrimination and we will take this as our example. One version of the argument is based on theories about investments in 'human capital'.[1]

---

1 See, generally, G.S. Becker, *Human Capital* (3rd edn., 1993).

This is economists' shorthand for education or training which makes a worker more productive. Let us imagine the case of someone deciding whether or not to go to university. He or she must weigh the cost of getting a degree against the salary he or she will be able to secure as a graduate. If the salary is likely to be sufficient to pay off student loans and to make up for three years without earnings, the rational person will do a degree. Now imagine a woman who plans to leave the labour market after a couple of years in order to raise a family. She will only earn the higher salary for a short period of time, so she may calculate that it would not be rational to go to university because the costs of doing so would be higher than the benefits. On this theory, many of the women in the labour market will be less well-qualified than men. As a result, they will end up in lower-paid jobs. But this is due to the choices they have made, not to discrimination.

Another version of the theory focuses less on human capital and more on the degree of effort men and women are willing to expend on their jobs.[2] This approach starts with the assumption that although women now participate in the labour market to a very great extent, they still retain primary responsibility for childcare and housework. This means that their energies are divided between labour market work and domestic work. Two results follow. First, women expend less energy when they are at work. Because they are less productive than men, they earn less. Second, women seek jobs that are less energy-intensive. This explains why many women seek part-time work, or avoid jobs that involve foreign travel. These jobs tend to be lower-paid. Again, therefore, women's disadvantage in the labour market can be explained by their choices and may not be the result of discrimination.

Not surprisingly, the rational choice approach has prompted a furious reaction from critics. One response is to argue that women's choices may be made in the light of the discrimination they expect to encounter in the labour market[3] (a possibility acknowledged by Becker in his account of the effort theory[4]). For example, a woman may be aware that because of employers' prejudices, she is unlikely to be promoted beyond a certain level in the firm. It would not be rational for her to seek additional qualifications when she is unlikely to get a better job which would enable her to recoup her training costs. Another response is to argue that women's so-called 'choices' are in fact constrained by various factors such as social attitudes.[5] A woman's 'choice' of a part-time job located near her home might reflect the fact that her partner, family and friends assume that she will have primary responsibility for her children. She might prefer a different job, but her choice is *constrained* by the need to fulfil social expectations about the role of a mother. Whichever approach is adopted, the underlying argument is the same: discrimination, not women's choices, is the cause of women's disadvantage.

2 G.S. Becker, 'Human capital, effort, and the sexual division of labor' (1985) 3 *Journal of Labor Economics* S33–S58.
3 S. Fredman, *Women and the Law* (1997), p. 406.   4 Becker, 'Human capital'.
5 Fredman, *Women and the Law*.

In fact, most economists acknowledge some force in their opponents' claims. The real debate turns on how much of women's disadvantage to attribute to non-discriminatory factors and how much to discriminatory ones. A number of empirical studies have sought to disentangle women's choices from the discrimination they encounter, but given the complexity of the issues involved, these studies are rarely conclusive.[6] For our purposes, the important point is that few would deny the existence of *some* discrimination.

Nevertheless, not all would acknowledge that discrimination is a problem that requires a legal solution. Many economists claim that discrimination will ultimately be eliminated by market forces. Again, the pioneering work on this issue has been done by Becker.[7] He argues that discrimination is a 'taste' or preference for which employers are willing to pay. For example, a homophobic employer might be willing to pay an extra £2 per hour (called a 'discrimination coefficient') in order to obtain a workforce made up entirely of heterosexuals. This might mean paying £10 an hour to heterosexual workers, but only hiring a gay or lesbian worker if he or she was willing to accept less than £8 per hour. According to Becker, this situation is not sustainable over the longer term. The employer's products must compete in the market. A non-discriminating competitor could easily take advantage by employing gay and lesbian workers at £8 per hour. The competitor's products would be cheaper and would ultimately drive the discriminating firm out of the market.

The main criticism of Becker's theory is that it is not supported by the empirical evidence. Discrimination against homosexuals and other disadvantaged groups has persisted over time, and although it has become less prevalent in many cases, it has not been eliminated altogether. There are some obvious explanations for this. First, Becker's model assumes that employers know that the workers from the favoured and unfavoured groups are equally productive. In reality, however, employers' prejudices may lead them to think that certain groups are less productive than others.[8] The government's policy that gays and lesbians could not be employed in the armed forces was based, in part, on the claim that their presence would impede operational efficiency.[9] Where employers hold beliefs of this nature, they will not perceive any advantage in employing members of the unfavoured group, even at a lower wage. Second, Becker's model assumes that there is perfect competition in the employer's product market. Any tiny difference in labour costs could make or break a firm's fortunes. However, this may not be the case in practice.[10] Some firms may have a monopoly or may sell in markets in which consumers' decisions are not based solely on price.

6 For a critique, see B.R. Bergmann, 'Does the market for women's labor need fixing?' (1989) 3 *Journal of Economic Perspectives* 43.

7 G.S. Becker, *The Economics of Discrimination* (1957).   8 Fredman, *Women and the Law*.

9 See *R v. Ministry of Defence, ex p. Smith* [1996] QB 517.

10 See Bergmann, 'Does the market for women's labor need fixing?', p. 50.

Arguments which might support legal intervention

Some economists have produced alternative explanations of discrimination in labour markets which may be more supportive of legal intervention. The theory of 'statistical discrimination' suggests that discrimination may benefit employers. This means that it is unlikely to disappear unless the law intervenes. But it also suggests that anti-discrimination laws would impose costs on employers. The 'crowding model' demonstrates that discrimination is inefficient for society as a whole. This theory supports legal intervention more clearly because it identifies a positive economic benefit that would flow from anti-discrimination policies.

When an employer is making a hiring decision, it gathers information about each applicant. But information-gathering is costly, so employers make some decisions based on the average characteristics of the group to which the person belongs. These decisions are accurate in themselves, but they discriminate against anyone in the group who does not share the average characteristics. This is the theory of 'statistical discrimination'.[11] Imagine that the employer is looking for someone to do a job involving heavy lifting. The employer considers that it would be too expensive to conduct a medical check on all applicants. But the employer has evidence that people over the age of fifty are more likely to have health problems which make them unsuitable for physical work. As a result, it decides to exclude all applicants who are fifty or over. This discriminates against anyone in that group who is physically fit enough to do the job.

The statistical discrimination theory presents employers as the beneficiaries of discrimination. Their use of statistics sometimes means that they miss out on productive workers who do not fit the characteristics of their group. But this is not a hiring mistake on the part of the employer. The employer is acting rationally because the benefits of identifying that worker are not sufficient to outweigh the costs of more comprehensive investigations at the hiring stage. Employers only make hiring mistakes on this theory when they use out-of-date or inaccurate statistics. The theory could be used to justify legal intervention in the sense that it shows that employers have no incentive to combat discrimination by themselves: why would they seek to eliminate it if they are its beneficiaries? However, it also shows that anti-discrimination laws impose costs on employers. Instead of making stereotypical assumptions about individuals on the basis of their membership of a group, employers would be obliged to seek detailed information about each individual as part of the hiring process. In our example, the employer would be forced to conduct costly medical checks.

Another theory of discrimination is the 'crowding model'.[12] This theory focuses on the empirical evidence that women and members of the ethnic

---

11 One of the earliest versions is E.S. Phelps, 'The statistical theory of racism and sexism' (1972) 62 *American Economic Review* 659. For refinements, see D.J. Aigner and G.G. Cain, 'Statistical theories of discrimination in labor markets' (1977) 30 *Industrial and Labor Relations Review* 175. See also L.C. Thurow, *Generating Inequality* (1976), Chapter 7.

12 See B.R. Bergmann, *The Economic Emergence of Women* (1986), Chapters 5 and 6.

minorities have often found it difficult to enter certain jobs (often ones which are well-paid) and tend to end up 'crowded' into other (usually low-paid) occupations. A simple model will help to explain the theory. Imagine that there is a workforce of sixty men and sixty women, and three jobs: truck driver, car mechanic and childminder. There is an equal demand for workers to do each of the three jobs, so ideally there should be around forty workers in each job. But employers make the stereotypical assumptions that women are bad drivers and cannot fix cars but are good at caring for children. This means that the sixty men will be employed either as truck drivers or as car mechanics (say thirty of each) and the sixty women will be employed as childminders. Because the men are in short supply, they will receive high wages. And because there are too many women fighting over the childminding jobs, their wages will be low.

What would happen if anti-discrimination laws were passed? Assuming that the laws were effective, women workers would be able to move into the hitherto forbidden occupations of truck driver and car mechanic. Since we assumed that the demand for labour in all three jobs was equal, the market should ultimately achieve the equilibrium position in which there are around forty workers in each job: ten women would give up childminding to become mechanics, and ten women would give up childminding to become truck drivers. At this point, the wages for all three occupations would be equal. Wages for childminders would increase because there would no longer be an oversupply of workers. Wages for car mechanics and truck drivers would decrease because there would no longer be a shortage of workers. Because men would lose out, it seems unlikely that the discriminating employers would bring about this change of their own accord: it would be too unpopular with their workers. Legislation would be required.

But the significant difference between the crowding model and the other theories we have examined is that it does identify an economic benefit from ending occupational segregation. It leads to a more efficient allocation of labour. When the twenty women leave childcare, there is a loss of output in that sector. But there is a gain in output in car mechanics and truck driving because of the extra ten women in each. Since the pay in these last two occupations is higher than was the women's pay when all the women were childminders, it is apparent that employers place a higher value on their output in these new jobs. In other words, the value to the employer of each extra mechanic or driver is greater than the value of additional childminders. If certain assumptions are made,[13] economists can demonstrate that this additional value to the employer is equal to the additional value to *society as a whole* of having more people working in those jobs. This is common sense: the artificial labour shortages created by discrimination cannot be good for the economy.

Of course, in the real world, these advantages might take some time to materialise. The simple model we have been using assumes that there are no

---

13 The key assumptions are perfect competition in the labour market and perfect competition in the market for the firm's products.

costs involved for the women in changing careers. But this is obviously not the case in practice. The women would have to acquire the necessary training in order to become mechanics or truck drivers. They might find that this training is unavailable to them because of discrimination. Or they might decide not to incur the costs of training in case they meet with prejudice and are unable to get a new job at the end of it. These concerns seem to be borne out by the empirical evidence, which shows that some careers remain heavily male-dominated, despite the longstanding prohibitions on discrimination contained in English law.

The statistical discrimination and crowding models are, of course, inter-related. Crowding may occur for many reasons. Some employers may simply be prejudiced: they may make assumptions about the capabilities of particular groups without any evidence at all to support their views. Others may contribute to crowding because of their use of statistical data. For example, an employer which has to provide costly training to its staff and needs them to stay in work for a considerable period in order to recoup those costs might decide not to employ young women because they are statistically more likely than other groups to take breaks from the labour market in order to have children. This might result in women being crowded into occupations which do not require much training.

The two theories we have considered in this section suggest that there may be economic costs and benefits if anti-discrimination laws are enacted. Employers may face greater hiring costs, but the value of outputs across the economy as a whole may be increased. However, even those who advocate anti-discrimination laws on economic grounds would probably accept the need to look to rights arguments as well. As we have seen, although the crowding model predicts some advantages if discrimination is ended, these advantages may take some time to materialise. In the meantime, employers' concerns about their increased hiring costs may come to seem overwhelmingly important. Rights arguments can help to combat these problems by supporting the enactment of legislation even if the economic benefits are insubstantial or delayed. And rights arguments are useful for another reason. Anti-discrimination legislation comes in many different shapes and sizes. Rights arguments can help us to choose among the various possibilities.

Rights perspectives

All the major international human rights instruments contain a right to equal treatment. The only significant difference between them lies in the groups they seek to protect. Some groups have secured public support relatively recently, so they are protected only by more modern instruments. But equality is not a simple concept, so we will need to draw on the literature and on some of the more detailed instruments in order to determine exactly what the right to equal treatment means.

Who is protected?

Most instruments offer a list of those groups who are deemed to be protected against discrimination. The traditional formulation is:

> race, colour, sex, language, religion, political or other opinion, national or social origin, property, birth or other status.[14]

A more modern and comprehensive list is to be found in the EU Charter, which states in Article 21(1) that:

> Any discrimination based on any ground such as sex, race, colour, ethnic or social origin, genetic features, language, religion or belief, political or any other opinion, membership of a national minority, property, birth, disability, age or sexual orientation shall be prohibited.

The inclusion of 'genetic features' is a useful illustration of how discrimination law needs to develop over time. It is only in relatively recent years that it has become possible for scientists to identify the genes which are responsible for particular medical conditions. This opens up the possibility that an employer might refuse to hire someone on the grounds that he or she is likely to develop an illness in later life.

The advantage of listing the groups to be protected is that it guides states in their efforts to comply with international standards, and judges in their attempts to interpret those standards. The disadvantage is that it can be inflexible, making it difficult to accommodate newly recognised victims of discrimination.[15] Most instruments deal with this by indicating that the list of prohibited grounds is not exhaustive. Article 14 of the ECHR begins its list with the phrase 'such as' (to show that the list is illustrative) and ends it with 'or other status' (to make clear that other grounds can be added). But in order to work out what else could legitimately be added to the list, we need to develop some understanding of what it is that the various recognised grounds of discrimination have in common.

It is clear when one looks at the historical development of discrimination law that political factors have played a key role in determining which characteristics would be included. Affected groups have secured the law's protection after mounting extensive lobbying campaigns.[16] Nevertheless, commentators continue to search for some underlying theoretical basis for discrimination law. A leading contender is the notion of 'immutability'.[17] We should ignore some characteristics because they cannot be changed by the individual concerned. The individual cannot do anything about his or her race, so we should not treat it as a relevant factor when making employment decisions. However, there are

---

14 UDHR, Art. 2; ICESCR, Art. 2(2); ICCPR, Art. 2(1).
15 S. Fredman, *Discrimination Law* (2002), pp. 67–8.
16 For history, see ibid., Chapter 2.
17 For discussion, see S.A. Marcosson, 'Constructive immutability' (2001) 3 *University of Pennsylvania Journal of Constitutional Law* 646.

two problems with immutability. First, some characteristics we usually ignore can in fact be changed: for example, religion, sex and political opinion. But a common response to this is to argue that although individuals can change these characteristics of their own volition, it would be wrong to compel them to do so, because the psychological costs would be enormous. This makes the characteristics immutable in practice. Second, we do sometimes use immutable characteristics when making employment decisions. Intelligence is the most obvious example. But the advocates of immutability explain this by saying that society could not function properly if this characteristic was ignored, because it is highly relevant to an individual's ability to do certain jobs.

Other theories about the underlying basis of discrimination law also exist. One is the irrelevance theory: that we disregard certain characteristics because they are not relevant to an individual's ability to do the job.[18] But as we shall see below, there are some exceptional cases in which a person's characteristics may be relevant. The irrelevance theory cannot explain these cases. Another approach is to say that we protect certain characteristics because those who have them have been victims of discrimination in the past. But if a new ground of discrimination were to emerge, like genetic features, this approach would require us to wait for people to suffer discrimination instead of taking preventative action.[19] Finally, some would argue that we should look to a more general, flexible criterion, such as whether the treatment of a particular group makes members of that group feel as if they are not valued by society.[20] You need to consider which of these various approaches you find most persuasive.

What constitutes discrimination?

Most of the major human rights instruments we have been considering prohibit 'discrimination' without specifying what is meant by this. At first sight, the answer might seem simple: discrimination occurs when two people who are equal in terms of skills and abilities are treated unequally because one of them has a particular characteristic (is female or Asian or gay or disabled, for example). The problem is that there are at least three different interpretations of what a government needs to do in order to ensure that people are treated equally.

The first is often labelled 'equality as consistency' or 'formal equality'. According to CEDAW, Article 1:

> 'discrimination against women' shall mean any distinction, exclusion or restriction made on the basis of sex which has the ... *purpose* of impairing or nullifying the recognition, enjoyment and exercise by women ... of human rights.[21]

18 J.H. Ely, *Democracy and Distrust* (1980), Chapter 6.
19 P.T. Kim, 'Genetic discrimination, genetic privacy: rethinking employee protections for a brave new workplace' (2002) 96 *Northwestern University Law Review* 1497, p. 1500.
20 Fredman, *Discrimination Law*, p. 82.
21 Emphasis added. See also ICERD, Art. 1, and ILO Convention 111 on Discrimination (Employment and Occupation) 1958, Art. 1.

This is the simple idea that likes should be treated alike. It helps to overcome blatant forms of discrimination, such as an outright refusal to employ the over-fifties. But commentators have pointed out the many limitations of this approach.[22] One is that it depends on finding a 'comparator', a similarly qualified person with whom to claim equal treatment. If an employer dismisses a woman because she is pregnant, we might intuitively respond that this should amount to unlawful sex discrimination. On a strict interpretation of equality as consistency, however, it does not: she cannot show that she has been treated less favourably than a similarly situated man because men cannot be similarly situated and there is therefore no comparator.[23] Another problem is that formal equality only requires equal treatment, not fair treatment. Thus, if the law condemns an employer for refusing to allow people with certain conditions to have access to employer-sponsored health insurance, the employer could respond either by permitting them to join or by ceasing to provide insurance for any of its employees. Both responses treat all the employees equally, but the latter is clearly a bad outcome for them.

A further limitation of formal equality leads us neatly to our second conception, equality of opportunity.[24] The relevant ILO Convention[25] provides:

> Each Member for which this Convention is in force undertakes to declare and pursue a national policy designed to promote, by methods appropriate to national conditions and practice, *equality of opportunity* and treatment in respect of employment and occupation, with a view to eliminating any discrimination in respect thereof.[26]

There is no point in saying that a particular job – say, as an architect – is open to people of all races if the educational system disadvantages young people from certain ethnic groups. Formal equality does nothing to help those individuals who have not been able to obtain the qualifications they need in order to apply for the job. Equality of opportunity seeks to solve this problem by creating what is often called a 'level playing field' between all groups in society. Governmental intervention would be designed to help people from disadvantaged groups to apply for jobs and to have a realistic prospect of success. The state would provide, for example, special training for women who wanted to enter traditionally male-dominated careers. Equality of opportunity often involves policies outside the scope of employment law, though employers may be encouraged to provide targeted training too.

The third interpretation is 'equality of results'.[27] This picks up on another limitation of equality of opportunity. Advocates of equality of results point out that the creation of a level playing field (even if the strategy was properly

22 Fredman, *Discrimination Law*, pp. 7–11.
23 A conclusion reached in the early case of *Turley* v. *Allders* [1980] ICR 66.
24 Fredman, *Discrimination Law*, pp. 14–15.   25 ILO Convention 111.
26 Ibid., Art. 2 (emphasis added). See also CEDAW, Art. 3; ICERD, Art. 2(2).
27 Fredman, *Discrimination Law*, pp. 11–14.

resourced by the government) would still not guarantee that more individuals from disadvantaged groups would secure particular jobs. They propose at least two solutions. The first and less radical option is to attack the criteria used by employers when selecting people for jobs. The concern is that employers might use criteria which comply with formal equality but in practice operate to the disadvantage of members of a particular group. To quote Article 1 of CEDAW again:

> 'discrimination against women' shall mean any distinction, exclusion or restriction made on the basis of sex which has the *effect* ... of impairing or nullifying the recognition, enjoyment and exercise by women ... of human rights.[28]

For example, the employer might require the individual to work all day on a Friday. This applies equally to workers from all religious backgrounds, but it may be harder for Muslims to comply with because it interferes with their obligation to attend Friday prayers. Under an equality of results approach, these criteria would be banned, because although they are formally neutral, they *result* in discrimination. As we shall see below, however, employers usually have the opportunity to justify their use of these criteria where they reflect a genuine business need.

Some writers would adopt an even stronger focus on the results of employers' practices. They advocate a second option: that employers should be required to engage in 'positive discrimination' or 'affirmative action'.[29] This means deliberately favouring members of under-represented groups during the recruitment process until equality has been achieved:

> Adoption by States Parties of temporary special measures aimed at accelerating *de facto* equality between men and women shall not be considered discrimination as defined in this Convention, but shall in no way entail, as a consequence, the maintenance of unequal or separate standards; these measures shall be discontinued when the objectives of equality of opportunity and treatment have been achieved.[30]

Affirmative action is controversial because it involves discriminating against one group in order to advance the interests of another group. However, its advocates point out that this is only unfair if the two groups are equal to start with. If they are unequal, there is nothing unfair about favouring the previously disadvantaged group. Affirmative action policies may take many different forms. One option is to favour the member of the disadvantaged group only where his or her qualifications are equal to those of applicants from the advantaged group. This can be justified by saying that since their qualifications are equal, it is impossible to choose between them as individuals. Selecting a person in pursuit of the social goal of equality is as fair as, if not fairer than, selecting a person at random. A more controversial option is to favour the member of the disadvantaged group where he or she is *sufficiently* qualified to do the job, even if there

---

28 Emphasis added. See also ICERD, Art. 1; ILO Convention 111, Art. 1.
29 See, generally, Fredman, *Discrimination Law*, Chapter 5.
30 CEDAW, Art. 4. See also ICERD, Art. 1(4); ILO Convention 111, Art. 5.

are other applicants from the advantaged group who are better qualified. This makes a greater inroad into the principle that jobs should be allocated on merit and is more likely to prompt claims on the part of members of the advantaged group that they are being treated unfairly. But its advocates offer at least two justifications. One is that members of disadvantaged groups find it difficult to obtain qualifications, despite equal opportunities policies, so this approach will help more people than the equal qualifications option. The other is that members of the advantaged group cannot complain of unfairness since they start from a position of privilege in society, even if they themselves have never been responsible for the discriminatory treatment of others.

Can discrimination ever be justified?

We have already seen that some commentators think that discrimination can be justified. 'Positive discrimination' can be viewed as discrimination against members of a previously advantaged group, but it is justified by the need to redress the balance in favour of members of a disadvantaged group. But the question with which we are concerned in this section is a slightly different one. Is it ever possible to justify discrimination against a *disadvantaged* group?

One circumstance in which discrimination may be justified is in the field of equality of results. We saw in our discussion above that employers might sometimes use selection criteria which seemed neutral but in fact resulted in discrimination against members of a particular group. Such criteria are prima facie discriminatory. But it is generally accepted that they may be used where they are genuinely related to the job in question. According to Article 1(2) of the ILO Discrimination Convention, 'any distinction, exclusion or preference in respect of a particular job based on the inherent requirements thereof shall not be deemed to be discrimination'. Thus, an employer would be allowed to use the criterion 'ability to lift heavy weights' for the job of construction worker – even though it would discriminate against women and those with physical disabilities – because it reflects an essential feature of that job.

Another situation in which discrimination might be permitted is where a person's characteristic (race, sex and so on) is what *qualifies* him or her to do the job in question.[31] This exception is also permitted by Article 1(2) of the ILO Convention, quoted above. There are some straightforward examples. If a theatre company is looking for someone to play King Lear, it should be allowed to advertise for a male actor. It would be absurd if this amounted to discrimination. More controversially, if a police force is looking for officers to work on an estate inhabited largely by a particular ethnic group, it might argue that it should be allowed to appoint officers from that group because they are more likely to understand the needs of, and to be trusted by, the residents. There is clearly some force in this argument,

---

31 Note that this differs from affirmative action, in which everyone's qualifications are assessed neutrally, and their characteristics are only used as a tiebreaker.

though it does run the risk of perpetuating stereotypes. It denies people from other ethnic groups the opportunity to demonstrate that they could do the job effectively. Arguments about qualifications always require careful scrutiny.

English law

English law does prohibit discrimination, so it is clear that policy-makers have not adopted two of the economics arguments we considered: that discrimination does not exist at all, and that discrimination will eventually be eliminated by market forces. Instead, the law reflects rights arguments and, more recently, a version of the crowding theory: the argument that employers will benefit if they can recruit from a wider pool of talent. We will concentrate on two key questions. To what extent does the law implement a rights approach, in the scope of protection it offers and in its definition of discrimination? And to what extent does the law reflect the economists' point that anti-discrimination policies might be costly for employers to implement, at least over the short term?

Who is protected?

As we saw in Chapter 5, we must always ask whether any particular piece of employment legislation protects employees or workers. English anti-discrimination legislation protects workers and uses the broadest possible definition of that concept.[32] Thus, it includes self-employed people where they undertake to perform the work personally, as well as employees and workers narrowly defined. This reflects the fact that fundamental human rights are at stake. The legislation applies to all aspects of the employment relationship: selection procedures, hiring decisions, terms and conditions of employment, opportunities for promotion and training, and detrimental treatment and dismissal.[33]

For many years, English law concentrated largely on protecting workers against race and sex discrimination. Other groups, if they were to be protected at all, had to bring themselves within these categories. Attempts were made to argue that sex discrimination laws protected against discrimination on grounds of sexual orientation,[34] and that religious discrimination could also constitute racial discrimination.[35] These arguments had varying degrees of success. In 1997, the EU's competences were extended to cover a wide range of possible grounds of discrimination.[36] This has led to the enactment of a Framework Directive on Discrimination[37] and to new implementing legislation in English law, broadening the scope of our law considerably.[38]

---

32 For example, EE(SO)R 2003, reg. 2(3).   33 For example, ibid., reg. 6.
34 See, for example, (C-249/96) *Grant* v. *South West Trains* [1998] ECR I-621; *Advocate General for Scotland* v. *Macdonald* [2003] UKHL 34; [2004] 1 All ER 339.
35 See, for example, *Mandla* v. *Dowell Lee* [1983] 2 AC 548.   36 Art. 13 EC.
37 Directive 2000/78/EC.
38 See, generally, S. Fredman, 'Equality: a new generation?' (2001) 30 *ILJ* 145.

Discrimination on all of the following grounds is prohibited in English law:

- Being male or female (SDA 1975, as amended, ss. 1 and 2; Article 141 EC; Directive 76/207/EEC (the Equal Treatment Directive), as amended).[39]
- Intending to undergo, undergoing or having undergone gender reassignment (SDA 1975, s. 2A[40]).
- Being married or in a civil partnership (but not being single) (SDA 1975, s. 3, as amended).
- Being pregnant or taking maternity leave (SDA 1975, s. 3A, as amended).
- Race (RRA 1976, as amended, s. 1; Directive 2000/43/EC).

Under s. 3(1) of the RRA 1976, discrimination on racial grounds includes discrimination on grounds of 'colour, race, nationality or ethnic or national origins'. The courts consider factors such as a shared history, a cultural tradition, geographical origin, language, literature and religion when deciding whether or not a particular group constitutes a 'race'.[41] The fact that the law prohibits discrimination on 'racial grounds', rather than on grounds of the *claimant's* race, is thought to protect people against discrimination based on the employer's (mistaken) perception of their race, and discrimination based on the race of their friends or family. A similarly broad formulation is used in the legislation on sexual orientation and religion, discussed below.

- Disability (DDA 1995, as amended, ss. 4 and 4A; Directive 2000/78/EC).

According to s. 1(1) of the DDA 1995, a person has a disability if he or she 'has a physical or mental impairment which has a substantial and long-term adverse effect on his ability to carry out normal day-to-day activities'. To count as long-term, the disability must have lasted or be expected to last for at least twelve months.[42] The definition includes those who would suffer from a disability were it not for medication,[43] and those who have a progressive condition (such as HIV or multiple sclerosis) which currently has minor effects but might lead to a disability in the future.[44] The ECJ has recently held that those who care for a disabled person are also covered.[45]

- Religion or belief (EE(RB)R 2003, as amended, reg. 2(1); Directive 2000/78/EC).[46]

---

39 The Equal Pay Act 1970 is also of relevance, but it will be considered in detail in Chapter 8. You should also review the discussion of maternity leave and parental rights in Chapter 6.
40 Inserted by the Sex Discrimination (Gender Reassignment) Regulations 1999 (SI 1999/1102), after the ECJ's decision in (Case 13/94) *P v. S and Cornwall CC* [1996] ECR I-2143.
41 *Mandla* v. *Dowell Lee*. See also *Dawkins* v. *Crown Suppliers* [1993] ICR 517.
42 DDA 1995, Schedule 1, para. 2.   43 Ibid., Schedule 1, para. 6.
44 Ibid., Schedule 1, para. 8.
45 (C-303/06) *Coleman* v. *Attridge Law* [2008] IRLR 722.
46 See L. Vickers, 'The Employment Equality (Religion or Belief) Regulations 2003' (2003) 32 *ILJ* 188.

These regulations protect people from discrimination on the grounds of 'religion', 'any religious or philosophical belief', or the absence of such belief.[47] Thus, they protect atheists as well as believers.

- Sexual orientation (EE(SO)R 2003, regs. 2(1) and 3; Directive 2000/78/EC).[48]

These regulations protect people from discrimination on the grounds of homosexual, heterosexual or bisexual orientation.

- Age (EE(A)R 2006, reg. 3; Directive 2000/78/EC).[49]

These regulations protect against discrimination on grounds of age or membership of a particular age group. In some circumstances they also protect against discrimination on the ground of a person's apparent age.

Article 14 of the ECHR also contains an anti-discrimination guarantee. This can be enforced in the English courts by virtue of the HRA 1998, so it is just as much a part of English law as the provisions we have been considering. However, a major caveat is in order before we consider the content of Article 14. The Article only protects against discrimination which occurs when an individual seeks to exercise one of the other Convention rights.[50] Thus, if an employer banned members of a particular political party from wearing their membership badges at work, a claim could be brought.[51] There is a prima facie breach of Article 10 (freedom of expression) and Article 14 (discrimination on grounds of political opinion). But if the employer refuses to give someone a job because she is a woman, it is difficult to show that a Convention right has been breached. As a result, Article 14 cannot be invoked.[52]

Although the potential of Article 14 is limited, its scope is very broad. It covers 'sex, race, colour, language, religion, political or other opinion, national or social origin, association with a national minority, property, birth or other status'. Thus, it adds a number of prohibited grounds to those we have been considering, such as property and political opinion. Perhaps most significantly, the Article 14 right is not a closed list: other grounds of discrimination can be added under the category of 'other status'. This could occur in one of two ways. First, the UK courts could be persuaded to add a new ground on their own initiative. Second, the UK courts are bound to take into account the Strasbourg jurisprudence when interpreting the Article, so they could be persuaded to adopt new grounds which

---

47 Art. 9 ECHR (as well as ECJ jurisprudence) may be relevant to the construction of these provisions.
48 See H. Oliver, 'Sexual orientation discrimination: perceptions, definitions and genuine occupational requirements' (2004) 33 *ILJ* 1.
49 See M. Sargeant, 'The Employment Equality (Age) Regulations 2006: a legitimisation of age discrimination in employment' (2006) 35 *ILJ* 209.
50 The Article prohibits discrimination in 'the enjoyment of the rights and freedoms set forth in this Convention'.
51 Subject to the issues about horizontal effect discussed in Chapter 4.
52 Protocol 12 to the ECHR contains a free-standing right not to be discriminated against. However, the UK has not ratified it.

have been added by the ECtHR. The Strasbourg court has included a number of other grounds, including sexual orientation[53] and illegitimacy.[54]

If we measure English law against one of the most up-to-date lists of grounds, that contained in the EU Charter, there are a few omissions. One of the most interesting is discrimination on the ground of a person's genetic features. A genetic predisposition to a particular disease is not protected under the DDA 1995, because that Act only applies once someone has a substantial impairment as a result of their disability (or a minor impairment in the case of a medical condition which is going to get worse). It might be possible to persuade the courts to construe the EU Framework Directive (which does not define disability) broadly,[55] or to include genetic discrimination within Article 14 ECHR. The government's view is that there is no need to introduce statutory protection since there is no evidence that employers are making extensive use of genetic testing in the workplace. However, this may change as the science develops.

What constitutes discrimination?

English law incorporates both formal equality (through what is often labelled 'direct discrimination') and a version of equality of results (through the concept of indirect discrimination).[56] But it does not satisfy many rights commentators because it does not require employers to apply equal opportunities policies or affirmative action.

According to reg. 3(1)(a) of the EE(SO)R 2003, A discriminates against B if 'on grounds of sexual orientation, A treats B less favourably than he treats or would treat other persons'. Thus, the court must find, first, that B has been treated less favourably than a comparator (who might be real or hypothetical), and second, that this has occurred because of sexual orientation. The comparator's circumstances must be 'the same, or not materially different' to those of the claimant.[57] Thus, where a female police officer had been suspended from the role of performing appraisals of more junior officers after complaints had been made about her, the House of Lords held that the appropriate comparator in her sex discrimination claim was a hypothetical male officer against whom similar complaints had been made.[58] Turning to the second part of the test, in *James* v. *Eastleigh BC*, a 'but-for' test was used to determine the reason for the treatment: but for the man's sex, would he have received the treatment of which he was complaining?[59] Some recent cases have focused more directly on the 'reason' for the treatment – was it on a prohibited ground?[60] This approach has been enshrined in statute in relation

---

53 *Salguiero da Silva Mouta* v. *Portugal* (2001) 31 EHRR 47.
54 *Marckx* v. *Belgium* (1979–80) 2 EHRR 330.   55 Directive 2000/78/EC.
56 The DDA 1995 defines these concepts in a different way to the other Acts, but space precludes a full discussion of its approach.   57 EE(SO)R 2003, reg. 3(2).
58 *Shamoon* v. *Chief Constable of the RUC* [2003] UKHL 11; [2003] 2 All ER 26.
59 *James* v. *Eastleigh BC* [1990] 2 AC 751.
60 *Shamoon* v. *Chief Constable of the RUC*, para. 11 (per Lord Nicholls).

to pregnancy, where the requirement to compare the employer's treatment of a pregnant woman with how the employer would have treated her had she not become pregnant has recently been repealed.[61] However, in looking at the reason for the treatment, it is important not to get sidetracked by the employer's motive. Direct discrimination is generally prohibited even if the employer had 'good' intentions, such as helping a disadvantaged group.[62] In practice, the 'reason' and comparison approaches may not be very different: to determine the reason for the treatment, it may be necessary to consider how other people would have been treated, thereby bringing in an element of comparison.

According to reg. 3(1)(b), indirect discrimination occurs where:

A applies to B a provision, criterion or practice which he applies or would apply equally to persons not of the same sexual orientation as B, but –

  (i) which puts or would put persons of the same sexual orientation as B at a particular disadvantage when compared with other persons,

  (ii) which puts B at that disadvantage, and

  (iii) which A cannot show to be a proportionate means of achieving a legitimate aim.

The first part of this definition describes the situation in which an employer is using apparently neutral selection procedures. The use of 'criterion or practice' is intended to capture not only formal selection requirements, but also more informal behaviour which might be discriminatory. For example, recruiting only from among the friends of existing employees instead of advertising vacancies may be discriminatory since it tends to perpetuate the composition of the existing workforce. Paragraph (i) seeks evidence that the criterion or practice has a disparate impact between groups. The phrase 'particular disadvantage' is intended to be less technical and statistical than the phrase 'considerably smaller proportion' which was used in earlier legislation. Paragraph (iii) will be considered below, in our discussion of justification.

The DDA does not contain a definition of indirect discrimination. Instead, it imposes on employers a duty to make reasonable adjustments under s. 4A(1):

Where –

  (a) a provision, criterion or practice applied by or on behalf of an employer, or

  (b) any physical feature of premises occupied by the employer places the disabled person concerned at a substantial disadvantage in comparison with persons who are not disabled, it is the duty of the employer to take such steps as it is reasonable, in all the circumstances of the case, for him to have to take in order to prevent the provision, criterion or practice, or feature, having that effect.

Thus, the employer might be obliged to make its premises more accessible, to allow a disabled worker to take additional time off to attend medical appointments or

---

61 SDA 1975, s. 3A, as amended, Sex Discrimination Act 1975 (Amendment) Regulations 2008 (SI 2008/656).

62 As in *James* v. *Eastleigh BC*. Though direct age discrimination can be justified (EE(A)R 2006, reg. 3(1)), as can some types of direct disability discrimination (DDA 1995, s. 3A).

to transfer that worker to a job with different responsibilities.[63] Tribunals will take into account factors such as the cost and practicality of making the changes in deciding what is 'reasonable'. The duty to make reasonable adjustments plays a similar role to the concept of indirect discrimination in that it challenges ostensibly neutral arrangements which make life more difficult for certain groups. However, because of the way it is formulated, it encourages employers to think more positively about ways in which they might accommodate disabled workers.

It was noted above that equal opportunities policies were largely beyond the scope of labour law, focusing as they do on education and training. But some training is provided by employers. As we saw above, training is one of the areas in which employers are obliged not to discriminate. But s. 48(1) SDA 1975 contains an exception which allows the employer to encourage members of the under-represented sex to apply for jobs and to favour them in the provision of training. Similar provisions are contained in other pieces of anti-discrimination legislation. However, these provisions do not satisfy rights theorists. They permit employers to help disadvantaged groups, but they do not oblige them to do so. Thus, they will only be of assistance where the employer has a commitment to equal opportunities.

Traditionally, affirmative action or positive discrimination has not been permitted in English law because most of our anti-discrimination legislation is 'symmetrical': it protects traditionally advantaged groups as well as traditionally disadvantaged groups. Thus, as we have seen, the SDA 1975 applies to men and women, and the EE(SO)R 2003 apply to homosexuals, heterosexuals and bisexuals. This means that a positive discrimination measure which favours a traditionally disadvantaged group, such as women or homosexuals, would be unlawful because it would discriminate against men or heterosexuals. The most significant exception to this is the DDA 1995, which applies only to people with a disability. This permits affirmative action in the sense that a person who did not have a disability would have no grounds for complaint if, for example, an employer advertised a job for disabled people only. At the time of writing, the government is proposing to permit affirmative action in the Equality Bill.[64] Where two candidates are equally qualified, the employer would be allowed (but not obliged) to choose between them in a way that would increase the representation of an otherwise under-represented group in the workplace. The employer would not be allowed to make this preference automatic, reflecting the ECJ's view that any individual who is likely to suffer as a result of affirmative action programmes should have an opportunity to argue that he or she ought to be offered the job despite being a member of the advantaged group.[65]

---

63 *Archibald* v. *Fife Council* [2004] UKHL 32; [2004] 4 All ER 303.
64 Lord Privy Seal, *The Equality Bill: Government Response to the Consultation* (2008) (Cm 7454), Chapter 5. For the position in Community law, see Directive 2000/78/EC, Art. 7; Directive 2000/43/EC, Art. 5; Art. 141(4) EC.
65 The leading cases are (Case C-409/95) *Marschall* v. *Land Nordrhein Westfalen* [1997] ECR I-6363; (Case C-158/97) *Badeck* [2000] ECR I-1875; (Case C-407/98) *Abrahamsson* v.

Rights theorists will probably give a cautious welcome to this development. They have long argued that English law's reliance on direct and indirect discrimination alone has not done enough to improve the position of disadvantaged groups. One problem, noted in our theoretical discussion, above, is that direct and indirect discrimination may not be powerful enough to overcome employers' (and society's) deep-seated prejudices about the abilities of those who belong to certain groups. Another problem is that direct and indirect discrimination laws must be enforced by individual litigants in the courts. Many potential complainants lack the resources to litigate and may feel that the odds are stacked against them.[66] The EHRC can assist complainants, but it too has limited resources and cannot take on every case. Affirmative action could help because it gives employers an active role in tackling discrimination. However, a key point to note about the proposed scheme is that – like the current law on training – it is permissive rather than mandatory. This means that only employers who already have a strong commitment to equality will use it. Thus, it may not make very much difference in practice.

Another radical strategy for tackling deep-seated discrimination is 'mainstreaming'. This involves imposing positive duties on employers to review their actions and policies in order to ensure that they do not discriminate.[67] It is potentially far-reaching because it does not depend on an individual complaint and it could lead to changes that would help many people in the relevant workplace. In England, Wales and Scotland, mainstreaming has been confined to public bodies. They are currently under a positive duty to promote equality in the fields of sex, race and disability.[68] The proposed Equality Bill would create a single duty covering all the main grounds of discrimination.[69] In Northern Ireland, mainstreaming has been extended to private employers. They are under a duty to review their employment of Catholics and Protestants, and to take affirmative action if the members of one community are not being treated fairly.[70] It is, of course, essential to monitor employers' compliance with this duty. This role is performed by the Northern Ireland Equality Commission.[71] The evidence suggests that the Commission's interventions have helped to encourage greater integration in Northern Ireland's workplaces.[72] The government currently has no plans to extend mainstreaming to private firms elsewhere in the UK.

Fogelqvist [2000] ECR I-5539. For discussion, see S. Fredman, 'Affirming affirmative action' (1998) *Cambridge Yearbook of European Legal Studies* 199.

66 Fredman, *Discrimination Law* , pp. 163–74.

67 Ibid., pp. 176–94; B.A. Hepple *et al.*, *Equality: A New Framework* (2000), Chapter 3.

68 RRA 1976, s. 71; SDA 1975, s. 76A; DDA 1995, s. 49A. Northern Ireland Act 1998, s. 75 requires public bodies in Northern Ireland to promote equality of opportunity more generally.

69 Lord Privy Seal, *The Equality Bill*, Chapter 2.

70 Fair Employment and Treatment (Northern Ireland) Order 1998 (SI 1998/3162), Art. 55.

71 Fredman, *Discrimination Law*, pp. 182–7, discusses enforcement issues.

72 C. McCrudden *et al.*, 'Legal regulation of affirmative action in Northern Ireland: an empirical assessment' (2004) 24 *OJLS* 363.

Can discrimination ever be justified?

English law permits discrimination in two main sets of circumstances. One is where someone's characteristics are a 'genuine occupational qualification' for the job in question. Thus, although it would normally be unlawful to offer a job only to a woman, an exception can be made where the job involves acting a female part in a film. The traditional approach to this exception is to list the circumstances in which it applies, thereby reducing the judges' discretion in interpreting it. Thus, the SDA 1975, s. 7, lists authenticity in dramatic performances, the need for decency and privacy, and the provision of personal welfare services, among others, as situations in which sex might be a genuine occupational qualification. More recent legislation takes a more flexible and discretionary approach. Thus, the EE(SO)R 2003, reg. 7(2), carves out an exception for cases in which the employer can show that it is 'proportionate' to treat sexual orientation as a 'genuine and determining' occupational requirement in a particular case. The addition of the word 'determining' indicates that the person's sexual orientation must be essential to the job, not just a desirable characteristic. And the proportionality test, to be discussed below, is relatively difficult to satisfy. This should ensure that the genuine occupational qualification exception is only used in the most limited circumstances and does not perpetuate stereotyping. The government plans to extend this more general approach to all the grounds of discrimination.[73]

A second respect in which discrimination can be justified is in relation to equality of results.[74] Here, the employer is generally forbidden from using criteria that have a disparate impact on a particular group, even if those criteria seem to be neutral. But the employer is permitted to justify the use of such criteria where it can be shown that they are necessary for the job in question. Thus, in *Clymo* v. *Wandsworth LBC*,[75] the council refused to permit the claimant and her husband (who was also employed by the council) to share her job when she returned from maternity leave. The court accepted the council's argument that the job was a management position involving the supervision of junior staff who needed continuity in the instructions they were given, and was therefore unsuitable for job-sharing. From a rights perspective, the scope of the justification test is crucial. If it is too wide, the right to equal treatment will be fatally undermined.

The justification test in English law is proportionality. This stems from the ECJ's decision in the *Bilka-Kaufhaus* case.[76] The Court held that discriminatory measures could only be justified where they 'correspond to a real need on the part of the undertaking, are appropriate with a view to achieving the objectives pursued, and are necessary to that end'.[77] The discrimination legislation now codifies this test. It provides that the employer discriminates where he applies a criterion

---

73 Lord Privy Seal, *The Equality Bill*, Chapter 8.
74 Direct age and (sometimes) disability discrimination can be justifiable: EE(A)R 2006, reg. 3(1) and DDA 1995, s. 3A.
75 *Clymo* v. *Wandsworth LBC* [1989] ICR 250.
76 (Case 170/84) *Bilka-Kaufhaus* v. *Weber von Hartz* [1986] ECR 1607.   77 Ibid., para. 37.

'which [he] cannot show to be a proportionate means of achieving a legitimate aim'.[78] If applied correctly, the test is relatively strict. It forces the courts to judge the validity of the employer's goals and to assess whether or not the employer could have achieved those goals by some other non-discriminatory means.

The justification test responds to a wide-ranging set of cost arguments being put forward by employers. The basic argument is that changing from a discriminatory practice to a non-discriminatory one will be less convenient and therefore more expensive.[79] This argument is familiar from our discussion of the statistical discrimination theory, in which we saw that employers might use statistical information during recruitment because it is easier and cheaper than finding out about individual candidates in detail. But employers' claims are by no means confined to increases in recruitment costs. In *Clymo* v. *Wandsworth LBC*, the council was concerned about the possible costs of a new way of organising a job. Most rights theorists are relatively dismissive of employers' claims about costs. They emphasise the fundamental nature of the right to equal treatment and argue that it should trump financial considerations. They also derive some support from the economists' crowding model, which shows that over the longer term, the ending of discrimination will benefit the economy as a whole. The problem is that the courts do not have the tools to measure these wider economic benefits, but they are acutely aware of each employer's arguments about the short-term, transitional costs. We will examine the justification test in more detail in Chapter 8, because it has been of particular importance in shaping the law on equal pay, so you may want to look at that discussion before forming a view on it.

Further reading

For detailed textbook accounts of this topic, see S. Deakin and G.S. Morris, *Labour Law* (4th edn., 2005), Chapter 6, or H. Collins, K.D. Ewing and A. McColgan, *Labour Law: Text and Materials* (2nd edn., 2005), Chapter 3. On the European material, see C. Barnard, *EC Employment Law* (3rd edn., 2006), Chapters 6 and 8.

For a readable introductory text, written largely from a rights perspective, see S. Fredman, *Discrimination Law* (2002). There are lots of questions to think about when considering the rights perspective. What conception of equality should the law adopt? Should it be based on equality at all? (On this last question, see also H. Collins, 'Discrimination, equality and social inclusion' (2003) 66 *MLR* 16.) In what circumstances, if any, can discrimination be justified? The most important

---

78 For example, EE(RB)R 2003, reg. 3(1)(b)(iii). The DDA 1995, s. 3A(3), uses a less stringent test, but the government plans to change it to a proportionality test in the Equality Bill (Lord Privy Seal, *The Equality Bill*, Chapter 11). For the approach of the English courts, see *Allonby* v. *Accrington and Rossendale College* [2001] EWCA Civ 529; [2001] ICR 1189.

79 Where there is no real inconvenience, the courts are more sympathetic to claimants. See, for example, *London Underground* v. *Edwards* (No. 2) [1999] ICR 494.

current debate from this perspective is around the role of affirmative action and positive duties. For discussion, see S. Fredman, *Human Rights Transformed: Positive Rights and Positive Duties* (2008), Chapter 7. What are the limits of labour law in combating discrimination? What other government policies are relevant?

One of the most famous neoclassical critiques of anti-discrimination laws is R. Epstein, *Forbidden Grounds: The Case Against Employment Discrimination Laws* (1992), especially Chapters 1–3. His work has a strong ideological basis in the doctrine of freedom of contract. What are the advantages of a market solution to the problem of discrimination? What assumptions does Epstein make in setting out his theory? Why might markets fail to eliminate discrimination? For a shorter piece focusing in particular on the costs of anti-discrimination laws, see R. Posner, 'An economic analysis of sex discrimination laws' (1989) 56 *University of Chicago Law Review* 1311. To what extent should we be concerned about the costs of anti-discrimination policies? Is there a case for saying that the costs should simply be ignored?

For an excellent introduction to the debate between neoclassical and new institutional economists, see M. Sawyer, 'The operation of labour markets and the economics of equal opportunities', in J. Humphries and J. Rubery (eds.), *The Economics of Equal Opportunities* (1995). In the same volume, I. Bruegel and D. Perrons, 'Where do the costs of unequal treatment for women fall?', give an account of the economic benefits for firms and for the economy as a whole which would flow from the elimination of discrimination. How do these writers arrive at such different conclusions to those of the neoclassical economists? What assumptions do they use? More generally, what are the advantages of justifying anti-discrimination laws on the grounds of their economic benefits? Are there any risks associated with this strategy?

The government's own view of discrimination law is heavily influenced by 'third way' arguments that diversity is good for business. For the government's most recent review of the law, see the 2007 consultation paper entitled *Discrimination Law Review: A Framework for Fairness: Proposals for a Single Equality Bill for Great Britain*. For an interesting discussion of the *Review* from the perspective of regulatory technique, see C. McCrudden, 'Equality legislation and reflexive regulation: a response to the Discrimination Law Review's Consultative Paper' (2007) 36 *ILJ* 255. At the time of writing (2008), the government is proposing to bring all the grounds of discrimination together into a single Equality Act. To what extent do you think that the various grounds of discrimination should be treated in the same way? For an interesting discussion of this issue in relation to sexual orientation, see H. Oliver, 'Sexual orientation discrimination: perceptions, definitions and genuine occupational requirements' (2004) 33 *ILJ* 1.

8

Wages

In the days of collective laissez-faire, a book on labour law would not have contained a chapter on wages.[1] Workers' pay was seen as pre-eminently a matter for collective bargaining between trade unions and employers. Even when the law did intervene, through the creation of Wages Councils to determine wage rates for the lowest paid, this was viewed as a substitute for collective bargaining rather than as a new approach to pay determination.[2] Nowadays, however, the position is very different. English law regulates pay in two ways. First, the National Minimum Wage Act 1998 (NMWA) seeks to ensure that all workers receive a minimum hourly rate for their work. This is intended to improve the working conditions of the lowest-paid workers. Second, the Equal Pay Act 1970 (EqPA) and the anti-discrimination legislation seek to ensure that workers who make an equal contribution to the firm are paid equally, and that no artificial distinctions are made on the basis of sex, race, religion and so on. The discussion of equal pay in this chapter will concentrate primarily on equality between the wages of women and men, because this has received most attention in the cases and the literature. However, it is important to bear in mind that unequal pay may affect other groups too, particularly the members of certain ethnic minorities.[3]

Neoclassical economists are hostile to legal regulation of wages. They argue that it is the function of markets to set wages, so any interference with the usual interplay of market forces will be counterproductive. The minimum wage will artificially inflate the wages of some workers to a level above their market value, leading to redundancies for some workers and an inefficient use of labour in the economy as a whole. Equal pay legislation is unnecessary because the market itself is capable of eliminating inequalities over time. In contrast, the new institutional economists welcome some regulation of wages, arguing that it is important to prevent firms from trying to compete on the basis of low wages in an

---

1 See Chapter 1.
2 O. Kahn-Freund, 'Legal framework', in A. Flanders and H. Clegg (eds.), *The System of Industrial Relations in Great Britain* (1954), discussed in P. Davies and M. Freedland, *Labour Legislation and Public Policy* (1993), pp. 27–34.
3 According to the EOC, Pakistani women working full-time earn 28 per cent less on average than white men working full-time: EOC, *Moving on Up? The Way Forward* (2006), p. 17. The pay gap for women generally is 17 per cent.

era of globalisation. Instead, firms should compete on the basis of quality and productivity. In turn, this involves harnessing the enthusiasm of the workforce by showing them how much they are valued. On this theory, it is essential to avoid very low wage levels and to ensure that equally productive workers are paid equally, regardless of characteristics such as race or sex.

The other main argument in favour of legal regulation comes from a rights perspective. It can be argued that low pay puts workers' dignity in jeopardy. The very essence of employment is the wage–work bargain: the individual offers to work for the employer in return for a wage. The individual's dignity is violated if he or she is obliged to work for less than he or she needs to live on, or for a lower wage than that earned by an equally productive person of the opposite sex or of another race. On this view, the law's role is to prevent exploitation.

Economics perspectives

We will discuss the minimum wage and equal pay separately, although there is some overlap between the arguments on each topic.

Minimum wages

In order to understand the economics argument against the minimum wage, we need to begin with a simple account of how wages are determined. Employers have a demand for labour, which is determined by a variety of factors, including demand for the products they are selling and the prices of the other resources they are using, such as machinery. In general, employers' demand for labour decreases as the wage rate rises. Workers' labour supply is again determined by a variety of factors, including their preferences for work or leisure and their income from other sources; but, in general, workers' supply of labour increases as the wage rate increases. The 'invisible hand' of the market guides employers and workers to the point at which the amount of labour being supplied equals the amount of labour employers want. This is the equilibrium wage. At this price, just enough workers enter the labour market to fulfil employers' demand.

Of course, this model is a simple one and assumes that markets are perfectly competitive.[4] Nevertheless, it helps us to understand the theoretical impact of a minimum wage. If the minimum wage is set at a rate below the equilibrium wage, it will have no impact at all. Employers are already willing to pay a higher rate. But this is unlikely to happen in practice, since the purpose of the minimum wage is to improve the conditions of the lowest-paid workers. Thus, the minimum wage will usually be set so that it is higher than the equilibrium wage. Where this

---

4 Where the employer is a monopsonist, the minimum wage might cause employment to increase by countervailing the employer's power to set wages at an artificially low level. See E.G. West and M. McKee, 'Monopsony and "shock" arguments for minimum wages' (1980) 46 *Southern Economic Journal* 883.

is the case, economists predict three main effects.[5] First, since the cost of labour has increased, employers will employ fewer workers. Some people – usually disadvantaged individuals on the fringes of the labour market – will lose their jobs.[6] Second, since the wage level has increased, more people will be willing to enter the labour market. This means that more people will now be looking for a job, so the number of unemployed people will increase. Third, the minimum wage creates allocative inefficiency. The workers who are made redundant as a result of the minimum wage will either not be able to find jobs at all or will only be able to find lower-paying jobs in sectors not covered by the minimum wage. The value of their output to society in their new job (if any) is lower than the value of their output to society before the minimum wage was introduced. Society as a whole loses out because workers are not being allocated to their most valued uses. Of course, employers might offset some of these effects by making savings in other respects: they might be able to keep their overall wage bill down by cutting fringe benefits. But while this might prevent some redundancies, advocates of the minimum wage would not welcome it because it does not leave workers any better off as a result of the wage increase.

There are two ways in which a new institutional economist might defend the minimum wage: the 'shock' theory and the 'efficiency wage' theory. Both theories focus on the role of wages in improving firms' productivity. This reflects the new institutionalists' macroeconomic concern with globalisation. They argue that UK firms cannot hope to compete with firms in developing countries on the basis of price, and should compete instead by being productive and by developing innovative goods and services.

The idea behind the shock theory is that employers might respond to the minimum wage by being 'shocked' into improving other aspects of their business so that the minimum wage does not have a damaging effect.[7] If a worker has to be paid £5 an hour instead of £4 an hour, the rational employer will seek to ensure that the worker becomes more productive so that it is worth paying that much for his or her output. This might involve investing in new machinery or providing training. However, critics point out that a firm that is selling in a competitive market will keep matters such as equipment and training under constant review in order to ensure that it is not outdone by its rivals. Thus, the shock theory would only work where a firm was not operating in a fully competitive market.

---

5 The literature is substantial. See, for example, J. Stigler, 'The economics of minimum wage legislation' (1946) 36 *American Economic Review* 358; J. Mincer, 'Unemployment effects of minimum wages' (1976) 84 *Journal of Political Economy* S87; P. Linneman, 'The economic impacts of minimum wage laws: a new look at an old question' (1982) 90 *Journal of Political Economy* 443. For critique and counter-arguments, see D. Card and A.B. Krueger, *Myth and Measurement: The New Economics of the Minimum Wage* (1995).

6 H. Hutchison, 'Toward a critical race reformist conception of minimum wage regimes: exploding the power of myth, fantasy and hierarchy' (1997) 34 *Harvard Journal on Legislation* 93, argues that the minimum wage in the USA is a form of institutionalised racism because it has an adverse impact on the employment levels of African American workers.

7 See, generally, A. Rees, *The Economics of Work and Pay* (1973), pp. 80–3.

And the effect of the shock might be to make the employer realise that it has too many workers, thereby leading to redundancies.[8]

The other possible way of justifying the minimum wage would be to treat it as an application of the efficiency wage theory.[9] This theory seeks to explain why it might sometimes be to an employer's advantage to pay workers more than the equilibrium wage. The traditional model of wage determination assumes that all workers are equally productive. The efficiency wage theory assumes that workers differ in their degree of productivity and that they can be motivated by higher wages to be more productive. Workers will value their jobs more highly if they are paid an efficiency wage. They will have more to lose if they are dismissed. This should deter them from being lazy or unproductive (often referred to as 'shirking').[10]

Some figures will help to illustrate the benefits to the employer. Under the traditional model, if the employer hires workers at a wage above the equilibrium wage, he or she will simply be increasing his or her costs unnecessarily, because equally productive workers could have been hired at the equilibrium wage. The rational employer would not hire a worker to produce four units of output for £6 an hour when he or she can get the same output at the equilibrium wage of £4 an hour. But now imagine that while the worker paid £4 an hour will produce four units of output, the worker paid £6 an hour will produce eight units of output. By paying an efficiency wage, the employer in fact makes a saving. Instead of paying two workers £4 an hour to get eight units, the employer can achieve the same number of units by paying one worker £6 an hour.

The efficiency wage theory was first used to explain employers' voluntary decisions to pay above the market rate, but it can be adapted in support of the minimum wage. Workers who receive low pay are, on this theory, unlikely to put much effort into their work. An increase in pay prompted by the introduction of a minimum wage will make jobs more valuable and encourage workers to be more productive in order to keep their jobs. Of course, the employer might decide to pay an efficiency wage to its workers without legislative intervention,[11] but the usual concerns about undercutting by competitors might prevent this.

However, the efficiency wage theory has been developed for a specific set of circumstances: the situation in which the employer cannot monitor or measure its employees' performance. Firms can usually find cheaper ways of preventing shirking. Many workers can be monitored: the output of workers on a production line in a factory can be checked by a supervisor. Or workers' pay can be

---

8 West and McKee, 'Monopsony and "shock"'.

9 R. Solow, 'Another possible source of wage stickiness' (1979) 1 *Journal of Macroeconomics* 79; C. Shapiro and T. Stiglitz, 'Equilibrium unemployment as a worker discipline device' (1984) 74 *American Economic Review* 433.

10 Some writers argue that efficiency wages can be used to combat other problems too, such as high employee turnover.

11 See C. Jolls, 'Fairness, minimum wage law, and employee benefits' (2002) 77 *New York University Law Review* 47.

related to performance. Traditionally, many workers have been paid piece rates: they are paid for each shirt they sew rather than for each hour they work. Other examples include offering performance-related bonus payments or giving workers the chance to be promoted if they perform well. Moreover, worker loyalty can be generated by pay and pension schemes which reward those who stay with the firm for longer.[12] For those who take the view that efficiency wages are helpful only on the rare occasions when these strategies do not work, a legally imposed minimum wage is an unduly costly way of improving productivity.

Equal pay

The standard neoclassical argument against equal pay laws is that they are unnecessary. Becker's 'taste for discrimination' model identifies discrimination as a preference for which employers are willing to pay.[13] Preferring an all-male workforce, they are willing to pay men a premium, and will only employ women if they are prepared to work at a lower wage. The difference between the wage offered to men and that offered to women is the 'discrimination coefficient'. However, Becker suggests that this behaviour cannot be sustained over time. Non-discriminating employers will take advantage of the supply of cheap female labour and will drive their discriminating competitors out of the market. Legislative intervention to require employers to pay men and women equally imposes unnecessary costs on employers. As we saw in Chapter 7, this theory has been much criticised for the fact that its predictions have not been borne out: women's average earnings remain considerably lower than men's, despite long-standing awareness of the issue of unequal pay.

Unequal pay might also be addressed through the 'crowding' analysis we explored in Chapter 7.[14] On this view, the problem is not that women are paid less than men even though they are equally productive; women are paid according to the value of their output to the employer (and to society as a whole). The problem is that due to discrimination, women are segregated into certain occupations instead of being equally represented throughout the economy. This means that there is an oversupply of workers in female-dominated occupations – which pushes their wages down – and an undersupply of workers in male-dominated occupations – which pushes their wages up. This theory can be used to support legal intervention to give women access to hitherto excluded jobs. The correction of crowding has benefits for employers and for society because it leads to a more efficient allocation of labour.

Interestingly, however, it also follows that the crowding model does *not* support legal intervention to raise women's pay. First, equal pay laws would not tackle the root cause of discrimination: occupational segregation. Second, such

12 J.M. Malcomson, 'Work incentives, hierarchy, and internal labour markets' (1984) 92 *Journal of Political Economy* 486.
13 G.S. Becker, *The Economics of Discrimination* (1957).
14 B.R. Bergmann, *The Economic Emergence of Women* (1986), Chapters 5 and 6.

laws would rarely be applicable in practice. If women are crowded into particular jobs, they will not be able to identify any men doing the same work who are being paid more than they are. They will not be able to demonstrate the existence of unequal pay. And third, if an equal pay law could be invoked, it would require the employer to pay the women workers above their market value, which would have the same harmful consequences as the minimum wage, discussed above. The crowding model only supports laws which seek to give women access to jobs that have previously been unavailable to them.

However, there are some economic justifications for equal pay legislation. Both the shock theory and the efficiency wage theory which we used to justify minimum wage legislation can also be employed here. A firm that was required by law to increase the pay of its female workers to the same level as that of its male workers might be 'shocked' into providing additional training to improve its productivity. Or, on the efficiency wage theory, if the women's pay was improved, they might become more productive because they would value their jobs more highly. Of course, the introduction of equal pay would not necessarily involve paying the women a wage which was above equilibrium in the new, non-segregated labour market. But it would involve paying them more than they had previously earned. It would also combat any resentment they might have felt at the unequal way in which they were being treated, which might have made them less loyal to the firm.

Rights perspectives

The right to a minimum wage appears in a number of economic and social rights instruments, but inevitably – given the different economic conditions in the sig-natory states – governments are given a substantial degree of discretion to deter-mine the rate and the criteria to be used in setting it. The right to equal pay is dealt with explicitly in economic and social rights instruments, and since it is a part of the right not to be discriminated against it can be read into civil and political rights instruments too. Again, however, the exact scope of the right is unclear.

Minimum wages

Article 7 ICESCR provides that there is a right to 'remuneration which provides all workers, as a minimum, with … a decent living for themselves and their fam-ilies'.[15] The key phrase here is 'decent living'. This requires the state to determine how much money a person needs in order to have a reasonable existence and to ensure that remuneration is determined accordingly. Article 23(3) of the UDHR is, if anything, more explicit in identifying the relevant standard. It specifies that the remuneration should be sufficient to ensure 'an existence worthy of human

---

15 Art. 4(1) ESC 1961 (which was unchanged in 1996) is in similar terms.

dignity'. But the most specific provision is Article 3 of the ILO's Minimum Wage Fixing Convention:

> The elements to be taken into consideration in determining the level of minimum wages shall, so far as possible and appropriate in relation to national practice and conditions, include –
>
> (a) the needs of workers and their families, taking into account the general level of wages in the country, the cost of living, social security benefits, and the relative living standards of other social groups;
> (b) economic factors, including the requirements of economic development, levels of productivity and the desirability of attaining and maintaining a high level of employment.[16]

This identifies in some detail the factors which must be taken into account when determining how much workers need to live on. The cost of living is clearly essential. An effective minimum wage must enable workers to fulfil basic needs such as food and accommodation. But the references to wage levels and other social groups suggest that the minimum wage should be about more than just survival. It should ensure some level of equity between different groups in society, so that the living standards of those on the minimum wage bear some relationship to the living standards of other groups. But the most significant feature of this provision is paragraph (b), in which attention is drawn to the potential costs of the minimum wage for employers and, indirectly, for workers. A minimum wage may result in redundancies for some workers, or may deter foreign firms from setting up business in the country. These effects are likely to increase the higher the wage is set. This provision cautions states not to set the minimum wage at too high a level and to balance its potential benefits against the potential costs.

States are generally given some discretion as to whether or not the entire responsibility for the minimum wage should fall on employers. Obviously, it is inherent in the idea of a minimum wage that it is paid by employers. But a state might decide to provide a decent standard of living through a combination of a minimum wage paid by employers and social security benefits paid directly by the state. This approach is accepted by the ILO. Article 3 of Convention 131 (quoted above) indicates that social security benefits are one of the factors to be taken into account when setting the wage level. The UDHR also makes clear that remuneration from employers can be 'supplemented, if necessary, by other means of social protection'.[17] This is a significant limitation on the use of human rights arguments to support a minimum wage. Employers can argue that the responsibility for upholding workers' rights need not fall entirely on them.

---

16 ILO Convention 131 on Minimum Wage Fixing 1970, Art. 3, not ratified by the UK. The other relevant ILO convention is Convention 26 on Minimum Wage-Fixing Machinery 1928, originally ratified by the UK but denounced in 1985.
17 UDHR, Art. 23(3).

Equal pay

We saw in Chapter 7 that the right not to be discriminated against is a fundamental right which features in all the major human rights instruments we are considering. Pay inequality is, of course, a particular type of discrimination, just like discrimination in hiring or promotion prospects, so it is covered by these more general guarantees. But because of the prevalence of unequal pay, many economic and social rights instruments include a specific right to equal remuneration. We will consider these rights here in order to see whether they offer us any more detailed guidance as to what workers are entitled to in this sphere.

The vast majority of instruments focus on pay inequality between men and women. This is true of the ESC, the EU Charter and, inevitably, CEDAW.[18] The ICESCR obliges signatories to implement the principle of equal pay for men and women 'in particular', which implies that states should also give consideration to the issue of whether any other groups deserve particular attention in this respect.[19] Article 5 of ICERD refers to equal pay, thus identifying it as an area in which discrimination might take place on the grounds of race. But the most general right is Article 23(2) of the UDHR, which provides that 'everyone, without any discrimination, has the right to equal pay for equal work'.

The instruments tend to adopt one of two formulations in order to define workers' entitlement. One is 'equal pay for equal work', and the other (which is more common) is 'equal pay for work of equal value'. The former carries the risk that it might be given a narrow interpretation. 'Equal work' implies that the work done by the woman and the person with whom she seeks equality must be the same. Thus, a female catering worker would have to compare herself with a male catering worker doing exactly the same job. This creates particular difficulties where women are 'crowded' into particular occupations. If their job is female-dominated, there may be no men doing the same job for them to compare themselves with. This will prevent them from bringing a claim. The concept of 'work of equal value' is much more radical. It implies that jobs can be allocated a value even if they are ostensibly different. Thus, the job of a female catering worker might involve the same degree of responsibility, effort, skill and so on as the job of a male mineworker, even though the two jobs are quite different. On this approach, a woman might be able to claim equal pay with a man doing a different job, provided that their jobs are of equal value. This makes it easier for women in female-dominated occupations to bring a claim. The ILO's Equal Remuneration Convention requires states to take measures, where necessary, 'to promote objective appraisal of jobs on the basis of the work to be performed'.[20] This is intended to assist in the application of the equal value principle.

---

18 ESC 1961, Art. 4(3) (not accepted by the UK); ESC 1996, Art. 4(3) (not ratified by the UK); EU Charter, Art. 23; CEDAW, Art. 11(1)(d).
19 ICESCR, Art. 7(a)(i).
20 ILO Convention 100 on Equal Remuneration 1951, Art. 3 (ratified by the UK in 1971).

Importantly, the ILO Convention gives employers a defence to an equal pay claim:

> Differential rates between workers which correspond, without regard to sex, to differences, as determined by such objective appraisal, in the work to be performed shall not be considered as being contrary to the principle of equal remuneration for men and women workers for work of equal value.[21]

This means that where the work performed by men and women is not the same, the employer may reflect this in their pay. Thus, if the jobs of catering worker and mineworker were rated equally in an appraisal, but the mineworkers had to spend some nights on call in case of an emergency at the mine, the mineworkers could be paid extra. This is a relatively straightforward defence, but it is of interest because it is narrowly defined. The only excuse it allows is a difference 'in the work to be performed'. As we shall see, English law permits employers to rely on a wider range of factors in defence.

English law

The rights perspective is evident in several aspects of English law on the minimum wage and on equal pay. Considerable efforts have been made to ensure that the rights are available to as many people as possible regardless of their employment status. In relation to the minimum wage, the rights and economics perspectives come into sharp conflict when we consider the way in which the rate is determined and the level at which it has been set. In relation to equal pay, controversy surrounds the availability of the 'material factor' defence, which allows employers to argue that unequal pay can be justified where it is the result of market forces.

The national minimum wage

The National Minimum Wage Act 1998 created, for the first time in the UK, a minimum wage which applies across all parts of the country and almost all sectors of the economy.[22] The government supported the measure using both rights and economics arguments.[23] In terms of rights, the government argued that a minimum wage was necessary in order to combat the poverty faced by the lowest-paid workers, and to tackle unequal pay, since a high proportion of

---

21 Ibid., Art. 3(3).
22 For analysis, see B. Simpson, 'A milestone in the legal regulation of pay: the National Minimum Wage Act 1998' (1999) 28 *ILJ* 1; 'Implementing the national minimum wage: the 1999 Regulations' (1999) 28 *ILJ* 171; 'The national minimum wage five years on: reflections on some general issues' (2004) 33 *ILJ* 22.
23 See the statement by Margaret Beckett to the House of Commons on 18 June 1998 in response to the Low Pay Commission's first report (available at www.berr.gov.uk/employment/pay/national-minimum-wage/page12598.html).

the beneficiaries would be women and workers from ethnic minority groups.[24] In terms of economics, the government argued that the minimum wage would contribute to the macroeconomic goal of a high-wage, high-productivity economy. Critics argued that the minimum wage would cause unemployment and would discourage firms from investing in Britain.

Entitlement and enforcement

The rights approach to the minimum wage is most apparent in the legislative provisions on entitlement to be paid the minimum wage and on the mechanisms for enforcing that entitlement. Considerable efforts have been made to ensure that the minimum wage is available to the vast majority of working people, and to ensure that it is effectively enforced.

The minimum wage must be paid to all 'workers'.[25] This term is defined in s. 54(3) of the Act to exclude those who are genuinely self-employed. The Act also makes specific provision for certain groups who would not otherwise fall within this definition. These groups include agency workers who do not have a worker's contract with either the agency or the user,[26] and homeworkers who do not necessarily undertake to perform the work personally.[27] Moreover, in s. 41, the Secretary of State is given a power to extend the Act to other groups who do not count as workers. This gives the Secretary of State the opportunity to close loopholes in the coverage of the Act.[28] The breadth of coverage indicates that the minimum wage is seen as a fundamental right which should be secured to as many workers as possible.

As we have seen in previous chapters, the enforcement of employment rights is generally a matter for the affected individual. He or she must bring a case before the Employment Tribunal. This is also one mechanism for the enforcement of the minimum wage.[29] However, those workers who are likely to benefit from the minimum wage are among the most disadvantaged people in society. It was not considered reasonable to expect these individuals to bear the entire burden of enforcing this basic entitlement. Two main mechanisms have been employed to assist them.[30] First, the government sought to ensure that employers would comply with the minimum wage voluntarily, without the need for enforcement. Thus, the introduction of the minimum wage was surrounded by considerable publicity, and changes to the minimum wage rate must be advertised.[31] The choice of a single hourly rate for all regions and sectors was intended to make the law easy to understand. However, commentators argue that this strategy has not been entirely successful.[32] For example, the government abandoned a plan to oblige

24 See S. Fredman, *Women and the Law* (1997), pp. 263–71, for the relationship between the minimum wage and equal pay.
25 Simpson, 'A milestone in the legal regulation of pay', pp. 4–5.   26 NMWA 1998, s. 34.
27 Ibid., s. 35.   28 See Chapter 5.   29 NMWA 1998, ss. 17, 18, 28.
30 See, generally, P. Skidmore, 'Thinking about enforcement: the minimum wage in practice', in H. Collins *et al.*, *Legal Regulation of the Employment Relation* (2000).
31 NMWA 1998, s. 50.
32 Simpson, 'Implementing the national minimum wage', pp. 180–1.

employers to give workers a statement with their pay explaining how they were being paid the minimum wage.[33] Employers argued that this would be too costly to administer, but it would clearly have helped workers to understand – and to challenge – their employers' calculations.

The government's second strategy for ensuring that the minimum wage would be enforced was to grant enforcement powers to a public body, the Inland Revenue.[34] Revenue officials can identify employers who may be in breach of the NMWA 1998, either by acting on information from disadvantaged workers or by looking at tax records, and can investigate those employers, using an array of statutory powers to gather evidence.[35] Where a breach is identified, the Inland Revenue can issue a 'notice of underpayment' requiring the employer to pay workers any arrears they are owed.[36] The notice will normally also require the employer to pay a penalty to the Secretary of State.[37]

The rate

The most controversial aspect of the minimum wage is, of course, the rate at which it is set. Despite the rights arguments and new institutional economics arguments adopted by the government in its advocacy of a minimum wage, the rate as finally set reflects to a considerable extent the concerns of those economists who are hostile to the policy. The relatively weak positions taken by international human rights instruments mean that it is difficult to construct a powerful human rights critique of the minimum wage rate.

The minimum wage is set at £5.73 per hour, which works out at £275.04 per week on the basis of the maximum forty-eight-hour week set by the WTR 1998.[38] From a human rights perspective, the test must be whether this sum is sufficient to ensure a 'decent' standard of living for the worker and his or her family. Not surprisingly, this is very difficult to determine. The government sets the 'poverty line' at 60 per cent of the median income of the population as a whole (£377 per week in 2006–7),[39] which means that those who earn £226 per week or less are officially living in poverty. Of course, in working out these figures it is important to take into account the number of people making up the household that must live on this income. The official figures are calculated for couples. This means that £275.04 per week is enough to take either a single person or a childless couple above the poverty line. However, the picture changes when we take account of the needs of households with children. Government figures enable us to calculate the 'real' value of £275.04 per week to different sizes of

---

33 NMWA 1998, s. 12, but no regulations have been issued thereunder.
34 See Simpson, 'The national minimum wage five years on', pp. 35–9.
35 NMWA 1998, ss. 14–15.   36 Ibid., s. 19.
37 Ibid., s. 19A. The process has been simplified by amendments introduced by the Employment Act 2008, s. 9.
38 From 1 October 2008.
39 *Households Below Average Income* survey (available at www.dwp.gov.uk/asd/hbai/hbai2007/pdf_files/chapters/chapter_2_hbai08.pdf).

household.[40] Thus, for a couple with two children aged 5 and 14, the poverty line is £346 per week.

Nevertheless, it is difficult to say that the minimum wage is not enough to fulfil the criteria set by international human rights instruments.[41] First, our picture of household income was deliberately simplified. For example, we assumed that the household only had one income. A household with two minimum wage earners would be less likely to fall below the poverty line. Second, we did not take into account the social security benefits to which low-income families are entitled. The system of tax credits is designed to help those in work who have low incomes, and other social security benefits may also be available.[42] As we saw above, international standards permit the government to provide a minimum wage in part by supplementing workers' wages with social security benefits. Third, the ILO standard requires states to take into account the economic consequences of fixing the minimum wage at too high a level. When the minimum wage was first introduced, the government made very clear that it was seeking to set the wage at a level that would not create unemployment. Many commentators felt that the government had given too much credit to employers' claims that they might have to make workers redundant. Nevertheless, a sensible human rights argument must allow for the relevance of these concerns.

The delicate balance between workers' rights and economic concerns is highlighted particularly clearly by the government's decision to introduce separate rates for younger workers. Those aged 18–21 are entitled to £4.77 per hour (£228.96 for a forty-eight-hour week) and those aged 16–17 are entitled to £3.53 per hour (£169.44 for a forty-eight-hour week). The government made two main claims in favour of this approach. First, it was argued that those under the age of twenty-one should be encouraged to stay in education for as long as possible by making work unattractive to them. This can be linked to new institutional economics arguments about creating a highly skilled and therefore productive workforce. Second, it was argued that employers should be encouraged to hire younger workers in order to ensure that those who did enter the labour market did not experience unemployment. This reflects neoclassical concerns with the costs of the minimum wage. The minimum wage is expressly excluded from the law on age discrimination.[43] If separate rates for younger workers were challenged on this ground, it is not clear whether the ECJ would accept that they were a proportionate means of achieving the government's stated goals.[44]

---

40 Using the data in *Households Below Average Income* survey, Table 2.3.
41 Though it is regarded as inadequate by the European Committee of Social Rights, *Conclusions XVIII-2 (UK)* (2007), p. 13.
42 See, generally, N. Wikeley *et al.*, *The Law of Social Security* (5th edn., 2002).
43 EE(A)R 2006, reg. 31.
44 See M. Sargeant, 'The Employment Equality (Age) Regulations 2006: a legitimisation of age discrimination in employment' (2006) 35 *ILJ* 209, pp. 222–3.

From a rights perspective, the most obvious problem with separate rates for younger workers is that the right to a decent living applies universally in the human rights instruments, regardless of age.[45] It is not clear that the underlying goal of protecting workers' dignity is met where two workers doing the same job can be paid different rates because of their age. Moreover, these differentials may be problematic from a new institutionalist perspective. The aim of pursuing a high-productivity economy in which workers' loyalty is secured through the payment of a decent wage may not be met where equally productive workers are paid different rates, or where employers are tempted to find a way of dismissing workers once they become entitled to the main rate.

A final feature of the NMWA 1998 that has been much criticised by commentators is that there is no obligation on the government to review the rate. One option would have been to index-link the rate, so that it would have risen (or fallen) automatically in line with inflation. Another, less radical, option would have been to place the Secretary of State under a statutory duty to review the minimum wage on a regular basis. However, the government did not pursue either of these options and retains complete discretion over the rate. The Low Pay Commission was created to advise the government on the minimum wage, but there is no obligation to follow its recommendations.[46] In practice, the rate has been revised in October of each year, broadly in line with the Low Pay Commission's findings, but there is no legal requirement for this approach to continue. It seems possible to criticise this from virtually any of the perspectives we have been examining. In a situation of high inflation, the minimum wage might cease to provide a decent living or to act as an incentive to workers to be productive. In a situation of low inflation, the minimum wage might become a burden on business and a cause of unemployment. Of course, it is to be hoped that the government would use its discretion to alter the rate in these circumstances, but the absence of any legal safeguards to ensure that this takes place must be seen as a flaw in the Act.

Equal pay

English law appears to adopt the rights perspective on equal pay. It makes an equal pay claim available not only to women but to other groups as well, and adopts a broad definition of those workers who can bring such a claim. However, commentators have argued that the law places too many technical hurdles in the way of those seeking equal pay, and gives too much credit to neoclassical economic arguments about the cost of implementing equal pay.[47] They point out that

---

45 It has been condemned by the ESC Committee as a breach of Art. 7(5) (the right of young persons to a fair wage). See K.D. Ewing, 'The Council of Europe's Social Charter of 18 October 1961: Britain and the 15th cycle of supervision' (2001) 30 *ILJ* 409.

46 www.lowpay.gov.uk

47 See, generally, Fredman, *Women and the Law*, Chapter 6, and 'Reforming equal pay laws', (2008) 37 *ILJ* 193.

limited progress has been made in tackling pay inequalities. In 2006, women's average hourly pay (excluding overtime) was still 17.2 per cent less than that of men.[48] Our discussion will focus in particular on the Equal Pay Act 1970 (EqPA), which must be read in the light of the Equal Pay Directive.[49] A woman may also base a claim directly on Article 141 EC.

Eligibility and enforcement

According to s. 1(6)(a) EqPA 1970, the Act applies to workers broadly defined, so it includes employees, workers and those self-employed people who undertake to perform work personally. Sex discrimination is the only field in which a separate statute governs pay issues. The other anti-discrimination legislation protects individuals against unequal pay alongside other forms of discrimination, such as unfairness in hiring or promotion. Thus, although many international human rights instruments concentrate on the problem of unequal pay faced by women, English law protects people against pay discrimination on grounds of race, sexual orientation, religious belief and so on. As we saw in Chapter 7, the broad worker definition is used in these contexts too. The main mechanism for enforcing equal pay is individual litigation, though some claimants may be able to get help from the Equality and Human Rights Commission or from their trade union.

To bring a claim under EqPA 1970, a woman must show that she is doing 'like work' or 'work of equal value' to that of a man 'in the same employment' (her 'comparator').[50] The concept of 'like work' covers the situation in which the woman is doing the same or broadly similar work to her comparator.[51] The concept of 'work of equal value' applies where their jobs are different but can be rated as equivalent in terms of effort, skill, responsibility and so on.[52] A major difficulty faced by women seeking to bring a claim lies in identifying a man 'in the same employment' with whom they can compare their pay. The man must be a real person. The woman cannot argue that she has been treated less favourably than a hypothetical man *would have been* treated.[53] And the man must be employed by the same employer or an associated employer and must work at the same establishment.[54] The woman can only compare her treatment with that of a man at one of the employer's other establishments if 'common terms and conditions of employment' are observed at both.[55] Community law may allow a broader range of comparison across establishments and firms, but only where there is a 'single source' responsible for the discrimination: in other words, where

---

48 Source: National Statistics, *Annual Survey of Hours and Earnings.* This figure is the internationally comparable mean.

49 Directive 75/117/EC. The Directive is, of course, directly effective against public sector employers.

50 EqPA 1970, s. 1(1) and (2).   51 Ibid., s. 1(4).

52 Ibid., s. 1(2)(c).

53 (C129/79) *Macarthys* v. *Smith* [1980] ECR 1275. This type of comparison is permitted under the other discrimination legislation, even for pay issues. See below.

54 EqPA 1970, s. 1(6).

55 See *Leverton* v. *Clwyd CC* [1989] AC 706; *British Coal* v. *Smith* [1996] 3 All ER 97.

there is one decision-maker who can introduce equal pay for the woman and her comparator.[56]

Another related problem with the comparator requirement is that it only entitles the woman to claim *equal* pay with the male comparator, not proportionate pay. If her work is found to be less valuable (say 70 per cent of his), but she is paid even less than the value of her work (say 60 per cent of his pay), she cannot claim the 10 per cent difference. If her work is found to be more valuable than his, she cannot claim more pay. The only claim the courts have allowed is a claim for equal pay where her work is more valuable than that of her comparator. Thus, a woman whose job was rated at 120 per cent of her comparator's, but whose earnings were only 80 per cent, would be able to claim equal pay.[57] This would leave her better off, but still underpaid. To get the 'right' pay, it is vital that the woman is able to find the 'right' comparator.

Of course, it is the very essence of a claim based on formal equality that the woman is seeking to compare her treatment with that of someone else: she is seeking equality *with* her male comparator. But the need for a real comparator is highly problematic when we consider the degree of occupational segregation in the labour market. Many women have few options for comparison. Imagine a woman working as a carer in a nursing home. All the other carers are women. Her employer owns another home at which some of the carers are men, but she cannot use them as comparators because they have different terms and conditions. Thus, even if she suspects that her pay is low and that if there were any male carers in her workplace they would be paid more highly, she cannot prove that she is being treated unequally.

Rights theorists tend to favour more radical equal pay laws that would allow women a broader range of comparisons. One of the least controversial options would be to permit comparisons to be made with hypothetical male workers.[58] This is permitted under the SDA 1975 and the other anti-discrimination legislation, so it is only women seeking to bring an equal pay claim who are precluded from adopting this strategy. A more controversial option would be to allow women greater freedom to compare themselves with men working in other establishments or firms, even where there is no 'single source' of discrimination.[59] However, a difference between the pay of women working for one firm and men working for another might be attributable to a wide range of factors other than discrimination, such as the different market conditions faced by the two firms. Thus, even if the legislation made such a claim possible, it might be very difficult to persuade a court of its validity.

56 (C320/00) *Lawrence* v. *Regent Office Care* [2002] ECR I-7325; (C256/01) *Allonby* v. *Accrington and Rossendale College* [2004] ECR I-873. A collective agreement may constitute a single source for these purposes (*South Ayrshire Council* v. *Morton* [2002] SLT 656 (Inner House)), but multi-employer collective agreements are rare outside the public sector nowadays.

57 *Redcar and Cleveland BC* v. *Bainbridge* [2007] EWCA Civ 929; [2008] ICR 238.

58 Department for Communities and Local Government, *Discrimination Law Review* (2007), pp. 58–9, rejected this proposal.

59 See Fredman, *Women and the Law*, pp. 247–50.

A very different solution is suggested by the crowding model. From this perspective, equal pay laws – however radical – are doomed to failure because they do not tackle the root cause of women's disadvantage. Because of discrimination, women are 'crowded' into certain sectors of the economy. The oversupply of women in these sectors drives down their pay. Equal pay laws do not help because men tend not to work in 'women's' jobs, so women rarely have an obvious comparator. Instead of trying to strengthen the equal pay laws, we should focus on anti-discrimination legislation and other policy measures that would improve women's access to hitherto excluded jobs. Pay inequalities would disappear as women workers became more evenly distributed throughout the labour market.

Employers' defences

Perhaps the most direct conflict between the rights and economics perspectives comes when we consider the defence an employer may raise when faced with a prima facie claim of unequal pay. The ILO position is that the employer should only be able to pay a woman less than a man where this reflects a genuine difference in the work they do.[60] Otherwise, unequal pay is a breach of fundamental rights and cannot be defended. But for many economists, there is the overriding concern that the cost of implementing equal pay will be unsustainable for firms, leading to redundancies for the very women the legislation was seeking to help.

Under s. 1(3) EqPA 1970, the employer can escape the obligation to pay the man and the woman equally where it can prove that the difference in their pay is 'genuinely due to a material factor which is not the difference of sex'.[61] This clearly includes a difference in the work they are doing. However, judicial interpretations have revealed that it is much broader. In the case of *Rainey* v. *Greater Glasgow Health Board*, for example, the employer wished to expand the prosthetics service at a particular NHS hospital.[62] To do so, it needed to recruit new staff from the private sector. They had much higher salaries than those who were already working for the NHS. The vast majority of the private sector workers were men; the vast majority of the NHS workers were women. The hospital offered higher salaries to the new recruits. This gave rise to a prima facie case of unequal pay, because the female NHS workers remained on their old lower salaries, but the hospital successfully invoked the material factor defence. The fact that the men would not have joined the NHS if they had not been offered more money was a 'material factor' justifying the difference in pay.

---

60 ILO Convention 100 on Equal Remuneration 1951, Art. 3(3).
61 The test must be interpreted in the light of the objective justification requirement laid down by the ECJ in (Case 170/84) *Bilka-Kaufhaus* v. *Weber von Hartz* [1986] ECR 1607.
62 *Rainey* v. *Greater Glasgow Health Board* [1987] AC 224. In (Case C-127/92) *Enderby* v. *Frenchay HA* [1993] ECR I-5535, the ECJ indicated that the additional pay offered to attract someone to a job should be proportionate.

For rights theorists, this decision makes a mockery of the equal pay legislation, in at least two respects. First, the fact that the right to equal pay can be defeated by business considerations indicates that it is not being regarded as a fundamental right at all. A genuine right is one that 'trumps' other factors instead of giving way to them. Second, the courts are slow to identify possible instances of discrimination. In *Rainey*, the court assumed that it was an accident that most of the private sector workers were men. But as Fredman points out, women may have been unable to obtain lucrative private sector jobs because of discrimination.[63] If so, the *Rainey* decision allowed the NHS to perpetuate this discrimination.

For those economists who are concerned with the costs of equal pay legislation, the material factor defence is an important acknowledgement of the risks of redundancies and business failures associated with a strict insistence on equal pay. In the *Rainey* case, the NHS would not have been able to expand its prosthetics service to the same extent if it had had to increase the pay of its female staff. This would have harmed the users of the service and prevented the creation of new job opportunities in the economy. From this perspective, employers are seen as the 'victims' of market forces: the fact that the invisible hand of the market leads the employer towards a pay structure that is discriminatory should not be regarded as the employer's fault. The burden of reshaping the market should not fall on particular employers against whom claims are brought.

The material factor defence highlights a more fundamental feminist critique of the equal pay legislation. The legislation insists that equality must be achieved within the confines of the existing labour market. But many feminists argue that the market undervalues the jobs which have traditionally been done by women.[64] Jobs such as nursing and childcare are seen as unskilled work which women are inherently able to do because of the caring role they play within the family. The market systematically ignores the degree of responsibility associated with these jobs and the skills they require. This claim is difficult for economists to understand. Economists value jobs by looking at the wages people are prepared to work for and the wages employers are prepared to pay. If employers offer childcare workers low pay but they are prepared to accept it, that is the value of their job. It is not possible to put some other 'objective' value on the job which is higher than its market value. Taken to extremes, the debate about the rights and economics perspectives on equal pay becomes a debate about the very foundations of a market economy.

Further reading

For detailed textbook accounts of this topic, see S. Deakin and G.S. Morris, *Labour Law* (4th edn., 2005), 4.41–4.56 and 6.71–6.96, or H. Collins, K.D. Ewing and A. McColgan, *Labour Law: Text and Materials* (2nd edn., 2005), 3.10 and 4.4.

---

63 Fredman, *Women and the Law*, pp. 256–7.   64 Ibid., pp. 241–4.

There is very little theoretical discussion of the minimum wage from a rights perspective, but for a detailed analysis of the NMWA's provisions, see B. Simpson, 'A milestone in the legal regulation of pay: the National Minimum Wage Act 1998' (1999) 28 *ILJ* 1, 'Implementing the national minimum wage: the 1999 Regulations' (1999) 28 *ILJ* 171, and 'The national minimum wage five years on: reflections on some general issues' (2004) 33 *ILJ* 22. Perhaps the most accessible introduction to neoclassical arguments is J. Stigler, 'The economics of minimum wage legislation' (1946) 36 *American Economic Review* 358–65. The new institutional economics arguments are summarised in the Low Pay Commission's *First Report* (1998), Chapter 1 (www.lowpay.gov.uk). Does it matter whether the minimum wage is justified on a rights or a new institutional economics basis? Is it preferable to justify the minimum wage using a social justice perspective? What factors should be taken into account when defining a 'decent' wage? What is the appropriate role of cost considerations? Is the minimum wage currently set at an acceptable level? Should there be different rates for younger workers?

S. Fredman, *Women and the Law* (1997), Chapter 6, introduces the topic of equal pay from a rights perspective. Is it helpful to think about pay discrimination separately from other kinds of discrimination? To what extent should it be possible for an employer to justify unequal pay? What would the implications be for employers if the 'market forces' defence was not allowed? Should the enforcement strategy applied to the minimum wage be used in relation to equal pay? Or should employers be placed under a positive duty to promote equal pay (see Chapter 7, and S. Fredman, 'Reforming equal pay laws' (2008) 37 *ILJ* 193)? Or does the problem lie in the way in which pay is determined? On the last question, see A. McColgan, 'Regulating pay discrimination', in H. Collins *et al.*, *Legal Regulation of the Employment Relation* (2000). Finally, do equal pay laws tackle the right set of issues, or is occupational segregation or 'crowding' the real problem? Many of the suggestions for further reading in Chapter 7 also discuss the issue of equal pay, so you may find it helpful to review them when considering these questions.

9

Dismissal

Most people place a high value on their jobs. Even if they do not enjoy their work, they need the income their jobs bring in. If they do enjoy their work, their jobs are a source of personal fulfilment and social contacts. And most employers value their workers. Their labour helps to make the firm productive and profitable. But this does not necessarily mean that the employer will want to keep the same individuals in their jobs for life. A downturn in the business might lead to a reduction in the firm's demand for labour. Or an individual worker might stop being productive, through illness or even laziness. Sometimes, individuals leave their jobs of their own volition, when they retire or move on to a better opportunity at another firm. It is when the employer wants to terminate a worker's employment against that worker's wishes that the interests of the firm and the interests of the worker come into sharp conflict.

Neoclassical economists would resolve this conflict in favour of the employer. The law should not seek to control the circumstances in which an employee is dismissed, because to do so would impose additional costs on the employer and make it more difficult to run a productive business. Legal intervention would ultimately harm other workers and the economy as a whole. In contrast, new institutionalists would argue that some legal control over dismissal could benefit employers. These writers suggest that employers have an interest in providing a degree of job security, because it will make their workers more loyal and, as a result, more productive. The difficulty is that employers may sometimes forget this long-term goal and dismiss people to save money in the short term. The law can play an important role in preventing employers from giving in to this temptation.

Few international human rights instruments even consider the issue of dismissal. Nevertheless, many commentators have tried to identify an underlying human rights basis for laws on this topic. The most radical approach involves arguing that a job is a form of property. This would suggest that employees could not be deprived of their jobs without their consent and would therefore limit employers' freedom considerably. Other writers have invoked principles such as dignity and autonomy in order to advocate a lesser degree of job security which does allow the employer to dismiss employees, provided that there is a good reason for doing so and provided that fair procedures are followed.

Economics perspectives

Arguments against regulation

One of the most strident critics of controls on the employer's power to dismiss is Epstein. In a well-known article, he challenged the trend in many states of the USA to abandon 'employment at will' (in which the employer may dismiss employees at any time and for any reason) and to replace it with legal regulation of dismissals.[1]

According to Epstein, the employment at will doctrine has three main attractions for employers: it motivates employees, it is flexible and it is cheap to administer. We will consider each in turn. Epstein's first point about motivation is fairly obvious. If employees know that they can easily be dismissed for a poor performance, they will work harder. If the law grants them job security, they will be more tempted to shirk. The second major advantage from the employer's perspective is flexibility. The employer needs to respond to changes in its product markets. For example, the market price might fall because of the entry of a new competitor with lower production costs. In this situation, the employer would need to reduce its expenditure by selling machinery and dismissing workers. Any constraint on dismissals would reduce the employer's ability to remain competitive. The third advantage is that the employment at will doctrine is cheap to administer because no-one can challenge the employer's decisions. An unfair dismissal law would allow aggrieved employees to sue. The employer might incur substantial costs in defending litigation even if the claimant did not have a good case.

An obvious criticism of employment at will is that while it benefits employers, it does not benefit employees at all. They are vulnerable to dismissal at any time and for any reason, good or bad. But Epstein argues that employees do have job security under employment at will because market forces prevent employers from behaving arbitrarily. According to Epstein, the employer would face two main disadvantages if it dismissed a productive employee for a bad reason. First, the employer would lose the benefit of that person's skills and would have to incur the costs of hiring and training a replacement. Second, the employer's reputation would suffer. Members of the current workforce who saw that the employer had dismissed someone arbitrarily might decide to look for a new job elsewhere with a better employer. Alternatively, they might decide to reduce their level of effort: there is no point in working hard if it is no guarantee of job security. Outside the workplace, people looking for work might find out about the employer's behaviour and decide not to apply for vacancies. This would reduce the employer's chances of being able to choose from among the best candidates when recruiting. These problems should be enough to deter employers from dismissing employees without a good reason. On this view, job security laws are unnecessary.

Neoclassical economists also claim that job security laws may be positively harmful to employees, because they lead to cuts in wages and a reduction in the

---

1 R.A. Epstein, 'In defense of the contract at will' (1984) 51 *University of Chicago Law Review* 947.

demand for labour. This argument is developed by Harrison in particular.[2] As we saw above, job security laws increase employers' costs, because of the higher risk that dismissed employees might bring a claim. These costs are likely to be passed on to employees through cuts in their wages. Thus, whether a job security law benefits employees depends on whether they value job security more highly than the pay they will lose. Moreover, job security laws may make it more difficult for the unemployed to find work. Under employment at will, if there is a rise in demand in the employer's product market, it would hire additional workers and dismiss them if demand dropped again. Under a job security law, the employer may decide to delay hiring the additional workers until it is sure that the rise in demand is likely to be of long duration. This is because the law puts obstacles in the way of dismissing workers who are no longer needed. Thus, job security laws are potentially counterproductive for employees.

Arguments in favour of regulation

Those economists who argue in favour of legal regulation generally do so by attacking one or more of Epstein's underlying assumptions. We will consider arguments that challenge his suggestion that the rational employer would never dismiss a productive employee, his arguments about harm to the employer's reputation, and his claim that employment at will is a good way to motivate employees.

Some writers have argued that – contrary to Epstein's claims – there are at least two situations in which it would be rational for the employer to dismiss a productive employee. Both involve 'opportunism' on the part of the employer: ignoring long-term goals, such as maintaining a good reputation, in order to make a saving in the short term. First, when an employee is accused of misconduct, Epstein would argue that the employer should investigate the allegations in order to decide whether or not the employee is productive and, thus, whether or not he or she ought to be retained. But an investigation imposes immediate and obvious costs on the employer, whereas the benefits of keeping the productive employee will manifest themselves over the longer term. So the employer might respond to short-term imperatives and dismiss the employee without investigation.[3]

A second situation in which the employer might dismiss a productive worker arises where the employer has adopted what economists sometimes refer to as 'deferred benefit' payment schemes. A simple example is a bonus to be paid to the salesperson when an order is delivered to a new customer. The salesperson works to obtain the order but does not receive the bonus until the deal has been finalised. A more complex example is the payment of workers on a salary scale which increases with length of service. Workers at the top of the scale may be paid more than they are worth to the employer in productivity terms. But the

---

2 J.L. Harrison, 'The "new" terminable at will employment contract: an interest and cost incidence analysis' (1984) 69 *Iowa Law Review* 327.
3 H. Collins, *Justice in Dismissal* (1992), pp. 110–11.

purpose of the scheme is to motivate those at the bottom of the scale to remain loyal to the company and to work hard, in the hope of retaining their jobs and rising to the top of the scale. In both these situations, the employer can make a short-term cost saving by dismissing a worker before he or she becomes entitled to the bonus or to the higher salaries at the top of the scale.[4] Again, the employer has an incentive to behave opportunistically by dismissing a productive worker.

Epstein's response to these arguments would be to point to the damage such behaviour would do to the employer's reputation. If job applicants find out that the employer dismisses people without investigating the circumstances, they will look for a job with a fairer employer. If workers know that they are likely to be dismissed before they receive a bonus, they will realise that the promised payments are a trick and they will not be motivated by them. The second step in the counter-argument must therefore be to challenge Epstein's claims about reputation. Although Epstein's theory works when all parties have perfect information, this underlying assumption does not hold true in practice.[5] Prospective employees may not be able to find out very much information about a firm's hiring and firing practices. Even those who currently work for the firm may not know about the employer's behaviour. The employer may be able to disguise opportunistic dismissals as redundancies, for example, so that workers do not realise the true motivation behind them. Thus, it can be shown that opportunism is a real threat and that it is unlikely to be corrected by market forces. This might justify legal intervention to control the employer's power to dismiss.

Another way to challenge Epstein's arguments is to reconsider his claim about the motivation of employees. Epstein suggests that employment at will is a good motivator: employees will work hard in order to avoid being dismissed. But Fox argues exactly the opposite.[6] If employees feel insecure, they will do the minimum required of them and seize opportunities to shirk. He claims that employees respond best in a high-trust environment. If they feel that the employer trusts them to do a good job, they will repay that trust by working hard and doing their best for the firm. The employer can create a high-trust environment by giving employees discretion instead of continuously checking up on them, and by avoiding a situation in which they feel that they are constantly under threat of dismissal. From this perspective, it is arguable that some legal control over the power of dismissal could benefit employers by improving workers' loyalty and productivity.

Rights perspectives

The literature on unfair dismissal is littered with rights terminology. As we shall see, it is sometimes argued that individuals have a right to job security, or even to the 'ownership' of their jobs. Even those theorists who make the more

---

4 Note: 'Employer opportunism and the need for a just cause standard' (1989) 103 *Harvard Law Review* 510.
5 Ibid.
6 A. Fox, *Beyond Contract: Work, Power and Trust Relations* (1974), especially Chapter 1.

moderate claim that individuals should be treated fairly when their dismissal is being considered often base this on a right to be treated with dignity and respect. Nevertheless, the right not to be unfairly dismissed does not feature heavily in the international instruments, and the ILO has only relatively recently made it the subject of a detailed convention.

Perhaps the most basic right an employee can have is a right to notice: to be warned in advance that he or she is going to be dismissed. Although this does not offer any control over the employer's reason for dismissal, it does at least enable the employee to start looking for another job. Article 4(4) of the ESC requires states to recognise the right of all workers to a 'reasonable' period of notice before their employment is terminated.[7] A similar right is afforded by Article 11 of the ILO Termination of Employment Convention, although it contains two significant exceptions.[8] First, the employee may be given compensation instead of notice. This is more flexible for employers since it gives them the opportunity to make immediate changes to the workforce. Moreover, it may not disadvantage the employee, since he or she may be able to live on the compensation until he or she has found a new job. Second, the employee need not be given notice at all if he or she is guilty of serious misconduct (stealing from the employer, for example). This exception is relatively uncontroversial because the employer cannot be expected to continue employing someone it no longer trusts.

The right to notice does not protect the employee against arbitrary decision-making by the employer. To do this, the law must control the employer's reason for dismissal. Only one international instrument, the ESC 1996, provides a detailed right of this kind. Article 24 provides:

> With a view to ensuring the effective exercise of the right of workers to protection in cases of termination of employment, the Parties undertake to recognise:
>
> (a) the right of all workers not to have their employment terminated without valid reasons for such termination connected with their capacity or conduct or based on the operational requirements of the undertaking, establishment or service;
> (b) the right of workers whose employment is terminated without a valid reason to adequate compensation or other appropriate relief.
>
> To this end the Parties undertake to ensure that a worker who considers that his employment has been terminated without a valid reason shall have the right to appeal to an impartial body.[9]

This gives workers a right to stay in their jobs unless the employer can identify a valid reason for dismissing them. It also enables workers to enforce this right

---

7 This features in the ESC 1961 as well as the ESC 1996 and has been accepted by the UK.
8 ILO Convention 158 on Termination of Employment 1982. The UK has not ratified this convention. For detailed discussion, see B. Napier, 'Dismissals – the new ILO standards' (1983) 12 *ILJ* 17.
9 This provision does not appear in the ESC 1961 and has not therefore been ratified by the UK. The EU Charter, Art. 30, also grants a right to protection against unfair dismissal 'in accordance with Community law and national laws and practices'.

by challenging employers' dismissal decisions before an independent body and receiving a remedy if they are successful. We will examine each of these elements in turn.

The list of legitimate reasons for dismissal is drawn directly from the ILO Convention.[10] The first two reasons – capacity and conduct – relate to the characteristics of the employee to be dismissed. 'Capacity' applies where the employee is no longer able to do the job, for example, because of illness. Article 6 of the ILO Convention provides that 'temporary absence from work because of illness or injury shall not constitute a valid reason for termination'. This means that the employer can only dismiss on grounds of incapacity where it lasts or is likely to last a long time. 'Conduct' applies where the employee has disobeyed the employer's rules. Article 7 provides that where a worker's employment is to be terminated on grounds of 'conduct or performance', the worker should usually be given an opportunity to defend him- or herself. This is analogous to the fundamental right to a fair trial. The third reason for dismissal permitted by the ESC and the ILO Convention is the 'operational requirements' of the firm. This covers cases in which the firm is experiencing a downturn in business, and can no longer afford to retain all its staff. It allows the employer to dismiss individuals on economic grounds, even though there is nothing wrong with their work.

The ILO Convention also highlights certain reasons that *cannot* be relied upon by the employer when dismissing an employee.[11] Some of these forbidden reasons feature in other international human rights instruments, even ones which do not deal with unfair dismissal per se. Examples include dismissing an employee because she is pregnant or taking maternity leave,[12] dismissing an employee on discriminatory grounds, such as race or religion,[13] and dismissing an employee because he or she has sought office as a trade union or workforce representative. These cases highlight an important point about dismissal. It is that protection against dismissal may be necessary to ensure that other rights are upheld. There is no point in providing women with a right to maternity leave if the employer can dismiss them as soon as they take the leave. Thus, as well as being important in itself, the right not to be unfairly dismissed is an important component in the protection of workers' rights in general.

The second component in the ESC right, quoted above, is that the worker should be able to challenge his or her dismissal before an impartial body. The ILO Convention allows states to choose whether this should be a 'court, labour tribunal, arbitration committee or arbitrator'.[14] If the dismissal is found to be unlawful, the ESC states that the worker should be given 'compensation or other appropriate relief'. The ILO Convention also accepts the possibility of compensation as a remedy, but seeks to make it secondary to the remedy of reinstatement.

10 ILO Convention 158, Art. 4.   11 Ibid., Art. 5.
12 CEDAW, Art. 11(2)(a); ESC 1961 and 1996, Art. 8(2) (not accepted by the UK); EU Charter, Art. 33(2).
13 ESC 1996, Art. 20 (sex discrimination).   14 ILO Convention 158, Art. 8(1).

However, the provision is drafted relatively weakly and does not impose any particular obligation on the state to make reinstatement available:

> If the bodies referred to in Article 8 of this Convention find that termination is unjustified and if they are not empowered or do not find it practicable, in accordance with national law and practice, to declare the termination invalid and/or order or propose reinstatement of the worker, they shall be empowered to order payment of adequate compensation or such other relief as may be deemed appropriate.[15]

The Convention does not offer further guidance on how the 'adequacy' of compensation is to be determined.

The ESC right is simply described as a right for 'workers', but the ILO Convention offers more specific guidance as to the limitations states may place on who is protected.[16] It permits states to exclude three main groups: workers on fixed-term contracts (provided that employers are not permitted to use these contracts as a means of evading unfair dismissal laws), workers serving a reasonable period of probation, and casual workers. The state may, after consultation with the social partners, exclude other groups where certain conditions are met – for example, where they work for a small business.

Despite – or perhaps because of – the lack of emphasis on the right not to be unfairly dismissed in the human rights instruments, there is a considerable literature on the topic which does seek to attribute a powerful human rights basis to unfair dismissal laws. The most radical approach is to argue that workers have 'ownership' of their jobs in the same way as they own any other piece of property.[17] It is usually suggested that workers acquire this ownership over time just as a squatter can eventually acquire prescriptive rights over land. Of course, workers' contribution to the firm is rewarded with the payment of wages. But advocates of job property argue that this is not enough to compensate workers for their efforts. Workers may have learnt skills that are only useful in that particular firm. They may also have spent time finding out how the firm works and getting to know other members of staff. These investments will only be rewarded if they are allowed to keep their jobs for a reasonable period of time.

But what does it mean to say that a worker 'owns' his or her job? The fact that I own my car means that I can sell it to whomever I choose. But a worker cannot 'sell' his or her job to another person when he or she does not want it any more. Even those who advocate the job property approach would not make this claim. It would force the employer to form an employment relationship with a person chosen by the former employee, a person who might not even be qualified to do the job. The fact that I own my car also means that no-one is entitled to take it away from me without my consent. This is both the virtue and the downfall of

---

15 Ibid., Art. 10.   16 Ibid., Art. 2.
17 See, for example, D.H.J. Hermann and Y.S. Sor, 'Property rights in one's job: the case for limiting employment-at-will' (1982) 24 *Arizona Law Review* 763.

the job property theory.[18] If employees own their jobs, the employer cannot take them away without the employees' consent. This gives employees a very high level of protection against dismissal. But a moment's reflection reveals that it goes too far. It would not allow the employer to dismiss an employee who was incapable of doing the job, or even an employee who was flatly refusing to do any work at all. This would clearly benefit the employee, but it would cause harm to the employer, and consequently to the firm's other employees and to the economy as a whole. Some theorists have acknowledged that a realistic conception of job property would have to allow employers to dismiss on the three grounds listed in Article 24 of the ESC.[19] But these theorists have made such a big concession that it no longer seems appropriate to describe them as advocates of 'job property'.

Since the property approach is problematic, theorists have looked for some other way of linking the right not to be unfairly dismissed to more general human rights. The challenge is to find a basis which gives the employee some job security but (unlike the property approach) also allows the employer to dismiss the employee where there is a good reason for doing so. In an important analysis of the English law of unfair dismissal, Collins has identified dignity and auton-omy as the two key principles which underlie the right to job security.[20] We will examine each in turn.

The employee's right to be treated with dignity requires that the employer's decision to dismiss should have a rational basis. A dismissal that has no rational basis infringes the employee's dignity by showing that he or she is at the mercy of the employer's whims. This approach rules out dismissals for bad reasons, such as on the ground of an employee's sexual orientation or because the employee has sought to enforce his or her entitlement to the minimum wage. It also rules out dismissals for potentially good reasons where the employer has not investigated the circumstances properly. If an employee is accused of persistent lateness, for example, the employee's dignity is respected only where the employer investigates the accusations and gives the employee a chance to defend him- or herself. But it does not rule out all dismissals. If the employer has a good reason for dismissing the employee – he or she has been caught stealing, for example – the employee's dignity is not affronted because there is no irrational behaviour on the part of the employer.

The second principle advocated by Collins is respect for the employee's autonomy. This helps to acknowledge the fact that work is an important way in which people bring meaning to their lives. The employer is under an obligation to respect this aspiration insofar as it is compatible with running an efficient business. For example, Collins argues that the rules which govern the workplace should be published. This allows employees to guide their behaviour accordingly.

18 Collins, *Justice in Dismissal*, pp. 9–12.
19 Hermann and Sor, 'Property rights in one's job', p. 767.
20 Collins, *Justice in Dismissal*, pp. 15–21.

He also argues that the employer should not, in general, seek to interfere with what employees do outside their working time. Both requirements show respect for employees as autonomous individuals who need to be able to plan their lives. The employer can set limits in the interests of the business, but these limits must be appropriate. Again, therefore, the employer is obliged to behave in certain ways but is not forbidden from dismissing an employee altogether. An employee who disregarded work rules that were well-publicised and fair could be dismissed without any violation of his or her autonomy.

The principles of dignity and autonomy help to strike a balance between employees' and employers' interests, and offer a middle way between the employment at will and job property approaches. However, the principles are not self-executing: they require interpretation to decide what they mean in particular situations. For example, it is not clear whether the vindication of an employee's dignity requires that he or she should get his or her job back after an unfair dismissal, or whether a substantial award of compensation would be a sufficient remedy. These controversies will become apparent in our discussion of English law.

English law

English law offers two types of claim when a person's employment is terminated: wrongful dismissal and unfair dismissal. In a *wrongful* dismissal claim, the employee alleges that the employer is in breach of the terms of the contract of employment. For example, if the contract states that the employee is entitled to four weeks' notice before dismissal, and the employer fails to comply, a wrongful dismissal claim would be available. In an *unfair* dismissal claim, the employee alleges that the employer has failed to comply with the statutory requirements concerning dismissal set out in ERA 1996. These govern the employer's reason for dismissal and the procedure it adopts before deciding who to dismiss. The two claims have advantages and disadvantages, depending on the employee's circumstances, so we will compare and contrast them under four headings: eligibility to claim, controls over the employer's reason for dismissal, controls over the employer's dismissal procedure, and remedies.

From a rights perspective, the law presents a mixed picture. It rejects the two extreme positions: employment at will and job property. But in trying to strike a balance between the interests of employers and employees, the legislators have given considerable weight to the argument that dismissal laws impose costs on employers. The government has been particularly concerned by the high number of unfair dismissal claims, which made up around 20 per cent of the employment tribunals' workload in 2005–6.[21] Thus, the issue for rights theorists adopting the dignity and autonomy perspective, and for economists concerned with

---

21 Employment Tribunals Service, *Annual Report 2005–06* (HC 1303) (2006), p. 9.

preventing opportunism and promoting productivity, is whether the law offers employees *enough* job security in order to fulfil the values they are advocating.

Eligibility to claim

The law of dismissal largely protects employees, rather than workers. This stems from the fact that much of the legislation dates from the 1960s and 1970s, long before the needs of the wider category of workers had been recognised.

Wrongful dismissal claims are based on the employer's breach of the express or implied terms of the contract. A claim based on the express terms of the contract is a straightforward one whether the individual is an employee or a worker. However, the employee is better protected because ERA 1996, s. 86, sets out the minimum period of notice the employee must be given, depending on how long he or she has worked for the employer. No such minimum standards apply in a worker's contract. If a worker's contract did not contain a notice clause, it would be up to the courts to decide how much notice the worker was entitled to.[22] It seems unlikely that the courts would find that casual workers were entitled to long notice periods, given the inherent instability of their jobs.

The law of unfair dismissal applies only to employees. According to s. 94(1) ERA 1996, 'an employee has the right not to be unfairly dismissed by his employer'. Moreover, in most cases the employee must have worked continuously for one year for the employer before a claim can be brought.[23] The use of a qualifying period is permitted by the ILO Convention.[24] The usual justification is that it allows the employer a period of time in which to decide whether or not the employee is suitable. Critics point out that the law of unfair dismissal would not stop the employer dismissing an unsuitable employee, so that the law could apply from the beginning of the employment. But the counter-argument is that an employer might still have to incur the costs of defending a claim, and that job creation in the economy would be stifled as a result. The only exceptions to the one-year rule are those cases in which the employer's reason for dismissal is prohibited under any circumstances, for example, where the employee is dismissed because she is pregnant.[25] These exceptions fit neatly into the dignity rationale suggested by Collins. The employee's dignity is violated when he or she is dismissed for a prohibited reason, regardless of length of service.

For many commentators, the absence of any protection against unfair dismissal is one of the most serious gaps in the law relating to workers. Unlike employees, they are constantly at the mercy of the whims of their employer. But the suggestion that the law should be extended to them is highly controversial. As we saw above, even the ILO Convention allows states to exclude various kinds

---

22 For discussion of the courts' likely approach to such cases, see S. Deakin and G.S. Morris, *Labour Law* (4th edn., 2005), pp. 400–1.
23 ERA 1996, s. 108.   24 ILO Convention 158, Art. 2.
25 ERA 1996, s. 99; MPLR 1999, reg. 20.

of atypical workers. You may find it helpful to review Chapter 5 once you have considered the law of unfair dismissal in more detail.

Controls over the employer's reason for dismissal

The law of wrongful dismissal focuses largely on the procedure adopted by the employer when dismissing the employee, and in particular on the notice he or she is given. It is only the law of unfair dismissal which attempts to control the employer's reason for dismissal. The employer's reason may be automatically fair, automatically unfair or potentially fair. It is automatically fair to dismiss an employee who is taking unofficial industrial action, a concept which will be discussed further in Chapter 12.[26] For now, we will concentrate on the other two categories.

Automatically unfair reasons are those which can never be relied upon by the employer, whatever the circumstances. They include dismissals on discriminatory grounds,[27] for pregnancy or taking maternity leave,[28] for taking other forms of parental leave,[29] for participating in trade union activities[30] or acting as a workers' representative,[31] and for asserting statutory rights such as the right to be paid the minimum wage or to work no more than forty-eight hours per week.[32] They reflect the argument made by Collins that certain grounds for dismissal violate the employee's dignity and should not be permitted. They also reflect the role of unfair dismissal law in protecting other fundamental rights, such as the right to the minimum wage. There is little point in providing employees with these rights if the employer is allowed to dismiss them whenever they bring a claim. English law is largely in compliance with Article 5 of the ILO Convention in this area.

Potentially fair reasons for dismissal are those which the employer can rely on provided that it has acted 'reasonably' in dismissing the employee for that reason. The law offers four options: conduct, capability, redundancy and 'some other substantial reason' that would justify the dismissal of the relevant employee.[33] Space precludes a full discussion of all four reasons, so we will concentrate instead on tribunals' general approach. The first stage in the process is the identification of the employer's reason for dismissal.[34] This is a simple factual inquiry: what motivated the employer to dismiss the employee?

Then the tribunal must ask whether the employer acted reasonably in treating this as a justification for dismissal.[35] This second stage is governed by a test laid down in *Iceland Frozen Foods* v. *Jones*, which requires the tribunal to ask

---

26 TULRCA 1992, s. 237.
27 For example, SDA 1975, s. 6(2)(b). Equivalent provisions are contained in the other anti-discrimination legislation.
28 ERA 1996, s. 99; MPLR 1999, reg. 20.   29 Ibid.   30 TULRCA 1992, s. 152.
31 ERA 1996, s. 103.   32 Ibid., ss. 104A and 101A respectively.
33 Ibid., s. 98. These standards reflect Art. 4 of ILO Convention 158 quite closely.
34 Ibid., s. 98(1).   35 Ibid., s. 98(4).

whether the dismissal was 'within the band of reasonable responses' open to the employer.[36] This suggests that the employer has a large area of discretion when deciding how to respond to the situation and that the tribunal should only interfere when the employer's reaction is extreme. The approach is analogous to the test of unreasonableness in administrative law.[37] It has led many commentators to suggest that tribunals are not performing their intended role under the Act.[38] Instead of setting standards for employers which indicate how employees' dignity and autonomy should be respected, tribunals are simply reflecting 'normal' behaviour on the part of employers.

The HRA 1998 adds some new possibilities here. Where the employee's Convention rights (such as privacy or free speech) are affected by the dismissal, the reasonableness test may have to be read so as to require the employer to respect those rights, in accordance with s. 3 HRA 1998. However, the case law so far suggests that even in cases of this kind, the courts will still afford considerable respect to employers' views of what is necessary for their business.[39]

For many commentators, then, the only control exercised over the employer's reasoning is when a prohibited ground such as sex discrimination is the motivation behind the dismissal. On the one hand, this approach can be seen as offering inadequate protection to employees' rights, and an insufficient deterrent to employers who are tempted to make opportunistic dismissals. On the other hand, it can be argued that the employer is best placed to assess the needs of its own business, and that interference from the tribunal would come too close to the unsustainable job property approach.

Controls over the employer's procedures

If the law offers limited control over the employer's reason for dismissal, attention inevitably shifts to the employer's procedures. The law of wrongful dismissal controls the employer's procedures in various ways. First, it requires the employer to give the employee notice before he or she is dismissed. ERA 1996 s. 86 specifies that those who have worked for between one month and two years should have a week's notice. The entitlement increases gradually up to twelve weeks for those who have worked for twelve years or more. The contract may expressly provide for a notice period, but it must be at least as long as the employee's statutory entitlement.[40] The employee may waive his or her right to notice or accept a payment in lieu,[41] but the employer can only dispense with notice where the employee has committed a repudiatory breach of the contract, often known as

---

36 *Iceland Frozen Foods* v. *Jones* [1983] ICR 17.

37 *Associated Provincial Picture Houses* v. *Wednesbury Corporation* [1948] 1 KB 223. See P.L. Davies and M.R. Freedland, 'The impact of public law on labour law, 1972–1997' (1997) 26 *ILJ* 311.

38 For example, Collins, *Justice in Dismissal*, pp. 37–40; A. Freer, 'The range of reasonable responses test: from guidelines to statute?' (1998) 27 *ILJ* 335.

39 *Pay* v. *Lancashire Probation Service* [2004] ICR 187.　　40 ERA 1996, s. 86(3).　　41 Ibid.

'gross misconduct'.[42] For example, a shop worker caught in the act of stealing from the till could be dismissed without notice. These various provisions are in line with ILO standards.

A second respect in which the law of wrongful dismissal controls the employer's procedures is where the contract itself specifies that the employee can only be dismissed after a certain procedure has been followed. Many public sector employees have detailed contractual entitlements of this kind which the courts will uphold.[43]

Third, where the employer does conduct a disciplinary procedure (whether voluntarily or because of a contractual obligation), the employer's actions will be governed by the implied term of 'mutual trust and confidence'. This term is implied into every contract of employment by the courts and requires both parties to behave in ways which preserve the relationship of mutual trust and confidence between them.[44] Among other things, this term forbids arbitrary behaviour on the part of the employer. In *Johnson* v. *Unisys*, the House of Lords held that the term did not apply to the employer's decision to dismiss, largely on the grounds that this would subvert Parliament's intentions in creating the doctrine of unfair dismissal and its associated remedies.[45] However, in *Eastwood* v. *Magnox Electric*, it was held that the term did apply to the conduct of any disciplinary procedures, even if they ultimately led to dismissal.[46]

Even so, the law of unfair dismissal provides better procedural protection because it requires all employers to follow a fair procedure (not just to give notice), regardless of whether or not any such procedure has been voluntarily included in the contract of employment. At the time of writing, the law on procedures is in a state of flux.

Guided by the ACAS Code of Practice on Disciplinary and Grievance Procedures, tribunals developed a substantial jurisprudence on procedural fairness. If the employer failed to follow a fair procedure – failed to investigate allegations and give the employee a hearing, for example – a tribunal would generally find that the dismissal was unfair. The only exception to this was that laid down in the *Polkey* case: the dismissal would not be unfair where a reasonable employer would have dispensed with the procedure – for example, because the employee had admitted to very serious wrongdoing.[47]

The EA 2002, which came into force in 2004, sought to formalise the procedural aspects of dismissal law. It created statutory disciplinary and grievance procedures and required both employer and employee to comply with

---

42 Ibid., s. 86(6).
43 See the discussion of remedies, below.
44 See, generally, D. Brodie, 'Beyond exchange: the new contract of employment' (1998) 27 *ILJ* 79.
45 *Johnson* v. *Unisys* [2001] UKHL 13; [2003] 1 AC 518.
46 *Eastwood* v. *Magnox Electric* [2004] UKHL 35; [2005] 1 AC 503. See also *GAB Robins (UK) Ltd* v. *Triggs* [2008] EWCA Civ 17; [2008] ICR 529.
47 *Polkey* v. *AE Dayton Services Ltd* [1988] AC 344.

them.[48] Under the disciplinary procedure, the employer had to inform the employee of the case against him, arrange a meeting to discuss the issue, and provide the employee with a possibility of appeal against the initial decision. Under the grievance procedure, the employee had to inform the employer of his or her complaint in writing, and the employer had to arrange a meeting to discuss the issue and provide a possibility of appeal if the employee was unsatisfied with the outcome of the initial meeting. Harsh penalties applied if the requirements were not met. If the employer failed to use the disciplinary procedure, the dismissal was automatically unfair.[49] If the employee failed to send a written statement of his or her grievance to the employer, he or she was barred from bringing an unfair dismissal claim to a tribunal.[50] If either party failed to complete the procedure, this could be reflected in an adjustment to the award of damages.[51]

The government's aim in introducing these provisions was to reduce the number of claims which reached a tribunal hearing – by encouraging the parties to resolve their problems themselves through the procedures – and consequently to reduce the costs faced by employers in defending unfair dismissal claims.[52] However, critics argued that employers, and employees in particular, might not be aware of the penalties they faced if they ignored the procedures.[53] This meant that the penalties would not be an effective deterrent and would in fact operate unfairly. Also, the procedures were seen as inflexible, imposing a 'one size fits all' model on large and small firms alike.

The Employment Act 2008, s. 1, repeals the EA 2002 procedures.[54] The procedural fairness of dismissals will fall to be assessed in accordance with a (revised) ACAS Code of Practice. Failure by the employee to invoke a grievance procedure will no longer mean that unfair dismissal proceedings might be barred. Failure by the employer to follow a disciplinary procedure will not render a dismissal automatically unfair. Instead, the tribunal will have to decide whether or not it was reasonable for the employer to dismiss the employee without using a procedure, applying the *Polkey* test discussed above. However, under s. 3 of the 2008 Act, inserting a new s. 207A into TULRCA 1992, tribunals will have the power to adjust damages awards upwards or downwards if they consider it 'just and equitable' to do so where it appears that the employer or the employee respectively has unreasonably failed to follow the relevant parts of the ACAS Code. The aim

---

48 EA 2002, s. 29 and Schedule 2.   49 ERA 1996, s. 98A.   50 EA 2002, s. 32.
51 Ibid., s. 31.
52 For discussion of the government's rationale, see B. Hepple and G.S. Morris, 'The Employment Act 2002 and the crisis of individual employment rights' (2002) 31 *ILJ* 245. A similar concern is evidenced by the introduction of an arbitration procedure for unfair dismissal claims under the Employment Rights (Dispute Resolution) Act 1998, noted by R. Lewis, 'The Employment Rights (Dispute Resolution) Act 1998' (1998) 27 *ILJ* 214.
53 Hepple and Morris, 'The Employment Act 2002'.
54 See M. Gibbons, *A Review of Employment Dispute Resolution in Great Britain* (2007); DTI, *Resolving Disputes in the Workplace: A Consultation* (2007).

is to give the parties an incentive to follow procedures (and to resolve matters for themselves) while regulating their conduct in a more flexible manner. It remains to be seen how this approach will operate in practice: whether it will strike a good balance between upholding employees' dignity and reflecting economic concerns about the cost to employers of unfair dismissal litigation.

Remedies

The remedy offered by the law to an employee who has been wrongfully or unfairly dismissed is an important indicator of the value placed by the law on the employee's rights. For example, if a substantial award of compensation is given when an employee's dignity has been violated, it can be regarded as clear condemnation by society of the employer's behaviour. Substantial remedies are also important from the new institutional economics perspective: if employers are to realise the benefits of providing job security to their employees, they need to be deterred from opportunistic dismissals. However, most commentators agree that the remedies are relatively weak: Epstein's concerns about costs have prevailed again.

The remedies for wrongful dismissal are those available in the law of contract. If an employee has been wrongfully dismissed without notice, he or she can claim the wages that would have been paid during the notice period. However, the usual contract rules apply, so the employee must mitigate his or her loss by seeking another job. The damages will be reduced if he or she finds another job or if the court considers that he or she has not made enough of an effort to do so. The sums available on this approach are relatively small for most claimants.

As we have seen, some employees are fortunate enough to have contractual terms which require the employer to follow a procedure before dismissing them. These employees have access to a more advantageous set of remedies at common law. First, they may be able to claim additional damages if the employer does not go through the contractual disciplinary procedure. Logically, the damages should consist of the wages the employee would have received while the disciplinary procedure took place, and some compensation for the loss of the chance that the employee might not have been dismissed. However, while the courts have accepted the former element, they have not so far seen fit to include the latter.[55] Second, the employee may be able to seek an injunction to force the employer to conduct the disciplinary procedure. The employee must act quickly to show that he or she has not accepted the employer's repudiatory breach of contract so that the contract remains in existence.[56] Then the court will grant an injunction if there is still a relationship of mutual trust and confidence between the parties so that it is not unfair to the employer to be required to keep the employee

---

55 *Gunton v. Richmond LBC* [1981] Ch 448; *Boyo v. Lambeth LBC* [1994] ICR 727.
56 See *Gunton v. Richmond LBC*.

on. This sounds like an impossible hurdle, but in practice the courts have been quite willing to find that mutual trust and confidence are present.[57] By forcing the employer to go through the disciplinary procedure, the employee not only gets his or her wages during that period, but also gets a chance to show that he or she has not done anything to deserve dismissal. This offers a strong protection for the employee's dignity-based right to have the issue of dismissal carefully considered by the employer.

Finally, we saw above that it may be possible to claim for breaches of the implied term of mutual trust and confidence in the time leading up to the dismissal, even though it is not possible to claim for breaches of that term arising out of the decision to dismiss itself. In accordance with normal contractual principles, the employee may only recover for financial losses and not for injury to feelings. Thus, in *Eastwood*, the claimants had an arguable case because they alleged that the employer's conduct had led to psychiatric illness rendering them unable to work.[58]

Two remedies are available to the employee who brings a successful unfair dismissal claim: re-employment and damages.[59] In principle, re-employment offers a high level of protection to employees because it allows the court to *override* the employer's decision to dismiss. Job property theorists view it as an important instance of their approach: the employee has been unfairly deprived of his or her property and should be given that property back. However, re-employment is the remedy in a tiny fraction of cases, so it does not operate as a strong remedy in practice.[60] Some critics argue that this is one of the legislation's failings. Tribunals are too ready to find that it is not 'practicable' for the employer to take the employee back,[61] and even when they do order re-employment, the employer who breaches the order is only required to pay a small amount of additional compensation, which is insufficient to act as a deterrent.[62] Others argue that the remedy is unrealistic and should be abandoned. Returning to the workplace after an acrimonious dismissal is an unattractive option for many people, and this is borne out by the fact that few claimants request re-employment.[63] On this view, it is more realistic to compensate employees and deter employers by using substantial awards of damages.

An award of damages for unfair dismissal is made up of two elements: the basic award and the compensatory award.[64] The basic award is calculated using a formula which reflects the claimant's age, length of service with the employer

---

57 *Irani* v. *Southampton AHA* [1985] ICR 590; *Jones* v. *Gwent CC* [1992] IRLR 521.
58 *Eastwood* v. *Magnox Electric.*
59 The statute provides for the employee to be reinstated in his or her old job (ERA 1996, s. 114) or re-engaged by the employer in comparable employment (ERA 1996, s. 115). 'Re-employment' does not appear in the statute, but is a useful umbrella term.
60 In 2006–7, re-employment was awarded in a mere 23 out of a total of 3,870 successful tribunal applications. Source: Employment Tribunals Service, *Annual Statistics 2006–7* (2007).
61 ERA 1996, s. 116(1)(b).   62 Ibid., s. 117.   63 Ibid., s. 116(1)(a).
64 The figures used to calculate these awards must be revised once a year by the Secretary of State in line with the retail price index: ERA 1999, s. 34. The amounts applicable from 1 February 2008 are set out in the Employment Rights (Increase of Limits) Order 2007 (SI 2007/3570).

and usual weekly wage,[65] up to a limit of £330 per week.[66] The maximum available under this heading is £9,900. This means that employees who earn more than £330 per week cannot be fully compensated. The second element is the compensatory award.[67] This is a sum that the tribunal considers 'just and equitable', normally up to a maximum limit of £63,000. The purpose of this award is to compensate the employee, not to punish the employer, so the tribunal usually looks quite closely at the employee's losses. Non-pecuniary losses are not recoverable.[68] Again, awards under this heading tend to be relatively low. In 2006–7, the average compensation for unfair dismissal was £7,974.[69] These modest awards help to keep employers' costs down. But they can be criticised for failing to vindicate employees' rights and for failing to encourage employers to maintain a policy of job security. They also help to explain why some employees, like the claimants in *Johnson* and *Eastwood*, have tried to pursue their claims at common law as well.

In some circumstances, tribunals may be able to make higher awards of damages to reflect the seriousness of the employer's actions. The maximum limit on the compensatory award does not apply in cases of discrimination on grounds of sex, race and so on. Where the employer has dismissed the employee on trade union grounds[70] or for acting as a workforce representative,[71] a minimum basic award of £4,400 must be awarded, regardless of the individual's length of service. These provisions fit well with the dignity rationale suggested by Collins. Because they apply when a forbidden reason for dismissal is used, the employee's dignity is violated and particularly strong condemnation is required.

Under the EA 2002, where the employer has failed to complete a disciplinary or grievance procedure, the employee's damages must be increased by 10 per cent and may be increased by up to 50 per cent unless exceptional circumstances apply.[72] Where the failure is attributable to the employee, his or her unfair dismissal damages must be reduced by 10 per cent and may be reduced by up to 50 per cent, unless exceptional circumstances apply.[73] These rules were intended to encourage the parties to use internal procedures and thus to resolve their differences without recourse to a tribunal. However, critics pointed out that they could operate unfairly, particularly when one party (most likely the employee) was unaware of the importance of following procedures.[74] Under the Employment Act 2008, the government has introduced a softer version of this approach, in which the employee's compensation can be increased (or reduced) by up to 25 per cent where the employer (or the employee) unreasonably fails to comply with the ACAS Code of Practice. Much will turn on tribunals' interpretation of unreasonableness in this context.

---

65 ERA 1996, ss. 119–122.   66 Ibid., s. 227.   67 Ibid., ss. 123–124.
68 *Dunnachie v. Kingston upon Hull CC* [2004] UKHL 36; [2005] 1 AC 226.
69 Source: Employment Tribunals Service, *Annual Statistics 2006–7*.
70 TULRCA 1992, s. 156.   71 ERA 1996, s. 120.   72 EA 2002, s. 31(3) and (4).
73 Ibid., s. 31(2) and (4).   74 Hepple and Morris, 'The Employment Act 2002'.

A final point to note is that the statute provides compensation for those who are made redundant even where the redundancy is fair.[75] This compensation is calculated in exactly the same way as the basic award in unfair dismissal, described above.[76] It is commonly regarded as a way of acknowledging to employees that a dismissal for redundancy, though justified, is not their fault. However, it can be questioned whether the payments are sufficient to do this, given the relatively low level at which they are set.[77] Moreover, the payments may not be enough to deter employers from behaving opportunistically and ignoring the longer-term goal of job security. In contrast, Collins is critical of the very existence of redundancy payments, arguing that it is in the interests of the economy as a whole that employers should not be deterred from reorganising their businesses.[78]

Further reading

For detailed textbook accounts of this topic, see S. Deakin and G.S. Morris, *Labour Law* (4th edn., 2005), Chapter 5, or H. Collins, K.D. Ewing and A. McColgan, *Labour Law: Text and Materials* (2nd edn., 2005), Chapter 5.

H. Collins, *Justice in Dismissal* (1992), is a thought-provoking study of dismissal laws which draws on both rights and economics arguments. For a critique, see G. Pitt, 'Justice in Dismissal: a reply to Hugh Collins' (1993) 22 *ILJ* 251. What methodology does Collins adopt? Are there problems with it? How does he classify dismissals? What flaws does Pitt identify in his classification? Are the economics arguments he uses primarily neoclassical or new institutional? Do you agree with the balance he strikes between the rights to dignity and autonomy, and cost considerations? Do you find these rights persuasive as the basis for dismissal law, or would you prefer to see it justified in some other way? For a modern take on the job property approach, see W. Njoya, *Property in Work* (2007).

At EU level, 'flexicurity' (flexibility and security combined) is a major part of the policy agenda. The idea is that workers should view their security more in terms of being employable in the labour market, rather than staying in the same job for a long period of time. This is closely linked to new institutionalist arguments about training workers so that they are highly skilled and therefore adaptable. See European Commission, *Towards Common Principles of Flexicurity: More and Better Jobs through Flexibility and Security* (2007). How big a role does security play in flexicurity?

In the UK, the government's main concern is with the costs associated with unfair dismissal claims, particularly for employers: see DTI, *Resolving Disputes in the Workplace* (2007). Is the government right to be concerned? What is the

---

75 ERA 1996, s. 135.   76 Ibid., s. 162.
77 For critique, see R. Fryer, 'The myths of the Redundancy Payments Act' (1973) 2 *ILJ* 1.
78 Collins, *Justice in Dismissal*, Chapter 5.

best regulatory strategy for addressing litigation costs? Can it be done without limiting employees' rights? For interesting empirical evidence on the incidence of dismissal disputes, see K.G. Knight and P. Latreille, 'Discipline, dismissals and complaints to employment tribunals' (2000) 38 *BJIR* 533.

The most accessible account of the neoclassical perspective is R.A. Epstein, 'In defense of the contract at will' (1984) 51 *University of Chicago Law Review* 947. What assumptions does Epstein make in formulating his argument? What do you think motivates people to work hard? Does it depend on the job? Are Epstein's critics right to identify real risks of employer opportunism? Do those risks fully justify English unfair dismissal law or do we need to use other arguments too?

In the light of these competing arguments, you may find it helpful to revisit the issue of the worker/employee distinction discussed in Chapter 5. Should workers benefit from unfair dismissal laws?

10

Collective representation

This chapter is the first of three chapters dealing with the collective dimension of labour law: in other words, its approach to *groups* of workers. Trade unions are, of course, the classic example of workers grouping together in order to bargain with the employer about terms and conditions of employment. As we saw in Chapter 1, the labour law of the 1950s was designed to support collective bargaining. Today, the law continues to play this role to some extent. However, collective bargaining is no longer the sole mechanism through which workers may present their views to the employer. Duties derived from EC law to consult with employees also form an important part of labour law. Consultation may involve trade unions, but it need not do so.[1] This chapter will address the two main controversies that arise in this area: whether workers should have a say in the running of the workplace at all and, if so, what form their participation should take.[2]

Human rights instruments generally support some form of worker participation. Civil and political rights instruments usually contain a right to form and join trade unions 'for the protection of [the individual's] interests'. Commentators have argued that this phrase could be used to support a right to engage in collective bargaining, but interpretations (for example, by the ECtHR) have not always confirmed this view. Economic and social rights instruments usually contain an express right to collective bargaining. Consultation is a recent innovation and makes an appearance only in the most modern economic and social rights instruments, such as the EU Charter and the revised ESC 1996.

The economics literature on the role of collective bargaining is substantial and often quite polarised. At the one extreme, there are those who feel that unions are damaging to the national economy and to the interests of individual workers. They argue that unions secure 'rents' for their members: in other words, higher

---

1 This chapter will focus mainly on general duties to consult or bargain. Sometimes, consultation can be used to vary obligations contained in legislation – for example, on working time. This will not be considered in detail in this chapter, but many of the points made here are applicable to this process too.
2 Some countries require companies to have worker representatives as board members. For reasons of space, this will not be discussed in this chapter. For detail, see M. Biagi and M. Tiraboschi, 'Forms of employee representational participation', in R. Blanpain (ed.), *Comparative Labour Law and Industrial Relations in Industrialized Market Economies* (9th edn., 2007).

pay than the market would justify. This reduces firms' profits, limits the number of workers they can afford to employ, and increases inequality between unionised and non-unionised workers. At the other extreme, there are those who argue that unions have a positive effect. Unions improve communication between employers and workers. They increase firms' productivity by supplying information to management about how working practices might be improved and by reducing the turnover of employees (thus lowering firms' hiring and training costs). Duties to consult employees have not been so fully studied by economists. Some versions of consultation may be closely related to collective bargaining – where a trade union is involved and similar issues are covered – and may therefore have the same balance of advantages and disadvantages. But, as we shall see, the effect of consultation is more difficult to predict the further away we move from collective bargaining.

Rights perspectives

Collective bargaining

Civil and political rights instruments tend not to address the question of collective bargaining. Article 11 of the ECHR is typical: 'Everyone has the right to freedom of peaceful assembly and to freedom of association with others, including the right to form and join trade unions for the protection of his interests'.[3] The phrase 'for the protection of his interests' has been invested with considerable significance by some commentators.[4] They have argued that if the trade union is to protect its members, it must have certain rights, such as the right to engage in collective bargaining and the right to strike. Such rights should therefore be seen as implicit in the right to freedom of association. In the *National Union of Belgian Police* case, the ECtHR appeared to support this view, holding that 'what the Convention requires is that under national law trade unions should be enabled ... to strive for the protection of their members' interests'.[5] But later cases have not required national governments to protect a right to collective bargaining. In the *Swedish Engine Drivers' Union* case, it was held that a trade union had no right to enter into a collective agreement with the employer,[6] and in *Wilson* v. *UK*, it was held that there was no obligation on the state to maintain a statutory procedure for the recognition of trade unions.[7]

The absence of a right to collective bargaining in civil and political rights instruments reflects their focus on rights for *individuals*. The right to freedom

---

3 See also Art. 22 of the ICCPR.
4 For discussion, see T. Novitz, *International and European Protection of the Right to Strike* (2003), pp. 225–40; K.D. Ewing, 'The Human Rights Act and labour law' (1998) 27 *ILJ* 275, pp. 279–80.
5 *National Union of Belgian Police* v. *Belgium* (1979–80) 1 EHRR 578, p. 591.
6 *Swedish Engine Drivers' Union* v. *Sweden* (1979–80) 1 EHRR 617.
7 *Wilson* v. *UK* (2002) 35 EHRR 20.

of association can be interpreted as a purely individual right to join associations. The only obligation this right imposes on others (such as employers) is to refrain from discriminating against people because of the associations they have joined. However, some would argue that this approach ignores the reasons which lead individuals to join organisations. In the case of trade unions, individuals often join because they want to use their collective strength in order to bargain with the employer for better terms and conditions. If the individual's right to join the union is to be rendered truly effective, the union itself must have the rights it needs in order to further its members' interests.

Economic and social rights instruments are more open to the possibility of rights which attach to groups, as well as individuals, which is why they are more likely to contain a right to collective bargaining. Let us look at some examples. Article 28 of the EU Charter states that:

> Workers and their employers, or their respective organisations, have, in accordance with Community law and national laws and practices, the right to negotiate and conclude collective agreements at the appropriate levels and, in cases of conflicts of interest, to take collective action to defend their interests, including strike action.

The ESC (in both the 1961 and 1996 versions) protects a right to bargain, but through more indirect means. Article 6 states that:

> With a view to ensuring the effective exercise of the right to bargain collectively, the Parties undertake:
>
> ... 2. to promote, where necessary and appropriate, machinery for voluntary negotiations between employers or employers' organisations and workers' organisations, with a view to the regulation of terms and conditions of employment by means of collective agreements.

In the ILO, collective bargaining is governed by two conventions. The first, Convention 98 on the Right to Organise and Collective Bargaining 1949, provides in Article 4 that:

> Measures appropriate to national conditions shall be taken, where necessary, to encourage and promote the full development and utilisation of machinery for voluntary negotiation between employers or employers' organisations and workers' organisations, with a view to the regulation of terms and conditions of employment by means of collective agreements.

The UK has ratified this convention.[8] Further detail is provided in Convention 154 on Collective Bargaining 1981. Article 5 requires states to promote collective bargaining, and specifies in some detail the aims to be pursued. These aims include ensuring that collective bargaining is possible for all employers and groups of workers, extending the scope of collective bargaining to cover terms and conditions of employment and relations between employers and workers and

---

8 The ESC 1961, discussed above, draws heavily on this Article.

their respective organisations, encouraging the parties to agree procedural rules for collective bargaining, and ensuring that collective bargaining is not hindered where no procedural rules have been agreed. This provides the most detailed international statement of the state's responsibilities in relation to collective bargaining, but it has not received widespread support. It has been ratified by a mere thirty-eight countries, not including the UK.

All these rights clearly oblige the state to refrain from preventing or interfering in collective bargaining voluntarily undertaken by employers and unions. The obligation to 'promote…machinery' for collective bargaining is, however, rather more difficult to interpret. The use of phrases such as 'appropriate to national conditions' and 'in accordance with…national laws and practices' indicates that states have substantial discretion in the way that they implement this obligation. The ILO Freedom of Association Committee has held that the state may not make bargaining compulsory, because this would infringe the fundamental requirement that bargaining should be voluntary.[9] Nor does the duty to promote collective bargaining permit the state to force employers and unions to use conciliation or arbitration when they cannot resolve their disputes. The state may provide such machinery, but recourse to it should be a matter of choice for the employer and union.[10] Finally, the state may help the parties to gain access to information that would assist them in bargaining.[11]

Consultation

Consultation is a relative newcomer and therefore features only in the most recent instruments. The EU Charter contains a basic right to consultation:

> Workers or their representatives must, at the appropriate levels, be guaranteed information and consultation in good time in the cases and under the conditions provided for by Community law and national laws and practices.[12]

As we shall see, there is already a substantial body of EU law on consultation. This right reflects this body of law, and offers little guidance as to how it might be developed in the future. The revised ESC 1996 is the other instrument that contains consultation rights. The UK is not bound by these rights because it has only ratified the ESC 1961, which did not address the issue of consultation. A general right to information and consultation is set out in Article 21:

> With a view to ensuring the effective exercise of the right of workers to be informed and consulted within the undertaking, the Parties undertake to adopt or encourage measures enabling workers or their representatives, in accordance with national legislation and practice:
>
> a. to be informed regularly or at the appropriate time and in a comprehensible way about the economic and financial situation of the undertaking employing them,

---

9 ILO, *Digest of Decisions of the Committee on Freedom of Association* (2006), paras. 925–931.
10 Ibid., para. 932.   11 Ibid.   12 EU Charter, Art. 27.

on the understanding that the disclosure of certain information which could be prejudicial to the undertaking may be refused or subject to confidentiality; and

b. to be consulted in good time on proposed decisions which could substantially affect the interests of workers, particularly on those decisions which could have an important impact on the employment situation in the undertaking.

This right requires workers or their representatives to be provided with information about the state of the business on a regular basis, and to be consulted on specific issues affecting them, such as redundancies. Although it refers to national legislation and practice, it gives a clearer idea than does the EU Charter of the obligations it imposes. It is supplemented by Article 28, which requires states to support workers' representatives by protecting them against detrimental treatment, including dismissal, and by providing them with facilities to carry out their task.[13] The ESC 1996 also contains some more specific consultation rights. For example, Article 29 requires states to oblige employers to consult workers' representatives in the event of collective redundancies. It states that consultation should cover 'ways and means of avoiding collective redundancies or limiting their occurrence and mitigating their consequences'.

One of the major contrasts between consultation and collective bargaining is reflected in the way in which these rights are framed. Collective bargaining requires the active participation of the relevant workers, who must form or join a trade union and seek recognition from the employer. As a result, the state's obligation is confined to providing mechanisms for the workers to use, rather than forcing the workers to use them. Information and consultation does not require the same level of participation. The workers need not join an organisation. They only need to elect representatives. Even if they do not want to do this, the employer can still provide them with information and ask them for their views as individuals. As a result, these rights are more strongly framed. States are required to 'adopt' measures or to 'guarantee' the relevant rights to workers.

This leads to a more profound question about the status of the right to be consulted. Some rights theorists are sceptical about its value to workers. They argue that collective bargaining offers a more effective form of participation because the presence of a trade union helps to equalise the bargaining power of workers and management. Consultation puts workers in a much weaker position. Therefore, consultation should only be promoted as a 'second-best' option when collective bargaining is not available. The two types of participation should not be given equal status by the law. Against this, it might be argued that the right to be consulted

13 Similar obligations are contained in ILO Convention 135 on Workers' Representatives 1971, which applies both to union representatives and to elected non-union representatives of the workforce. This reference to non-union representatives is unusual given the ILO's traditional focus on collective bargaining as the main mode of worker representation.

in an employment setting is linked to more general rights which *are* regarded as fundamental, such as the administrative law right to be given a hearing by a public authority, and even the fundamental human right to a fair trial. On this basis, the right to consultation is an important right to a fair hearing at work.

Economics perspectives

Trade unions have been a topic of considerable interest to economists. Neoclassical theorists argue that unions lead to unwarranted increases in wages, which have harmful consequences for firms, other workers and the economy as a whole. New institutionalists argue that trade unionism can benefit firms by reducing labour turnover and improving productivity. Consultation has not been studied so fully, but it is possible to speculate about its likely economic consequences.

Economic arguments against worker participation

An individual worker is unlikely to have much ability to bargain with the employer unless he or she has unique skills. The employer can easily hire a replacement if the worker demands improved terms and conditions. If workers join a trade union, however, the position changes. The larger the proportion of workers who are members of the union, the harder it is for the employer to hire replacements if they demand improved terms and conditions. Moreover, the union may be able to threaten strike action – which would disrupt the employer's business – if its demands are ignored. This enables unions to extract concessions from the employer. This may seem harmless: perhaps the employer is exploiting the non-unionised workers, using its superior economic muscle to pay them less than the market rate for their jobs. But economists do not analyse the situation in this way. If the employer was paying the non-unionised workers less than the market rate for the job, they would simply leave and find jobs elsewhere. So any concessions achieved by the union are 'rents': gains over and above the market rate for the job.[14] These rents are regarded as inefficient. They lead to a misallocation of labour. Because unionised firms will not be able to employ as many workers at the higher wage, some workers in that sector will lose their jobs. In turn, this reduces the output of the unionised sector: fewer workers mean that fewer goods are produced.

By comparing the wages paid to similarly qualified workers in unionised and non-unionised workplaces, economists are able to estimate the extent to which unions are able to secure rents in practice. There are some methodological difficulties with their calculations.[15] In particular, wages in the non-union sector are likely to be influenced by wages in the unionised sector. They may be pushed up

---

14 See F.A. Hayek, *The Constitution of Liberty* (1960), Chapter 18; R.A. Posner, *Economic Analysis of Law* (6th edn., 2003), pp. 335–42.

15 D.J.B. Mitchell, *Unions, Wages, and Inflation* (1980), Chapter 3.

by employers who want to protect themselves against union-organising drives. Or they may be pushed down, by the flood of workers into the non-unionised sector who have been made redundant because of wage rises in the unionised sector. A figure representing the difference between wages in the two sectors may therefore be a slight underestimate or overestimate of the union wage effect. Nevertheless, some idea can be given of the union wage effect for particular countries at particular points in time. In their classic study of trade unions, Freeman and Medoff found that in the 1970s, unionised workers in the USA were paid 20–30 per cent more than non-unionised workers.[16] More recent figures suggest that the effect for the USA in 2007 was still over 20 per cent.[17] However, the USA is not typical, and tends to show a greater effect than other countries, including the UK. We will examine data for the UK in our discussion of the legal provisions on collective bargaining, below.

Of course, the 'union wage effect' does not always manifest itself in practice. One reason for this is that unions do not pursue high wages at the expense of all other considerations. They are concerned with preserving their members' jobs as well as with securing better pay. So unions will not push for very high wages which would lead to substantial job losses. This is particularly likely to occur when the economy is in recession. If the firm's sales are declining, it may need to make some workers redundant in order to cut its costs and remain profitable. In these circumstances, the union may refrain from asking for a pay rise which would only make matters worse.

When the economy is enjoying a period of growth, the union wage effect is much more of a worry for neoclassical economists. If unions cannot be kept in check by fears about redundancies, some other way must be found to minimise the harm they can do to the economy. Many theorists argue that the law on trade unions can play an important role. It should be used to reduce the power of trade unions and to limit their bargaining power as against employers. For example, some legal systems allow the 'closed shop', in which all workers in a particular workplace can be forced to become members of the union. This makes the union very strong: the employer can hardly ignore the demands of all its workers. So a law which bans the 'closed shop' may help to reduce unions' ability to extract rents from employers. Similarly, unions' bargaining power is strengthened when they are able to make credible threats of strike action. Employers will be keen to avoid the disruption this may cause, so they will be more likely to accept the union's demands. Again, the law can intervene by placing obstacles in the way of strike action. Chapters 11 and 12 will explore these issues more fully.

The impact of consultation has not been analysed so extensively by economists. To begin with, we need to decide how similar consultation is to collective bargaining. If it is very similar, it is likely to have the same impact as collective bargaining: it will enable workers to extract benefits from the employer over

---

16 R.B. Freeman and J.L. Medoff, *What Do Unions Do?* (1984), Chapter 3.
17 US Department of Labor, Bureau of Labor Statistics, *Union Members in 2007* (2008).

and above those they would have achieved in the market. One important difference between the two processes is that consultation leaves the final decision firmly in the hands of the employer. In consultation, the employer asks workers for their opinion and then makes a decision which may or may not reflect their views. In collective bargaining, the aim is to reach an agreement with the union representatives – a 'collective agreement' – that will be respected by both sides. This suggests that consultation is less likely to affect market outcomes because employers can more easily ignore the opinions expressed during consultation. Another important difference between the two processes is that consultation, unlike collective bargaining, does not depend on the presence of a trade union to represent the workers. In collective bargaining, the threat of strike action helps to equalise the bargaining power between the workers and the employer. A similar threat could be used to enforce the demands of representatives in a consultation process. However, this is unlikely unless the workplace is unionised. As a result, the bargaining power of representatives in a consultation exercise may depend heavily on whether or not they have the support of a union. Again, this means that consultation may be a relatively harmless process in which the employer is hardly ever forced to make concessions to the workers.

Nevertheless, it seems unlikely that neoclassical economists would welcome, or even tolerate, extensive legal obligations on employers to consult with workers. Simply putting consultation procedures in place – supplying information to representatives, holding meetings and so on – costs money. They would see no justification for the imposition of these costs on employers.

Economic arguments in favour of worker participation

Two slightly different claims are commonly used to support the view that worker participation may be beneficial to firms. First, worker participation is said to improve a firm's ability to retain its employees. Second, worker participation may increase productivity by enabling the employer to harness workers' ideas for improving production processes. It might be expected that if these arguments were correct, employers would adopt worker participation mechanisms voluntarily, without the need for legal intervention. However, it is commonly argued that legislation is needed to protect 'good' firms from undercutting.

Firms with a high turnover of labour face increased costs because they have to hire replacements and train them to the required standard. Hiring costs include placing job advertisements and using managers' time to conduct interviews. Training costs may be considerable if the job requires firm-specific skills. Some theorists have argued that trade unions can reduce firms' labour turnover. Freeman and Medoff found that unionised firms had lower quit rates than non-unionised firms.[18] They estimated that this reduced firms' labour costs by 1–2 per cent. One explanation for this finding might be the union wage effect,

18 Freeman and Medoff, *What Do Unions Do?*, Chapter 6.

where it exists. For obvious reasons, workers who receive above-average pay are likely to value their jobs more highly. But Freeman and Medoff argued that unions reduced turnover rates even when the unionised and non-unionised firms they compared were paying the same wages. They attributed this to the union 'voice' effect. Workers in unionised firms chose to deal with their grievances by complaining ('voicing'), rather than simply looking for another job ('exiting').[19] This was because unions encouraged management to put in place grievance and arbitration procedures through which workers' concerns could be resolved. Consultation might have the same benefit if it provides workers with a means of voicing their concerns.

A second set of economic arguments in favour of worker participation is that it can improve the firm's productivity and performance. The government White Paper *Fairness at Work* contains a useful summary of these ideas:

> ... the returns from effective partnership to the business and its employees are real whether it operates in local or global markets:
>
> – where they have an understanding of the business, employees recognise the importance of responding quickly to changing customer and market requirements;
> – where they are taken seriously, employees at every level come forward with ways to help the business innovate, for example by developing new products; and
> – where they are well-prepared for change, employees can help the company to introduce and operate new technologies and processes, helping to secure employment within the business.[20]

The idea is that the employer can use either consultation or collective bargaining to build close relationships with worker representatives, often referred to as a 'partnership' approach. The representatives can then act as an important channel of communication between management and the workforce. They can inform management about workers' ideas for improving the firm's performance. And the representatives can inform workers about management's plans for the future of the business. The firm's productivity should improve, both as a direct result of workers' suggestions and indirectly because of workers' co-operation and enthusiasm.

If worker participation is as beneficial as the literature suggests, both in reducing turnover and improving productivity, it might be expected that firms would introduce it voluntarily out of self-interested motives. But it is often argued that legislation has an essential role to play, even when participation would benefit firms. First, legislation may educate employers. Economic theory assumes that employers always act rationally in order to maximise their profits. In the real world, employers may not realise the benefits of certain types of behaviour.

---

19 The terminology is from A.O. Hirschman, *Exit, Voice and Loyalty* (1970).
20 DTI, *Fairness at Work* (1998) (Cm 3968), p. 12.

Employers who are used to a hierarchical model of organisation may not be aware of what can be achieved through partnership. Thus, by requiring employers to respond to trade union requests for recognition or to set up consultation mechanisms, the law may trigger an interest in new ways of working. Second, legislation may help firms which are considering adopting a partnership approach but feel nervous about doing so. Partnership may require a considerable investment of time and effort over the short term in order to change the culture of the workplace. Firms may perceive the long-term benefits, but they might be afraid of being undercut by their competitors while they incur the short-term costs. Legislation may assist here by imposing some set-up costs on all firms and making it easier to adopt the long-term view.

But there are some problems with legally mandated bargaining or consultation. One study of firms which had implemented a 'partnership' approach found that 'achieving partnership at work is often difficult, requires high levels of commitment from all concerned, and can take a significant length of time to achieve'.[21] This suggests that the key to achieving lower labour turnover or higher productivity through worker participation lies in the attitudes of those involved. Although legislation may encourage positive attitudes in some firms, it may also provoke resentment. Where consultation or collective bargaining is grudgingly implemented by a reluctant employer, it seems unlikely to have many benefits.

The law on collective bargaining

Around 40 per cent of employees have their pay set through collective bargaining. Collective bargaining is more likely in larger workplaces, and in the public sector.[22] We will look at the various ways in which the law supports collective bargaining before examining the provisions from the rights and economics perspectives.

When an employer has agreed to engage in collective bargaining with a union, we say that the union has been 'recognised'. The recognition agreement will usually specify which aspects of the employment relationship the parties have opened up for bargaining. The law offers certain advantages to recognised trade unions, some of which will be discussed below. Under the traditional theory of collective laissez-faire, it is up to the union to secure recognition for itself. The union's main mechanism for doing this is to engage in, or threaten to engage in, industrial action. The impact of such action depends on factors such as the employer's ability to withstand the strike and the state of the labour market. These matters will be considered in detail in Chapter 12.

In 2000, the government reintroduced a statutory procedure to assist trade unions to obtain recognition where they are unable to secure it through their

21 J. Knell, *Partnership at Work* (1999), p. 27.
22 B. Kersley *et al.*, *Inside the Workplace* (2006), pp. 179–89.

industrial muscle alone.[23] The procedure is run by the Central Arbitration Committee (CAC).[24] Details are set out in Schedule A1 to TULRCA 1992.[25] A union can obtain automatic recognition if 50 per cent of the employees in a particular bargaining unit are members of the union.[26] It can also obtain recognition if a majority of those voting and at least 40 per cent of those eligible to vote have supported recognition in a secret ballot.[27] Once recognition has been achieved, the parties may negotiate as to how they will conduct collective bargaining, and if they fail to agree, the CAC may specify a procedure (called a 'method') for them.[28] The method takes effect as a legally binding contract which a court may enforce through an order for specific performance.[29] The bargaining must cover pay, hours and holidays, though the parties may add other matters by agreement.[30] So far there have been 630 applications for recognition, of which 374 were accepted by the CAC.[31] In 84 cases, recognition was ordered without a ballot. In 160 cases, a ballot was held, leading to recognition in 100 cases. In the vast majority of cases in which the union gained recognition, the parties agreed a method for collective bargaining, though the CAC has had to impose a method in 14 cases. It is important to note that many cases are withdrawn after the initial application and at various later stages of the process. Often this is because the employer has decided to recognise the union voluntarily. Indeed, research suggests that the statutory procedure has had a significant 'shadow' effect – in other words, unions have been able to persuade employers to recognise them simply because the procedure is a threat in the background.[32]

Once recognition has been obtained, whether by agreement or through the statutory procedure, the union must try to persuade the employer of the merits of its claims. Again, much will depend on the industrial muscle of the union, but the law does offer some indirect assistance to facilitate the bargaining process. Trade union representatives are entitled to a reasonable amount of paid time off

23 The Industrial Relations Act 1971, ss. 44–50, first introduced a recognition procedure into English law. A revised procedure was contained in the Employment Protection Act 1975, ss. 11–16. This was repealed in 1980.
24 The CAC is a statutory body with responsibility for various areas of collective labour law, including recognition and disclosure of information for collective bargaining (discussed below).
25 Inserted by ERA 1999, s. 1. For discussion, see B. Simpson, 'Trade union recognition and the law, a new approach – Parts I and II of Schedule A1 to TULRCA 1992' (2000) 29 *ILJ* 193; A.L. Bogg, 'The political theory of trade union recognition campaigns – legislating for democratic competitiveness' (2001) 64 *MLR* 875; T. Novitz and P. Skidmore, *Fairness at Work: A Critical Analysis of the Employment Relations Act 1999 and its Treatment of Collective Rights* (2001), Chapter 4. For discussion of the 2004 amendments to the procedure, see A.L. Bogg, 'Employment Relations Act 2004: another false dawn for collectivism?' (2005) 34 *ILJ* 72, pp. 75–82.
26 TULRCA 1992, Schedule A1, para. 22.   27 Ibid., Schedule A1, paras. 23–29.
28 Ibid., Schedule A1, para. 30; Trade Union Recognition (Method of Collective Bargaining) Order 2000 (SI 2000/1300).
29 TULRCA 1992, Schedule A1, para. 30(4) and (6).   30 Ibid., Schedule A1, para. 1(3) and (4).
31 CAC, *Annual Report 2007–8* (2008), p. 10.
32 See J. Blanden *et al.*, 'Have unions turned the corner? New evidence on recent trends in union recognition in UK firms' (2006) 44 *BJIR* 169.

work to prepare for and participate in collective bargaining,[33] and trade union members are entitled to a reasonable amount of unpaid time off for trade union activities, such as voting on the outcome of collective bargaining.[34]

The law also supports the collective bargaining process by giving recognised unions a statutory right of access to the employer's information. A strong union may be able to get information by negotiating for it, but where the union is weak, the employer may be able to frustrate collective bargaining by concealing relevant facts. Under s. 181(2) TULRCA 1992, the employer is under a duty to disclose information:

(a) without which the trade union representatives would be to a material extent impeded in carrying on collective bargaining with him, and
(b) which it would be in accordance with good industrial relations practice that he should disclose to them for the purposes of collective bargaining.

However, this offers limited guidance as to what information the employer is obliged to disclose.[35] The employer may also be able to rely on exceptions – for example, where the information is confidential or where its disclosure might damage the business.[36] The procedure for enforcement is through a complaint to the CAC,[37] but unions may be reluctant to invoke this, for fear that to do so might damage their future relations with the employer. Research by Gospel and Lockwood, who found that relatively few claims had been made under s. 181, seems to bear this theory out.[38] As the authors argue, however, the statutory right to information may have significant indirect effects. In other words, unions may be able to extract information from employers simply by threatening to invoke the statutory procedure.

The process of collective bargaining usually results in a collective agreement. Most collective agreements are not legally binding.[39] Employers and unions generally prefer to keep their agreements informal and flexible. If certain conditions are met, the terms of a collective agreement may be incorporated into the contracts of employment of the employees to whom it applies.[40]

From a rights perspective, much of this legislation is uncontroversial. The statutory procedure for obtaining information is an obvious way in which the state could comply with the obligation to promote voluntary collective bargaining. The recognition procedure could also be regarded as an important means of supporting collective bargaining. Collective bargaining is usually requested by the trade

---

33 TULRCA 1992, ss. 168–169.   34 Ibid., s. 170.
35 Some detail is provided in ACAS, *Code of Practice 2: Disclosure of Information to Trade Unions for Collective Bargaining Purposes* (1997), to which the CAC must have regard by virtue of s. 181(4) TULRCA 1992.
36 TULRCA 1992, s. 182.   37 Ibid., s. 183.
38 H. Gospel and G. Lockwood, 'Disclosure of information for collective bargaining: the CAC approach revisited' (1999) 28 *ILJ* 233.
39 TULRCA 1992, s. 179, contains a presumption that this is the case unless the parties expressly agree otherwise.
40 See S. Deakin and G.S. Morris, *Labour Law* (4th edn., 2005), pp. 261–9, for detail.

union, rather than by management. Many employers resist collective bargaining because it involves agreeing to *share* the power to determine terms and conditions of employment. Where the union has a high level of support but cannot persuade the employer to bargain, perhaps the law should intervene. Indeed, the ILO has argued that Schedule A1 does not go far enough, criticising (among other things) the fact that the procedure does not apply to small firms (with fewer than twenty-one workers) and the requirement that the union obtain either majority membership or a majority vote in the bargaining unit in order to secure recognition.[41] On another view, however, the recognition procedure could be regarded as wholly inappropriate. The right to bargain collectively is a right for employers as well as unions. The employer's right to negotiate should include a right not to negotiate.[42] Although the employer is only forced to take part in the procedure, and not to reach a particular agreement, it could be argued that the statutory recognition procedure conflicts with the very notion of voluntary collective bargaining, and is forbidden – not required – by the right to collective bargaining.

In order to examine the law from an economics perspective, it is helpful to begin by looking at whether or not there is any empirical evidence to support the neoclassical theorists' claims about the union wage effect. The most recent figures show that the hourly earnings of union members were around 15 per cent higher than those for non-members.[43] This is smaller than the differential in the USA, but it is still significant. However, it is important to note that in the public sector the differential is around 22 per cent, whereas in the private sector it is only 7 per cent.

Neoclassical theorists would find much to criticise in the current law. First, the law enhances unions' bargaining power (and thus their ability to secure higher wages) by helping them to gain access to information and, more seriously, by compelling employers to bargain with them. The recognition procedure obliges employers to listen to unions' demands. It is, however, important not to exaggerate its likely impact: it does not require the employer to reach an agreement with the union, or even to bargain in good faith. The procedure may not change the employer's decisions at all where it is determined to resist. Second, the law may impose significant costs on employers – for example, when a trade union representative is given paid time off to prepare for negotiations, the employer must find some other way of covering that person's work, while continuing to pay his or her wages.

But what about the argument that unions might have the beneficial effect of reducing labour turnover? The evidence indicates that unions do play a role in 'voicing' employees' grievances. Union representatives spend a considerable

---

41 ILO Committee of Experts, *Observations on Convention No. 98* (2006). For discussion, see R. Dukes, 'The statutory recognition procedure 1999: no bias in favour of recognition?' (2008) 37 *ILJ* 236.

42 See *Wilson* v. *UK* (2002) 35 EHRR 20, para. 44.

43 BERR, *Trade Union Membership 2007* (2008), p. 14.

amount of their time dealing with concerns about the treatment of employees and with disputes between employees and employers.[44] It is difficult to link this directly to employee turnover, though there is evidence that there is a lower incidence of voluntary resignations by employees in workplaces with a recognised union.[45] More generally, some studies have suggested that employees were happier when they believed that their union was effective and when they regarded management attitudes towards the union as favourable.[46] It seems reasonable to suppose that labour turnover would be reduced in these workplaces. However, it is not clear whether unions are able to voice employees' grievances where they have achieved recognition through the statutory procedure, because a hostile employer may stick closely to the required bargaining on pay, hours and holidays, and discourage the union from playing a broader role.

The empirical evidence on trade unions and productivity is problematic because productivity is itself quite difficult to measure. Most of the evidence suggests that productivity is roughly the same in unionised and non-unionised workplaces,[47] though there is some suggestion that productivity is worse where a union is recognised.[48] Again, the parties' approach to bargaining may well be relevant. Voluntary collective bargaining could conceivably be used as a forum for receiving employees' suggestions and communicating the firm's plans because its scope is a matter for agreement between the parties. But under statutory recognition, the employer may decide not to go beyond the strict legal requirement to discuss pay, hours and holidays.

The law on consultation

The law on consultation is largely derived from European directives[49] and has developed in a piecemeal fashion, starting with obligations to consult on particular issues (collective redundancies,[50] health and safety[51] and transfers of

---

44 Kersley et al., *Inside the Workplace*, pp. 149–54.
45 Ibid., p. 232.
46 A. Bryson and D. Wilkinson, *Collective Bargaining and Workplace Performance: An Investigation Using the Workplace Employee Relations Survey 1998* (2001), Chapter 5.
47 A. Bryson et al., 'High-involvement management practices, trade union representation and workplace performance in Britain' (2005) *Scottish Journal of Political Economy* 451, pp. 455–6.
48 Kersley et al., *Inside the Workplace*, p. 290.
49 There are three purely domestic duties to consult. One is to consult a recognised trade union where the employer proposes to contract out of the state earnings-related pensions scheme, under the Occupational Pension Schemes (Contracting Out) Regulations 1996 (SI 1996/1172), as amended. Another is to consult union or other representatives on certain changes to employer-run pension schemes, under the Occupational and Personal Pension Schemes (Consultation by Employers and Miscellaneous Amendment) Regulations 2006 (SI 2006/349). The third is to consult a union which has been recognised under the statutory procedure on training issues, under TULRCA 1992, s. 70B.
50 TULRCA 1992, ss. 188–192 (as amended). These provisions implement Directive 75/129/EEC as amended by Directive 92/56/EEC, now consolidated in Directive 98/59/EC.
51 See the Health and Safety at Work etc Act 1974, the Safety Representatives and Safety Committees Regulations 1977 (SI 1977/500), and the Health and Safety (Consultation with

ownership of a business[52]), and turning more recently to obligations to consult more generally on the state of the employer's business. We will begin by looking briefly at the redundancy consultation provisions as an example of the former approach, before looking at provisions of the latter type.

Under s. 188(1) TULRCA 1992, the obligation to consult on collective redundancies arises when the employer is 'proposing to dismiss as redundant 20 or more employees at one establishment within a period of 90 days or less'. The scope of the consultation is defined in s. 188(2):

> The consultation shall include consultation about ways of –
>
> a) avoiding the dismissals,
> b) reducing the numbers of employees to be dismissed, and
> c) mitigating the consequences of the dismissals,
>
> and shall be undertaken by the employer with a view to reaching agreement with the appropriate representatives.[53]

This uses a 'strong' definition of consultation – 'with a view to reaching agreement' – which suggests a process of negotiation similar to collective bargaining.

The selection of workforce representatives is governed by s. 188(1B) TULRCA 1992.[54] Where the employer recognises a trade union in respect of the employees who may be made redundant, the employer must consult the union representatives. Where no trade union is recognised, the employer may choose one of two options. One is to arrange for the affected employees to elect representatives. The other is to use representatives who have already been elected by the affected employees for another purpose – for example, where the employer has a consultative committee or works council already in place. These arrangements ensure that employers cannot bypass a recognised union and, at the same time, that consultation can take place in non-unionised workplaces.

The information to which the representatives must have access is set out in some detail in s. 188(4) TULRCA 1992. Among other things, the employer must disclose the reasons for the proposed redundancies, the numbers and descriptions of employees who may be dismissed, the proposed method of redundancy selection, and the proposed method of calculating the redundancy payments. However, recognised trade unions cannot use their right of access to information for collective bargaining in order to obtain information for consultation.[55]

The consultation process can be enforced through a complaint to an employment tribunal under s. 189 TULRCA 1992. Where the employer has breached a

---

Employees) Regulations 1996 (SI 1996/1513), and Directive 89/391/EC. The law here is domestic in origin but has been amended in response to the Directive.
52 Transfer of Undertakings (Protection of Employment) Regulations 2006 (SI 2006/246), regs. 13–16. The original directive was Directive 77/187/EC, as amended by Directive 98/50/EC, now consolidated in Directive 2001/23/EC.
53 See *Middlesbrough BC v. TGWU* [2002] IRLR 332.
54 For the history of this provision, see Deakin and Morris, *Labour Law*, pp. 863–5.
55 *R v. CAC, ex p. BTP Tioxide* [1981] ICR 843.

duty owed to the union or employee representatives – for example, by failing to disclose information in accordance with the provisions described below – they have the right to bring a claim. The affected employees may only claim where the employer has failed to comply with the election requirements. The burden of proof is placed on the employer to show that the chosen representative was appropriate[56] and that the election requirements set out in s. 188A were complied with.[57] If the tribunal finds that the employer has breached the consultation requirements, it may make a 'protective award' of remuneration to the employees who have been dismissed or whose dismissal is proposed.[58] This remuneration must be such as the tribunal considers just and equitable, up to a maximum of ninety days' payment.

More recent European directives have adopted a new approach. Instead of requiring consultation on specific issues, they require employers to create a mechanism for the consultation of workforce representatives on a regular basis. Initially, these duties applied only to pan-European firms under the Transnational Information and Consultation of Employees Regulations 1999.[59] Under these Regulations, 'Community-scale undertakings' are required to set up a European Works Council or equivalent consultation procedure if certain conditions are met. A Community-scale undertaking must have at least 1,000 employees within the Member States and at least 150 employees in each of at least two Member States.[60] The Information and Consultation of Employees Regulations 2004 (ICER) have extended the obligation to create a consultation procedure to national firms.[61] We will take the ICER as our example.

The ICER apply to firms employing at least fifty employees.[62] Importantly, the employees must trigger the process by asking the employer to initiate negotiations about information and consultation.[63] The request must come from at least 10 per cent of the firm's employees, subject to a minimum requirement of 15 signatures and a maximum of 2,500. The employer may also initiate negotiations of its own volition.[64]

---

56 TULRCA 1992, s. 189(1A).   57 Ibid., s. 189(1B).   58 Ibid., s. 189(2)–(4).

59 Transnational Information and Consultation of Employees Regulations 1999 (SI 1999/3323), implementing the European Works Councils Directive (94/45/EC). For discussion, see M. Carley and M. Hall, 'The implementation of the European Works Councils Directive' (2000) 29 *ILJ* 103. There are also obligations relating to employee consultation under the European Company statute (Reg. 2157/2001/EC), implemented in English law by the European Public Limited Liability Company Regulations 2004 (SI 2004/2326).

60 Transnational Information and Consultation of Employees Regulations 1999, regs. 2 and 4.

61 Information and Consultation of Employees Regulations 2004 (SI 2004/3426), implementing Directive 2002/14/EC, establishing a general framework for informing and consulting employees in the EC. For discussion of the Directive and the negotiating process, see B. Bercusson, 'The European social model comes to Britain' (2002) 31 *ILJ* 209. For the government's policy on implementation, see DTI, *High Performance Workplaces – Informing and Consulting Employees* (2003). For discussion of the Regulations, see K.D. Ewing and G.M. Truter, 'The Information and Consultation of Employees Regulations: voluntarism's bitter legacy' (2005) 68 *MLR* 626; M. Hall, 'Assessing the Information and Consultation of Employees Regulations' (2005) 34 *ILJ* 103.

62 ICER 2004, reg. 3.   63 Ibid., reg. 7.   64 Ibid., reg. 11.

The government was keen to ensure that where a firm already had consultation mechanisms in place, those mechanisms could continue. Thus, the Regulations provide that where there is a pre-existing agreement, negotiations on an information and consultation procedure can only be initiated where there is strong employee support.[65] One way to demonstrate this is where more than 40 per cent of the firm's employees have signed the request. Where this is not the case, the employer may organise a ballot. At least 40 per cent of the firm's employees and a majority of those voting in the ballot must vote in favour of triggering negotiations in order to displace the pre-existing agreement.

Once negotiations have been triggered, the employer must arrange for the employees to elect or appoint negotiating representatives.[66] The two sides then have a six-month period (which can be extended in some circumstances, including by agreement between the parties) within which to negotiate information and consultation arrangements. The legislation does not set out any limits to what the parties may agree. Importantly, they may choose either to set up a mechanism under which appointed or elected representatives will be consulted on behalf of the employees, or they may agree that the employees should be informed and consulted on an individual basis.[67]

If the employer refuses to initiate negotiations or if the parties cannot reach an agreement, the legislation lays down a default information and consultation procedure that must be used.[68] In theory at least, the default rules should act as a minimum standard for negotiated agreements. If the employer suggests a weak mechanism during negotiations, the representatives could choose not to agree to it and to wait instead for the default rules to take effect. The default mechanism provides for the election of representatives.[69] These representatives must be provided with information on 'the recent and probable development of the undertaking's activities and economic situation'.[70] They must be consulted, in the limited sense of 'the exchange of views and establishment of a dialogue'[71] on 'the situation, structure and probable development of employment within the undertaking and on any anticipatory measures envisaged, in particular, where there is a threat to employment within the undertaking'.[72] Finally, the representatives must be consulted 'with a view to reaching an agreement'[73] on 'decisions likely to lead to substantial changes in work organisation or in contractual relations', including redundancies,[74] but this obligation may cease to apply if the redundancy situation gives rise to a duty to consult under s. 188 TULRCA 1992 (discussed above) because the employer may choose to comply with that duty instead.[75]

Once the information and consultation procedure is in place (whether by agreement or by default), a complaint may be made by the representatives (or by the employees if no representatives have been elected) to the CAC if the employer

---

65 Ibid., reg. 8.   66 Ibid., reg. 14.   67 Ibid., reg. 16.   68 Ibid., reg. 18.
69 Ibid., reg. 19.   70 Ibid., reg. 20(1)(a).   71 Ibid., reg. 2.   72 Ibid., reg. 20(1)(b) and (3).
73 Ibid., reg. 20(4)(d).   74 Ibid., reg. 20(1)(c) and (3).   75 Ibid., reg. 20(5).

fails to comply with one of its provisions.[76] The CAC may issue an order telling the employer what to do. If such an order is made, the complainant may also ask the EAT to order the employer to pay a penalty to the Secretary of State in respect of the failure. This may not exceed £75,000. There are no other mechanisms for enforcing the Regulations.[77]

From a rights perspective, a number of criticisms can be made of these provisions. One is that the mechanisms are hard to enforce. The requirement to set up an information and consultation mechanism does not apply automatically, but instead must be triggered by the specified proportion or number of employees. This may be difficult to organise. If the employer fails to comply at any stage during the process, the need to complain separately to the CAC and the EAT is clumsy and the financial penalty may not be sufficient to deter the employer from breaching the provisions. Under the redundancy consultation provisions, the penalty of up to ninety days' pay for the affected employees is also regarded by many commentators as too limited. Indeed, some would argue that the only way to enforce consultation mechanisms is to provide that certain decisions, like redundancies, cannot take effect unless the employer has complied with the duty to consult.[78]

Another concern from the rights perspective is that the mechanisms do not do very much to ensure that the employer takes account of what the employees say. One problem with redundancy consultation is its timing. The Directive requires consultation when redundancies are 'contemplated', whereas domestic law (in breach of the Directive) only requires consultation when redundancies are 'proposed'.[79] It is generally agreed that 'contemplation' is an earlier stage in the process than 'proposal'.[80] Critics argue that the later the consultation takes place, the less likely it is that the employer's mind will be changed. Under the ICER, it is possible for the employees to be informed and consulted individually rather than collectively. Although this may work well as a means for the employer to provide information, it may be more difficult for the employees to get their point of view across under a mechanism of this type.

Another concern for many rights theorists is the relationship between consultation and trade union recognition.[81] Their concern is that workers' right to be represented by a trade union will be undermined by consultation, which they regard as a weaker form of participation than collective bargaining. The redundancy consultation provisions address this worry by providing that the employer must consult with trade union representatives where a union is recognised in the

---

76 Ibid., regs. 22–23.   77 Ibid., reg. 24.
78 See, for example, Deakin and Morris, *Labour Law*, p. 886. For a discussion of the difficulties with this idea, see *Griffin v. South West Water Services Ltd* [1995] IRLR 15.
79 Directive 98/59/EC, Art. 2(1); TULRCA 1992, s. 188(1).
80 *MSF v. Refuge Assurance* [2002] ICR 1365.
81 P. Davies and C. Kilpatrick, 'UK worker representation after single channel' (2004) 33 *ILJ* 121.

workplace. This prevents the employer from undermining the union by consulting with other representatives instead – an approach that was permitted until the law was amended in 1999. But the ICER do not give any special status to union representatives. It remains to be seen whether this will disadvantage unions. It is possible that unions will, in practice, benefit from the provisions because workers will regard union representatives as more expert than non-union representatives at negotiating with the employer.

Neoclassical economists are concerned about the ability of worker participation mechanisms to extract concessions from the employer that would not occur under normal market conditions. It is not possible simply to ask whether there is a 'consultation wage effect' comparable to the union wage effect because English law does not at present require consultation on wage rates. However, consultation does take place on issues that may require the employer to spend more money on the workforce – for example, by giving more generous redundancy payments. So it is still relevant to ask whether consultation enables worker representatives to extract concessions from the employer.

The answer depends in part on how consultation is defined. Consultation under the ICER is defined as 'the exchange of views and establishment of a dialogue'. This is a relatively weak obligation which simply requires the employer to provide information and to listen to the representatives' comments. The final decision is left firmly in the hands of the employer. The position is rather different for the stronger form of consultation required for collective redundancies. Here, the employer is obliged to consult 'with a view to reaching an agreement'. This model creates a greater expectation of joint governance by the employer and the representatives, and can be more readily compared with collective bargaining.

As we saw above, the ability of a union to extract concessions from an employer through collective bargaining depends on its bargaining power, which in turn depends on a multiplicity of legal and non-legal factors. It seems likely that the effect of consultation would vary in a similar way. However, from the neoclassical perspective, consultation seems less likely to have a damaging impact on the employer. Even if the employer is obliged to consult 'with a view to reaching an agreement', the final decision remains in the employer's hands. And – particularly where there is no union involvement in the consultation process – there is less likely to be any credible threat of industrial action on the part of the workforce to enhance the representatives' bargaining power.

Even if the consultation provisions are irrelevant to the employer's decision-making, they are still problematic from the neoclassical perspective. They may impose considerable costs on the employer. One of the most expensive mechanisms is the European Works Council (EWC). The EWC may involve substantial travel and interpreting costs, because representatives are drawn from different Member States of the EU and may not share a common language. A study of UK firms found that the average annual cost of an EWC (usually involving just one meeting per year) was £53,000.[82]

From the new institutionalist perspective, the key questions are whether the consultation mechanisms bring economic benefits in terms of reducing labour turnover and improving productivity. It is thought that consultation might reduce labour turnover by encouraging employees to voice and resolve their grievances rather than finding another job. Consultation might improve productivity by helping workers to adapt to change and by harnessing their ideas. From this perspective, it is important that the approach to consultation – and in particular the topics covered – allow for grievances to be raised and ideas shared. Here, an important difference emerges between consultation on a specific issue, like redundancies, and consultation under the ICER. In a redundancy situation, there seems little scope for the employee representatives to make suggestions about improving productivity, except where these might stave off the redundancies. Under the ICER, it is clear that a more wide-ranging consultation process is envisaged. Early evidence suggests that ICER consultation is being used as a means of airing the grievances of the workforce, albeit often grievances of a relatively trivial 'tea and toilets' kind.[83] It is also being used by management to provide information about the state of the business. This may help to build employee loyalty and adaptability. Representatives were less likely to have an opportunity to influence management decisions or to make suggestions for improving productivity. However, it is important to remember that these are early findings: consultation mechanisms may develop over time as employers get used to them and employee representatives become more adept at their task.

Further reading

For a detailed account of English law on consultation and collective bargaining, see S. Deakin and G. Morris, *Labour Law* (4th edn., 2005), Chapter 9, or H. Collins, K.D. Ewing and A. McColgan, *Labour Law: Text and Materials* (2nd edn., 2005), Chapter 8. The UK is unusual in not having a strong tradition of consultation, so you may find it helpful to look at some comparative material: M. Biagi and M. Tiraboschi, 'Forms of employee representational participation', in R. Blanpain (ed.), *Comparative Labour Law and Industrial Relations in Industrialized Market Economies* (9th edn., 2007).

To understand the debate about collective bargaining today, you need to have a more general appreciation of the challenges facing trade unionism. Like firms and governments, unions must respond to globalisation: see K. Klare, 'Countervailing workers' power as a regulatory strategy', in H. Collins *et al.*

---

82 T. Weber *et al.*, *Costs and Benefits of the European Works Councils Directive* (DTI URN 00/630) (2000), Chapter 4.
83 M. Hall *et al.*, *Implementing Information and Consultation: Early Experience under the ICE Regulations* (2007), esp. p. 52.

(eds.), *Legal Regulation of the Employment Relation* (2000). Others blame hostile governments for unions' decline: see F. Raday, 'The decline of union power – structural inevitability or policy choice?', in J. Conaghan *et al.* (eds.), *Labour Law in an Era of Globalization* (2002), and K.D. Ewing, 'The function of trade unions' (2005) 34 *ILJ* 1. Are unions still relevant today? Are they more under threat from changes in the economy or from the failure of governments to enact supportive legislation? Might there be a connection between governments' attitudes and economic factors? What strategies could unions adopt in order to reverse the decline? Chapters 11 and 12 will give you more ideas on these issues.

Unions have traditionally regarded consultation as an unwelcome development: P. Davies, 'A challenge to single channel' (1994) 23 *ILJ* 272. Unions' attitudes have changed, but there remains an important issue about whether – and if so how – to link new consultation mechanisms with traditional collective bargaining into an integrated system. For a thought-provoking discussion, see P. Davies and C. Kilpatrick, 'UK worker representation after single channel' (2004) 33 *ILJ* 121. Should unions be given a role in consultation mechanisms? Should this extend beyond recognised unions, as Davies and Kilpatrick argue? Where do the rights of those who are not union members fit in to these debates? Are they to blame for not joining a union? Or do they have a right to be heard which the law should uphold?

The neoclassical argument against collective bargaining is best captured in F.A. Hayek, *The Constitution of Liberty* (1960), Chapter 18, or R.A. Posner, *Economic Analysis of Law* (6th edn., 2003), pp. 335–42. But do these accounts oversimplify the aims of trade unions? For some ideas, see A. Flanders, 'Collective bargaining: a theoretical analysis' (1968) 6 *BJIR* 1.

The classic work on the economic benefits of collective bargaining is R.B. Freeman and J.L. Medoff, *What Do Unions Do?* (1984), especially Chapters 6 and 11; and see also S. Deakin and F. Wilkinson, 'The economic case for the Trade Union Freedom Bill', in K.D. Ewing (ed.), *The Right to Strike* (2006). For the government's view, see DTI, *High Performance Workplaces – Informing and Consulting Employees* (2003), Chapter 2. What are the conditions for effective 'partnership' between workers and employees? For some ideas, see J. Knell, *Partnership at Work* (1999) (DTI URN 99/1078). Are these various conditions likely to be realised when firms comply with the recognition procedure or with legislation on consultation? How important are the parties' attitudes? Does it matter what topics they are required to discuss? Do unions help or hinder the creation of effective partnerships? And what is an *effective* partnership from the perspective of the firm? Or from the perspective of the employees? For a critique of partnership from a rights perspective, see T. Novitz and P. Skidmore, *Fairness at Work: A Critical Analysis of the Employment Relations Act 1999 and its Treatment of Collective Rights* (2001), Chapter 1.

11

Trade union membership

In Chapter 10, we looked at what trade unions did: at the relationship between the union and the employer. In this chapter, we will examine the substantial body of law surrounding union membership. The law governs the relationship between the union member and the employer, and between the union member and the union itself. Although union membership has been declining since the 1970s, the issues to be discussed still affect many workers. In 2007, 28 per cent of UK workers were members of a union.[1] Moreover, both pro- and anti-union writers acknowledge that the law on membership plays an important role in encouraging – or discouraging – unionism.

A rights theorist would give this chapter the title 'freedom of association'. This denotes the right to form and join trade unions which features in civil and political rights instruments as well as economic and social ones. Rights theorists agree that the right is highly important, and they also agree on some aspects of its interpretation. For example, the right means that employers may not discriminate against workers on the grounds that they are members of a union, and that workers should be free to join a union if they want to. But other aspects of interpretation are much more controversial. Should employers be obliged to help unions by providing union officials with an office at the workplace? Can an individual be compelled to join a particular union? Can a union force its members to obey its instructions?

Economists tend not to write specifically about union membership. But, as we saw in Chapter 10, they are concerned about the role of unions. The law on union membership may strengthen – or weaken – unions. For example, if a union is allowed to discipline its members for failing to obey an instruction to go on strike, the union will be stronger. Its members will be more likely to comply with its orders, and its strike threats will be more credible as a result. The employer will be more likely to make concessions during collective bargaining. Thus, those economists who are hostile to collective bargaining are likely to be hostile towards any laws which help unions to increase their bargaining power. Those who argue that unions are beneficial will welcome laws which make them stronger.

---

1 BERR, *Trade Union Membership 2007* (2008), p. 3.

Rights perspectives

Freedom of association is a right common to instruments on civil and political rights and to those concerned with economic and social rights. Article 22(1) of the ICCPR is typical:

> Everyone shall have the right to freedom of association with others, including the right to form and join trade unions for the protection of his interests.

The right can be restricted on various grounds, including national security, public safety, public order and the protection of the rights and freedoms of others. Economic and social rights instruments tend to focus solely on freedom of association in unions, but the language used is surprisingly similar. Article 8(1)(a) of the ICESCR protects:

> The right of everyone to form trade unions and join the trade union of his choice, subject only to the rules of the organisation concerned, for the promotion and protection of his economic and social interests. No restrictions may be placed on the exercise of this right other than those prescribed by law and which are necessary in a democratic society in the interests of national security or public order or for the protection of the rights and freedoms of others.

We will look first at the implications of freedom of association for union members' relationships with their employers, before turning to the issues surrounding union members' relationships with their unions.

Freedom of association and employers

Imagine that the state allows workers to create unions, but hostile employers refuse to employ anyone who is a union member. This would render the workers' freedom to associate useless. Therefore, at a minimum, freedom of association implies that employers must be forbidden to discriminate against union members. This is confirmed by Article 1 of ILO Convention 98:

1. Workers shall enjoy adequate protection against acts of anti-union discrimination in respect of their employment.
2. Such protection shall apply more particularly in respect of acts calculated to –
   a) make the employment of a worker subject to the condition that he shall not join a union or shall relinquish trade union membership;
   b) cause the dismissal of or otherwise prejudice a worker by reason of union membership or because of participation in union activities outside working hours or, with the consent of the employer, within working hours.[2]

Thus, union members should be protected against discriminatory dismissal and hiring decisions, and against detrimental treatment during the employment

---

2 ILO Convention 98 on the Right to Organise and Collective Bargaining 1949 (ratified by the UK).

relationship. Paragraph (b) makes clear that workers are protected not just against discrimination on grounds of membership, but also on grounds of participation in union activities. Taking part in a strike is not covered by this provision because strikes, by their very nature, occur during working hours without the employer's consent. But other activities, such as attending meetings or voting in elections, are protected.

From a UK perspective, it is particularly important to note that the ECtHR strongly reinforced the requirement not to discriminate against union members in the *Wilson* decision.[3] This brought about changes in English law and may also have implications for judicial interpretation of the current law because of the HRA 1998. Mr Wilson's employer wanted to derecognise his union, so it promised pay rises to all those employees who were prepared to accept so-called 'personal contracts' not subject to collective bargaining by the union. Mr Wilson refused to give up his collectively bargained contract so he did not get the pay rise. He tried to claim that he had been discriminated against on the grounds of his union membership, but his claim failed in the English courts under the law as it then stood.[4] The ECtHR held that it was an essential part of union membership to have the union make representations on behalf of its members, so Mr Wilson had been discriminated against and the UK had failed in its Article 11 duty to protect his rights. The Court stated that:

> ... it is of the essence of the right to join a trade union for the protection of their interests that employees should be free to instruct or permit the union to make representations to their employer or to take action in support of their interests on their behalf. If workers are prevented from so doing, their freedom to belong to a trade union, for the protection of their interests, becomes illusory.[5]

The Court adopted what is sometimes called a 'dynamic' interpretation in which membership of a union is about more than just carrying a union card. It also includes getting help from the union in dealing with your employer.

Most unions are run by a combination of full-time officials, who are employed by the union itself, and part-time officials. These part-time officials – often known as shop stewards – do an ordinary job for the employer but also devote some of their time to representing the union in the workplace. Part-time officials deal with most of the day-to-day issues that arise in the workplace, with advice and assistance from full-time union officials on more important matters.[6] They are particularly vulnerable to discriminatory treatment by employers. Those employers who are hostile to unions may regard part-time union officials as 'troublemakers' who stir up discontent among ordinary union members. This concern is acknowledged in the international human rights instruments. The

---

3 *Wilson* v. *UK* (2002) 35 EHRR 20.   4 *Associated Newspapers* v. *Wilson* [1995] 2 AC 454.
5 *Wilson* v. *UK*, para. 46.
6 For empirical information about workplace representatives, see B. Kersley *et al.*, *Inside the Workplace* (2006), Chapter 6.

ESC 1996[7] and the ILO's Workers' Representatives Convention[8] both provide that states should take steps to protect representatives from dismissal or other detrimental treatment. These protections apply to worker representatives who are not union members too.

Many rights theorists would argue that while non-discrimination rights are necessary to protect freedom of association, they are by no means sufficient. If unions are to bargain effectively, they need positive legal support too. In Chapter 10, we saw that economic and social rights instruments fit in with this view because they include various explicit obligations on the state to help unions, particularly by promoting collective bargaining. Civil and political rights can be interpreted in this way too, but not everyone agrees – the ECtHR has been quite cautious, for example.

If we accept that employers should be obliged to help unions, this has important implications for the treatment of union members and representatives. Instead of just refraining from discriminating against them, employers could be obliged to support their activities – for example, union members could be given time off work to attend meetings. In fact, the international instruments focus mainly on facilities for union representatives. According to the ILO Workers' Representatives Convention, Article 2:

1. Such facilities in the undertaking shall be afforded to workers' representatives as may be appropriate in order to enable them to carry out their functions promptly and efficiently.
2. In this connection account shall be taken of the characteristics of the industrial relations system of the country and the needs, size and capabilities of the undertaking concerned.
3. The granting of such facilities shall not impair the efficient operation of the undertaking concerned.[9]

Facilities could include use of an office or meeting room and a telephone, or use of a noticeboard in order to communicate with union members. The drafting of the right reflects the need to take account of the interests of the firm and of the different conditions faced by different firms. States have a considerable degree of discretion as to its implementation.

Freedom of association and unions

Three main controversies arise in interpreting the right to freedom of association as between individual union members and their unions. First, can an individual be compelled to join a particular union? Second, to what extent can unions set their own rules on who can and cannot become a member? And third, once a

---

7 ESC 1996, Art. 28. The ESC 1996 has not been ratified by the UK.
8 ILO Convention 135 on Workers' Representatives 1971, Art. 1 (ratified by the UK).
9 Ibid., Art. 2. Art. 28 of the ESC 1996 is similar.

person has joined a union, can he or she be compelled to take part in the union's activities?

Very broadly, rights theorists adopt different views on these questions according to whether they are 'individualists' or 'collectivists'. Individualists believe that individuals are more important than groups.[10] They see freedom of association as a right for the individual to use as he or she chooses. The wishes of the group – to force the individual to join or to take part in a strike, or to exclude the individual from membership – are less important than the individual's choices. They argue that if we do not protect individuals' choices, they will be vulnerable to oppression by powerful groups. Collectivists believe that the interests of the group are more important than those of individuals.[11] They argue that groups are stronger if they are able to exercise some control over individuals: by forcing them to join or to go on strike, for example. And a powerful union will be better placed than a weak one to bargain with the employer. So although individuals may have to sacrifice their short-term choices, they should be better off in the long term.

Can an individual be compelled to join a union?

On a collectivist view, the decision to join a union need not be a matter of individual choice at all. If there is a strong union presence in the workplace, and if the employer agrees, it should be possible to have a 'closed shop' in which having a job is conditional on being a member of the union. The justification for the closed shop is that it preserves the strength of the union.[12] Although the individual may not want to join the union,[13] his or her best interests are ultimately served by doing so, because a strong union will be able to secure better terms and conditions of employment. Moreover, the closed shop helps to deal with the problem of 'free riders': workers who take the benefit of the terms and conditions negotiated by the union (because these are usually extended to all workers by the employer) but do not contribute to the union's work by paying union dues or participating in union action.

On an individualist view, by contrast, the very notion of *freedom* of association suggests that joining a union should be voluntary. Individuals should not be forced to join an organisation when they might not support its industrial relations goals or political views.[14] The union strength argument, although important, is not sufficient to justify so great a violation of individual freedom. If an individual is refused a job or dismissed because he or she is not a union member, the employer's action should be viewed as a form of discrimination which is just

---

10 For an extreme example, see F.A. Hayek, *The Constitution of Liberty* (1960), Chapter 18.
11 Lord Wedderburn, *The Worker and the Law* (3rd edn., 1986), Chapter 1.
12 W.E.J. McCarthy, *The Closed Shop in Britain* (1964), especially Chapter 11.
13 Systems which permit closed shops do sometimes provide exceptions for those with a conscientious objection to joining a union – for example, where their religion does not permit it.
14 C.S. Hanson, S. Jackson and D. Miller, *The Closed Shop* (1982), Chapter 1.

as unwarranted as discrimination against a person who is a union member. The right to join and the right not to join should carry equal weight. And this does not mean that unions will inevitably be weak. If they bring genuine benefits, people will join of their own volition.

The closed shop has caused some difficulty for international human rights instruments. This is because states' practices on this issue vary widely, with some outlawing the closed shop and others positively encouraging it. The clearest stance is that taken by the Universal Declaration, which simply states in Article 20(2) that 'no-one may be compelled to belong to an association'. But this provision was omitted from the ICCPR and ICESCR. Article 5 of the ICESCR has been held to contain a right not to join a union.[15]

ILO Convention 87 is also silent on the question of the closed shop.[16] This has been interpreted to mean that states have a discretion to prohibit or permit the closed shop as they choose.[17] The ILO Committee of Experts has stated that 'systems which prohibit union security practices in order to guarantee the right not to join an organisation, as well as systems which authorise such practices, are compatible with the Convention'.[18] The main qualification to this is that a closed shop will only be permitted where it results from a voluntary agreement between unions and employers. States are not allowed to impose closed shops through legislation.

The position of the ECtHR on this issue is of particular interest for our purposes, since English courts are obliged to uphold Article 11 of the Convention by virtue of the HRA 1998. There is some evidence from the *travaux préparatoires* that the drafters intended to adopt a neutral approach like that taken by the ILO:

> On account of the difficulties raised by the 'closed-shop system' in certain countries, the Conference in this connection considered that it was undesirable to introduce into the Convention a rule under which 'no one may be compelled to belong to an association' which features in [Article 20 para. 2 of] the United Nations Universal Declaration.[19]

However, this stance has not found favour with the ECtHR. In *Sigurjonsson* v. *Iceland*, the Court held that Article 11 protected the right not to join a trade union.[20] In *Sigurjonsson*, the closed shop had been imposed by law (contrary to ILO principles), and the claimant stood to lose his job as a result of his refusal to

---

15 For a review of the limited jurisprudence on Art. 22 of the ICCPR, see K.D. Ewing, 'Freedom of association and trade unions', in D. Harris and S. Joseph (eds.), *The International Covenant on Civil and Political Rights and UK Law* (1995).

16 ILO Convention 87 on Freedom of Association and Protection of the Right to Organise 1948.

17 International Labour Conference, 43rd Session, 1959, Report of the Committee of Experts, Report III (Part IV), para. 36.

18 ILO, *General Survey on Freedom of Association and Collective Bargaining* (1994), para. 100.

19 'Report of 19 June 1950 of the Conference of Senior Officials', in Council of Europe, *Collected Edition of the 'Travaux Préparatoires'* (1975–85), vol. IV, p. 262.

20 *Sigurjonsson* v. *Iceland* (1993) 16 EHRR 462, p. 479.

join. The Court held that his freedom not to associate had been infringed. In the recent case of *Sorensen* v. *Denmark*, the Court went further.[21] In *Sorensen*, the closed shop had been created by management and the union, and the claimants had applied for their jobs knowing that the closed shop was in operation and that they would have to join the union. But the Court still found that Article 11 had been infringed. Although in *Sorensen* the Court said that 'compulsion to join a particular trade union may not always be contrary to the Convention',[22] it also noted that closed shops were 'not an indispensable tool for the effective enjoyment of trade union freedoms'.[23] This suggests that the Court would uphold a closed shop only in exceptional circumstances.

Can unions set their own membership criteria?

In a system of voluntary union membership, should the individual be able to choose which union to join, or should the union be able to set rules on who is eligible to join? In other words, should the individual be able to force a union to admit him or her even if the union does not want to do so? The idea that membership of a particular union is a matter of choice for the individual – an 'extreme individualist' view – can be supported by arguing that unions are not simply private associations but have a quasi-public role. Because of their importance in the workplace, individuals should have a positive right to join the union of their choice, unless the union specialises in representing a particular job category or region to which the worker does not belong. The government should protect this choice by regulating union rules.

The more moderate view is that union membership should be voluntary for unions as well as individuals. 'Freedom' of association implies some element of mutuality, so that individuals should not have a right to associate with people who are unwilling to associate with them.[24] On this view, unions are private associations which should be free to set their own membership rules without government interference. This would enable them to exclude – for example – those who did not undertake to uphold the objectives of the union. Some controls might be imposed on public policy grounds, but these should be kept to a minimum.

International human rights instruments place considerable emphasis on the autonomy of unions and on protecting them from interference by the state. This suggests that it should be up to unions to decide who they want to admit to membership. ILO Convention 87 addresses this issue directly.[25] Article 2 provides that:

> Workers and employers, without distinction whatsoever, shall have the right to establish and, subject only to the rules of the organisation concerned, to join organisations of their own choosing without previous authorisation.

---

21 *Sorensen* v. *Denmark* (2008) 46 EHRR 29.   22 Ibid., para. 54.   23 Ibid., para. 75.
24 See *Cheall* v. *APEX* [1983] ICR 398, p. 405 (per Lord Diplock).
25 ILO Convention 87.

This emphasises individuals' freedom to choose which organisation to join, while at the same time making clear that it is acceptable for unions to restrict membership through their rules. The process of drafting union rules is governed by Article 3, which is also worth setting out in full:

1. Workers' and employers' organisations shall have the right to draw up their constitutions and rules, to elect their representatives in full freedom, to organise their administration and activities and to formulate their programmes.
2. The public authorities shall refrain from any interference which would restrict this right or impede the lawful exercise thereof.

It is therefore inappropriate for the government to interfere in the setting of union membership rules. There is, however, one important limitation on union autonomy. According to Article 8, workers and unions must 'respect the law of the land' in exercising their rights. For example, a government could prohibit union rules which discriminated on grounds of sex, race, disability and so on in the selection of members. A similar approach is adopted in ICESCR, Article 8.

The principle of union autonomy was also upheld by the ECtHR in its interpretation of Article 11 in the *ASLEF* case.[26] In *ASLEF*, the union had expelled a member who was a British National Party (BNP) activist, because it took the view that this was incompatible with the union's political objectives. At that time, English law made it unlawful for a union to exclude or expel a member because of his or her membership of a political party, so ASLEF was forced to compensate the expelled member.[27] The union complained to the ECtHR under Article 11. The government argued that the rules were necessary to protect the right of individuals to join the union of their choice and to engage in political expression. But the Court held that it was more important to protect the union's autonomy to set its own membership rules, particularly since the excluded member did not stand to suffer any particular harm as a result of the exclusion. This decision has led to changes in English law (discussed below) and may have broader implications because the domestic courts will have to take it into account under s. 2 HRA 1998.

Can unions compel their members to participate in union activities?

Once the individual has joined a union, a further set of issues arises concerning his or her freedom to choose whether or not to take part in union activities, such as strike action. On an individualistic interpretation, the individual should be able to decide his or her level of participation in any given situation.[28]

---

26 *ASLEF* v. *UK* (2007) 45 EHRR 34, and see K. Ewing, 'The implications of the *ASLEF* case' (2007) 36 *ILJ* 425.
27 For background, see David Mead, 'To BNP or not to BNP: union expulsion on ground of political activity – a commentary on *ASLEF* v. *Lee*' (2004) 33 *ILJ* 267; J. Hendy and K.D. Ewing, 'Trade unions, human rights and the BNP' (2005) 34 *ILJ* 197.
28 Department of Employment, *Trade Unions and their Members* (1987) (Cm 95), pp. 7–8.

An individual might have conscientious objections to a strike: for example, he or she might think that the employer's offer is reasonable and that the strike is unwarranted. Or the individual might have personal objections: workers are not paid during a strike, so he or she might feel that the economic sacrifice is too great. It might be argued that either or both of these excuses should be permitted, even if union members as a group have voted to support the strike.

On a collectivist view, the union should be able to compel its members to participate in lawful activities which have majority support,[29] by subjecting them to disciplinary action if they refuse.[30] Industrial action is, inevitably, much stronger if it has the full involvement of the workforce. Individuals who participate are much less exposed to victimisation by the employer if they do not have the option of continuing to work. And compulsion would address the problem of free riders, discussed above.

The issue of participation cannot be entirely separated from the issue of membership. On an extreme collectivist view, compulsion would be present at both stages: an individual could be forced to join the union and forced to go on strike. On an extreme individualist view, individual choice would prevail at both stages: the individual could choose whether or not to join and whether or not to go on strike. But middle positions are also possible. One option would be to allow unions to compel individuals to join, but then to give union members the choice of how much to participate in union activities. This solution combines the collectivist advantage of high levels of union membership with the individualist advantage that this would not entail anything more than carrying a union card unless the member chose to play a more active role. But it has the disadvantages of compulsion to join (for individualists) and of creating large numbers of passive members (for collectivists). The other option would be to allow individuals to choose whether or not to join a union, and then to subject them to compulsion once they had done so. The element of compulsion can be justified by arguing that the union member has chosen to join in the knowledge that this might involve participation in industrial action with which he or she does not fully agree. Moreover, it remains open to the individual to resign from the union if he or she feels sufficiently strongly opposed to the union's policies.

The human rights issues raised here are very similar to those considered above, since they raise again the question of the extent to which unions are free to set their own internal rules. Articles 3 and 8 of ILO Convention 87 allow unions complete autonomy in this regard, provided that they respect the law of the land. This suggests that it would be perfectly appropriate for unions to require their members to participate in lawful union activities. It is as yet unclear whether the ECtHR's recognition of union autonomy in the *ASLEF* case would extend to this

---

29 E. McKendrick, 'The rights of trade union members – Part I of the Employment Act 1988' (1988) 17 *ILJ* 141, pp. 147–50.

30 Of course, the individual would always retain the option of resigning from the union (though in a closed-shop situation this would lead to dismissal).

situation, particularly given the possibility that individuals might suffer harm if they are forced to strike. Some instruments, such as the ESC, provide an explicit right to take industrial action, including strike action, but they remain silent as to whether a union can make this compulsory.[31] On one view, a 'right' to strike inherently includes a choice as to whether or not to exercise the right. This would make 'compulsory' industrial action problematic. On another view, the right to strike should not be viewed as a matter of *individual* choice at all. Industrial action only makes sense when it is taken by unions or groups of workers. Thus, once workers as a group have decided in favour of industrial action – by a majority vote – then all members of the group should abide by that vote and should participate in the exercise of the right.

Economics perspectives

As we saw in Chapter 10, economists disagree quite radically about the impact of unions on the labour market. Some take the view that unions are damaging to the economy because they artificially inflate the wages of their members above the market rate.[32] This leads to unemployment and inefficiency in the allocation of labour. Others argue that unions can benefit firms by providing an important channel of communication between management and the workforce.[33] This can be used to improve productivity and to reduce labour turnover. Economists tend not to focus on the detailed law on union membership, but it has important implications for their analysis of the role of unions. This is because it influences unions' bargaining power.

The law on freedom of association as against employers may have an impact on union membership and on union activities. If workers are not protected against discrimination, they are unlikely to join a union. But if the law imposes sanctions on employers who discriminate against trade unionists, workers will feel more confident about joining. The level of protection afforded to union activists is particularly important because of the role they play in organising other workers. If they are not protected, it may be difficult for a union to start organising a workplace or to bargain with the employer. The facilities granted to union officials may also play a role in determining the union's impact. For example, if union officials have time off to prepare for negotiations, they may be better placed to secure concessions from the employer. If they have no facilities, they may prove to be ineffective at bargaining, and ordinary workers may decide that it is not worth supporting the union.

The union's relationship with its members is important in determining its bargaining power as against the employer. The closed shop is the most obvious example of this. If the law allows the closed shop, the union can maintain

31 ESC Art. 6(4), in both the 1961 version (ratified by the UK) and the revised 1996 version.
32 See, for example, R.A. Posner, *Economic Analysis of Law* (6th edn., 2003), pp. 335–42.
33 See, for example, R.B. Freeman and J.L. Medoff, *What Do Unions Do?* (1984).

100 per cent membership in the workplace. This obviously enhances the union's bargaining power because it is difficult for the employer to ignore an organisation that represents all the workers in a particular category, or even in the firm as a whole. Moreover, if the union threatens to call a strike, it is able to threaten severe disruption because of its high level of membership. The employer cannot rely on a few non-members to come to work and keep the business running during the strike. If the law prohibits the closed shop, the union may still be able to achieve 100 per cent membership, but it is less likely to do so. Some people may decide not to join, whether through opposition or indifference. And the smaller the proportion of union members in the workplace, the weaker the union is likely to be.

A similar analysis applies to the issue of whether unions should be free to set their own rules on membership and discipline. If they can set their own rules, they can discipline those who refuse to support the union's activities, particularly strikes. Again, this increases the value of the union's strike threat. If the employer knows that the union can pressurise all its members into taking part, the prospect of a strike may seem more worrying. It could lead to major disruption of the employer's business. This might prompt the employer to make concessions during bargaining. If the union cannot discipline its members, the employer might decide to take the chance that a strike would not be well supported and would not have much impact on the business.

As Chapter 10 explained, unions' bargaining power is affected by a number of factors, including the state of the employer's product market and the overall level of unemployment. But the law can play a role too. Those economists who are hostile to unions would argue that – for example – unions should have no power to discipline their members for refusing to go on strike. This would lessen the power of the unions and limit the economic damage they can cause. Those who identify benefits in trade unionism would obviously support a greater degree of protection – for example, they would argue that unions cannot play a constructive role in negotiations with the employer unless they have time to prepare and have suitable facilities in the workplace.

Freedom of association as against employers

Freedom of association as against employers has been a topic of some controversy in recent years. Although the law appears to protect the right not to be discriminated against, there are various loopholes in the provisions. Economics arguments have played a role in limiting the scope of trade unionists' rights.

Discrimination against trade unionists

Access to employment
TULRCA 1992, s. 137, tackles the employer's first opportunity to discriminate, at the hiring stage, by making it unlawful to refuse to employ a person on the

grounds of his or her union membership.[34] However, the section refers only to membership and not to activities. This omission was intended to allow firms to exclude from the workplace people who had a history of working as union organisers. The government took the view that an employer which did not want to engage in collective bargaining should be able to prevent a union from getting the opportunity to organise the workforce.[35] But rights theorists are strongly critical of this provision, arguing that union activists are particularly vulnerable to discrimination and that instruments such as the ESC and relevant ILO conventions, discussed above, demand that they be given more, not less, protection than ordinary trade unionists. After *Wilson* v. *UK*, it may be possible to persuade a court that Article 11 requires a broad interpretation of the concept of membership to include activities, using the duty to interpret legislation compatibly with Convention rights under s. 3 HRA 1998.[36]

How do employers find out about people's union activities? One possibility is that the employer might have access to a 'blacklist'. This term refers to a list of known union activists, perhaps shared among a group of employers, or drawn up by a firm or individual and sold to employers for profit. In ERA 1999, s. 3, the government took power to make regulations to prohibit the compilation, circulation and use of blacklists.[37] Draft regulations were issued in February 2003.[38] Among other things, the regulations would make it unlawful to refuse a person employment on the grounds that his or her name was included in a blacklist. From a rights perspective, this would go some way towards mitigating the narrowness of s. 137 TULRCA 1992. However, two limitations remain. First, the government argues that there is, at present, no evidence that blacklists are in use. It therefore proposes to refrain from enacting the regulations until there is proof that they are needed.[39] Second, even if the regulations were enacted, s. 137 TULRCA 1992 might still permit an employer to exclude a union activist from the workplace provided that the employer had found out about the person's union activities from a source other than a blacklist.

During employment

Discrimination during employment is addressed by a complex patchwork of provisions. They deal separately with detrimental treatment on grounds of union membership and activities, and inducements to give up union membership or

---

34 The remedy is an award of compensation up to the unfair dismissal maximum: s. 140 TULRCA 1992.

35 See comments by Patrick Nicholls, Parliamentary Under-Secretary of State for Employment, House of Commons, Official Report of Standing Committee D, 8 February 1990, col. 27.

36 See also *Discount Tobacco & Confectionery Ltd* v. *Armitage* [1995] ICR 431, though this was disapproved by the House of Lords in *Associated Newspapers* v. *Wilson*.

37 For discussion, see K.D. Ewing, 'Freedom of association and the Employment Relations Act 1999' (1999) 28 *ILJ* 283.

38 DTI, *Draft Regulations to Prohibit the Blacklisting of Trade Unionists: A Consultation Document* (2003) (URN 03/648).

39 DTI, *Review of the Employment Relations Act 1999* (2003), paras. 3.18–3.20.

collective bargaining. From a rights perspective, a key question is whether this aspect of the legislation – which was substantially amended in the light of the ECtHR's decision in *Wilson* v. *UK* – is fully in conformity with that decision.

Protection against detrimental treatment is contained in s. 146 TULRCA 1992. According to s. 146(1):

> A worker has the right not to be subjected to any detriment as an individual by any act, or any deliberate failure to act, by his employer if the act or failure takes place for the sole or main purpose of –
>
> (a) preventing or deterring him from being or seeking to become a member of an independent trade union, or penalising him for doing so,
> (b) preventing or deterring him from taking part in the activities of an independent trade union at an appropriate time, or penalising him for doing so,
> (ba) preventing or deterring him from making use of trade union services at an appropriate time, or penalising him for doing so, or
> (c) compelling him to be or become a member of any trade union or of a particular trade union or of one of a number of particular trade unions.

A preliminary point to note about this provision is that it protects workers as well as employees. From a rights perspective, this reflects the universal nature of the right to freedom of association set out in Article 11 ECHR and elsewhere. The provision also conforms to the 'dynamic' understanding of union membership set out in *Wilson* v. *UK*, in that it covers taking part in union activities and using union services as well as the mere fact of being a union member. But there are some important limitations.[40] First, the protection for activities only covers activities 'at an appropriate time'. It does not cover strikes because these take place when workers are supposed to be working. Protection for strikers depends on the law on industrial action, which we will consider in Chapter 12. Second, the definition of 'trade union services' for these purposes does not include collective bargaining.[41] This means that an employer is free to subject workers to detrimental treatment because they want their union to bargain on their behalf. This aspect of the legislation has been strongly criticised by rights theorists. Third, the provision only applies where the employer's attack on trade unionism is its 'sole or main purpose'. The government took the view that employers should be free to change their relationship with the workforce, for example, by derecognising a union and moving to a new pay and grading structure, without falling foul of these provisions.[42] It argued that employers needed 'flexibility…to reward and retain key staff, and to shape working patterns to specific or particular circumstances'.[43] So if the employer can prove that its main purpose was to

---

40 For an excellent analysis, see A.L. Bogg, 'Employment Relations Act 2004: another false dawn for collectivism?' (2005) 34 *ILJ* 72.
41 TULRCA 1992, s. 145B(4).
42 DTI, *Review of the Employment Relations Act 1999*, paras. 3.3–3.17.
43 Ibid., para. 3.12.

introduce new employment arrangements, it will not be found to have subjected union members to a detriment, even if a side effect of its actions was to disadvantage them. This aspect of the legislation highlights the role played by economics arguments in the government's thinking.

Two further provisions deal with 'inducements'. This is where (as in *Wilson* itself) the employer offers a bonus or pay rise in order to persuade workers to give up trade unionism. TULRCA 1992, s. 145A, deals with inducements aimed at encouraging workers to give up union membership, activities or services. This provision is similar to s. 146, and the comments made about that provision are also applicable here. TULRCA 1992, s. 145B, deals with inducements to give up collective bargaining. It provides:

(1) A worker who is a member of an independent trade union which is recognised, or seeking to be recognised, by his employer has the right not to have an offer made to him by his employer if –
   (a) acceptance of the offer, together with other workers' acceptance of offers which the employer also makes to them, would have the prohibited result, and
   (b) the employer's sole or main purpose in making the offers is to achieve that result.
(2) The prohibited result is that the workers' terms of employment, or any of those terms, will not (or will no longer) be determined by collective agreement negotiated by or on behalf of the union.

From a rights perspective, one problem with this provision is that it is not clear whether a union which has been derecognised by an employer (which was what was happening in *Wilson* itself) can be regarded as 'recognised, or seeking to be recognised'. However, a court might be able to interpret this phrase broadly. Another concern is that it might be difficult to prove that persuading the workers to give up collective bargaining was the employer's 'sole or main purpose'. But most problematic, as noted above, is that this is the only provision governing collective bargaining, so although workers may be protected against the employer's persuasive tactics, they are not protected against harm. This seems to be the wrong way round.[44]

The remedy for a breach of s. 146 is an award of compensation as the tribunal considers 'just and equitable'.[45] There is no maximum limit in the statute. The remedy for a breach of ss. 145A or 145B is an award of £2,900 (in 2008), though the worker may also be able to keep any inducement paid to him or her by the employer.[46] Commentators from a rights perspective have criticised these remedies, arguing in particular that it would be preferable to entrust enforcement to unions, because individuals may be reluctant to bring claims for fear of further intimidation by the employer. Indeed, it is arguable that since the ECtHR found

---

44 Bogg, 'Employment Relations Act 2004', p. 74.   45 TULRCA 1992, s. 149.
46 Ibid., s. 145E.

a violation of the union's rights in *Wilson*, English law is not in line with the Court's decision in the absence of a remedy for unions.[47]

We have seen that rights theorists have found much to criticise in these provisions, despite the fact that they are intended to give effect to *Wilson* v. *UK*. Bogg describes the changes as 'grudging and minimalist'.[48] Under the HRA 1998, it would be possible for a claimant to rely on *Wilson* v. *UK* in order to argue for a compatible interpretation of the statutory provisions, or for a declaration that they are incompatible with Article 11 ECHR.[49] However, it remains to be seen how the courts would respond to such arguments.

Dismissal

English law also addresses the possibility of discrimination when an employee is dismissed (s. 152 TULRCA 1992) or selected for redundancy (s. 153 TULRCA 1992). In line with the general law on unfair dismissal and redundancy, only employees – not workers – are eligible for this protection. However, a worker would be able to argue that the termination of his or her contract was a detriment within s. 146 TULRCA 1992. The prohibited grounds of discrimination under ss. 152 and 153 are union membership, taking part in the activities of an independent trade union 'at an appropriate time', making use of union services 'at an appropriate time' and refusing to accept an inducement in breach of ss. 145A or 145B.

These provisions offer advantages over ordinary unfair dismissal claims for those able to invoke them. First, employees are eligible to claim from the moment they start work. They do not have to complete a year of qualifying service. Second, a dismissal on union grounds is automatically unfair. Third, the remedies are slightly enhanced. Under s. 161 TULRCA, the employee may apply for interim relief. With the employer's consent, the employee may be re-employed pending the hearing of the claim. If the employer does not consent, the tribunal may make an order for the continuation of the contract of employment, which means that the employee will at least continue to get paid until the hearing. Under s. 156 TULRCA 1992, if the claim is successful, the employee is entitled to a minimum basic award, currently set at £4,400 (2008), regardless of his or her length of service. In contrast to claims for unfair dismissal on grounds of sex or race discrimination, however, union discrimination claims remain subject to the current upper limit of £63,000 on the compensatory award.

Duties to support union activities

Perhaps surprisingly, the rights perspective is more in evidence when we consider the law on employers' duties to support union activities. Employers are obliged to

---

47 See Joint Committee on Human Rights Thirteenth Report (Session 2003–4), Scrutiny of Bills: Sixth Progress Report (HL 102/HC 640), paras. 2.18–2.19.
48 Bogg, 'Employment Relations Act 2004', p. 73.   49 HRA 1998, ss. 3 and 4.

provide union members and officials with time off for union activities, provided that certain conditions are met. And as we saw in Chapter 10, employers may be obliged to bargain with unions under the statutory recognition procedure.

Under s. 168 TULRCA 1992, employees (not workers) who are union representatives are entitled to time off for negotiations with the employer about matters within the statutory definition of 'collective bargaining', for performing functions in relation to employees as agreed with the employer (such as informing them of the outcome of negotiations), and for training in connection with these roles. The representatives must be paid during these periods. Under s. 170, employees (not workers) who are union members are entitled to time off to take part in union activities (such as voting on the outcome of negotiations) or to act as union representatives. This time off need not be paid.

In both cases, the entitlement is to 'reasonable' time off with the employer's permission. This makes good economic sense. It allows the employer to control when and for how long union representatives and members can take time off, in the light of the needs of the business. It would be difficult to give effect to a more precise right (such as a right to a fixed amount of time off per week) given that negotiations may vary considerably in duration and complexity. However, the current right can be frustrated by a recalcitrant employer. If time off is refused, the affected representative or member must take a case to the employment tribunal to obtain a declaration or an award of compensation. This remedy is cumbersome, and although it may act as a deterrent, it does not help employees to secure time off when they need it.

The most significant limitation on these rights is that they are only available to members and officials of *recognised* trade unions. This means that the employer is only obliged to provide time off once it has agreed to engage in collective bargaining with the relevant union. From a new institutionalist perspective, there is much to be said for providing time off in this situation, since the bargaining process is likely to operate more smoothly if union representatives are well-prepared and union members well-informed. But these rights would also be of benefit to unrecognised unions which were seeking to recruit new members or to persuade the employer to negotiate with them.[50]

The ILO standards, quoted above, also refer to the provision of 'facilities' for union representatives. This is not addressed in TULRCA 1992 itself, but it is discussed in the ACAS Code of Practice issued under the Act.[51] Paragraph 38 suggests that employers should 'consider' providing meeting rooms, noticeboards, use of a telephone and even office space, taking into account the firm's resources and the amount of work carried out by union officials. These facilities may be just as important as the provision of time off to the ability of union officials to

---

50 If an unrecognised union invokes the statutory recognition procedure, it has a right of access to the workers at the balloting stage: TULRCA 1992, Schedule A1, para. 26.

51 ACAS Code of Practice 3, *Time Off for Trade Union Duties and Activities* (2003), issued under TULRCA 1992, s. 201. At the time of writing (2008), the government is conducting a review of this issue.

represent workers effectively. Rights theorists might prefer to see them enshrined in a precise legal right, but such a right would be difficult to draft given the need to take account of employers' particular circumstances.

To conclude, it can be seen that English law presents a mixed picture in terms of freedom of association against employers. Some aspects of the law are strongly rights-based, such as the duties on employers to facilitate union activities. The rules on discrimination against employees and workers on union grounds also reflect the rights perspective, but (despite recent reforms) these rules still have a number of loopholes. An important question to consider is whether what seems like a loophole from the rights perspective can be justified on some other basis – for example, that it provides a degree of flexibility for employers, as the government itself has argued.

Freedom of association between workers and trade unions

English law provides union members with a number of rights against their unions. It reflects the 'individualistic' view of freedom of association, discussed above, which emphasises individual choice over the needs of the group. The law is likely to be welcomed by those economists who are hostile to unions, because it does much to limit their powers. But it is heavily criticised by rights theorists in the collectivist tradition. They argue that individual rights weaken unions and harm individuals' interests in the long term.

Compulsory trade union membership

English law does not permit employers and unions to enforce the closed shop. It is no longer possible to insist that an individual be a member of a particular union in order to work for a particular firm. To understand how the law achieves this result, you need to understand how a closed shop is enforced. Although the closed shop involves compulsory union membership, it is enforced by the *employer*, acting at the union's request. In a pre-entry closed shop, the employer agrees to consider only those applicants who are already members of the union. In a post-entry closed shop, non-union candidates may apply for jobs, but must join the union if they are successful. The employer undertakes to dismiss any who refuse to join.

We saw above that the law forbids any discrimination against union members in recruitment, during the life of the contract and at dismissal.[52] These protections are symmetrical. In other words, they apply not only to union members but also to those who are not members. This means that it is unlawful for the employer to refuse to employ or to dismiss someone on the grounds that he or she is *not* a member of a union. As a result, the employer would be acting unlawfully if it tried to enforce the closed shop.

---

52 TULRCA 1992, ss. 137, 146 and 152–153.

From a neoclassical economics perspective, these provisions are to be welcomed. They limit unions' ability to get into a powerful position in the workplace and to extract significant rents from employers as a consequence. From a collectivist rights perspective, they are harmful for precisely the same reasons. From an individualistic rights perspective, they play an important role in protecting individuals' choice of whether or not to join a union. Theorists in this tradition receive the most support from international human rights instruments.

Trade union rules on membership

The human rights instruments discussed above set out relatively clearly the principle that unions should have the freedom to set their own membership rules. English law takes a much more individualistic approach. TULRCA 1992 controls unions' decisions on membership applications by setting out lists of permitted and prohibited criteria for membership.[53] Section 174 lists the four permitted grounds of exclusion: failure to satisfy an 'enforceable membership requirement'; where the union is regional, failure to work in the relevant part of the UK; where the union is employer-specific, failure to work for that employer; and conduct. Membership requirements are deemed enforceable under s. 174(3) if they relate to the occupation or qualifications of the applicant, thus allowing unions to focus on representing workers with specific skills.

The fourth permitted ground of exclusion, 'conduct', appears to give unions a wide discretion to reject applicants on the basis of union rules, but in fact this is not the case. By virtue of s. 174(4), unions are not allowed to consider certain types of 'conduct'. One is that the applicant is or has been a member of another union. This was intended as an attack on the Bridlington Principles, an agreement among TUC-affiliated unions that they would not 'poach' each other's members. Although the Principles still exist, they cannot be enforced by requiring unions to exclude 'poached' members. Another type of conduct that cannot be taken into account is any 'conduct' that would amount to 'unjustifiable discipline' within s. 65 TULRCA 1992. This provision is discussed in more detail below, but it includes bringing proceedings against the union or refusing to take part in industrial action. Thus, if someone who had been a member of the union in the past sought to join again, he or she could not be excluded because of these activities during the previous period of membership.

Most controversially, s. 174(4) provided (from 1993 onwards) that unions could not exclude members because of their membership of a political party. This prevented unions from requiring applicants to join a party they favoured or to resign from a party that was hostile to the union. In 2004, the government amended this provision to allow unions to exclude individuals for their political

---

53 At common law, the courts intervened only in exceptional circumstances. Compare *Faramus* v. *Film Artistes Association* [1964] AC 925, with *Nagle* v. *Feilden* [1966] 2 QB 633.

activities, but not solely for their membership of a political party.[54] However, as we saw above, the legislation was found to be in breach of Article 11 ECHR in the *ASLEF* case. The ECtHR stated that there was a clash between the freedom of expression and association rights of the individual and the freedom of association rights of the union. But it held that the clash should be resolved in favour of the union, given the importance of union autonomy. The Employment Act 2008, s. 19, amends s. 174 so that a union can now exclude or expel an individual for membership of a political party where certain conditions are met.[55] These are that the membership is contrary to a rule or readily ascertainable objective of the union, that the union follows some basic natural justice requirements, and that the affected individual does not 'lose his livelihood or suffer other exceptional hardship' as a result of the exclusion or expulsion. This will leave unions free to exercise their own discretion in this regard.

On the one hand, rights theorists in the collectivist tradition argue that this reform does not go far enough.[56] Although the *ASLEF* case only dealt with a union member's political affiliations, the principle of autonomy it enunciated could be regarded as more generally applicable. On this view, unions should have complete discretion over membership decisions, subject to basic controls such as anti-discrimination law. Further reforms are required to bring the law into line with the ECHR and with other international instruments such as the ESC.[57] Alternatively, the courts could be asked to interpret the legislation in line with *ASLEF* under s. 3 HRA 1998, or even to declare it incompatible under s. 4. On the other hand, from a more individualistic perspective, the decision is problematic because it allows the union to force individuals to choose between their political preferences and their right to be represented at work.[58] There are some advantages to being a member of the recognised union in the workplace, such as the ability to vote on and influence the outcomes of collective bargaining, but the loss of these advantages is not likely to amount to 'exceptional hardship' within the 2008 amendments.

An individual who feels that he or she has been wrongly excluded from the union can apply to the employment tribunal for a declaration and compensation.[59] The award is such as the tribunal considers 'just and equitable', up to a maximum (in 2008) of £72,900. Compensation may be awarded whether or not the individual is subsequently admitted to the union, but if the individual is not admitted, he or she must usually be given at least a minimum award of £6,900. These remedies (which are in some respects stronger than those for unfair

---

54 Employment Relations Act 2004, s. 33.
55 See DTI, *ECHR Judgment in* ASLEF *v. UK Case – Implications for Trade Union Law* (2007).
56 See, for example, Ewing, 'The implications of the *ASLEF* case'.
57 ESC Committee, *Conclusions XIII-3* (1996), pp. 107–11.
58 See Joint Committee on Human Rights (Session 2007–8), Seventeenth Report: Legislative Scrutiny (HL 95/HC 501), paras. 1.1–1.31.
59 TULRCA 1992, s. 176.

dismissal) reinforce the idea that it is for individuals to choose their union, rather than for unions to choose their members.

Union discipline and expulsion

So far, we have seen that the law is strongly individualistic: effectively outlawing the closed shop and giving applicants for union membership what amounts to a right to join the union of their choice. At this point, it might be expected that the law would switch to a collectivist mode, thereby putting in place one of the compromise positions set out above. Because individuals have made a free choice to join, they should obey the lawful orders of the union. However, English law remains strongly individualistic. Initially, protection for union members developed at common law through the courts' construction of the contract of membership. Now, the grounds on which unions can discipline or expel their members are governed by TULRCA 1992.

At common law, the courts were heavily influenced by the consequences of union disciplinary action for members. In particular, if the union decided to expel a member in a closed-shop situation, that member would lose his or her job.[60] The courts therefore held that they had jurisdiction to construe the membership contract between the individual and the union. Various techniques were adopted which ensured that the court's interpretation would protect the individual.[61] Perhaps the least controversial technique was to imply the rules of natural justice into the contract of membership. This served to ensure that members could not be disciplined or dismissed without proper notice of the charges against them and an opportunity to state their case. An example of this is *Edwards* v. *SOGAT*.[62] The union's rules provided that membership would terminate automatically if any member fell into arrears of more than six weeks with his or her subscriptions. The Court of Appeal held that this was a breach of natural justice, since it did not give the member the opportunity of putting forward any arguments as to why he or she should not be expelled.

More controversially, the courts have intervened in unions' substantive disciplinary decisions. Union rules commonly contain a general offence of 'unfitness to be a member', in addition to more specific offences such as falling behind with subscriptions. The general offence is often framed in a subjective manner: it is a matter of opinion for the relevant union committee. Such an offence was before the court in *Esterman* v. *NALGO*.[63] The applicable union rule provided for the expulsion of a member who was 'guilty of conduct which, in the opinion of the executive committee, renders him unfit for membership'. Instead of relying on the committee's opinion, the court looked at whether or not there was sufficient evidence to support the committee's findings. In other words, the court

---

60 See *Lee* v. *Showmen's Guild* [1952] 2 QB 329, p. 343 (per Denning LJ).
61 For a detailed discussion, see P. Elias and K. Ewing, *Trade Union Democracy: Members' Rights and the Law* (1987), Chapter 6.
62 *Edwards* v. *SOGAT* [1971] Ch 354.   63 *Esterman* v. *NALGO* [1974] ICR 625.

construed the apparently subjective term objectively. Ms Esterman had refused to obey a union order because she doubted whether the union had power to issue it. The court held that this did not render her unfit to be a member of the union.

Nowadays, union discipline and expulsion is extensively regulated by statute.[64] Expulsion from a union is dealt with under s. 174 TULRCA 1992, in the same way that exclusion, discussed above, is addressed. Thus, a member can be expelled if he or she ceases to work in the relevant trade or in the relevant part of the UK, but cannot be expelled for conduct amounting to 'unjustifiable discipline' under s. 65.

Where the penalty imposed on the individual is a lesser one than expulsion, such as being made to pay a fine or being denied access to union facilities, the case is governed by s. 64 TULRCA 1992, which grants union members a right not to be unjustifiably disciplined. This last phrase is defined in s. 65, which thus serves a threefold role of regulating exclusion, expulsion and discipline of union members. Some of the requirements in s. 65 are relatively straightforward. For example, s. 65(2)(j) protects a member who asserts his or her statutory rights against the union. This is analogous to provisions protecting employees from being victimised by their employers for bringing legal proceedings against them. Others illustrate the individualistic tenor of this area of the law. Under s. 65(2)(a), a member cannot be disciplined for 'failing to participate in or support a strike or other industrial action (whether by members of the union or by others), or indicating opposition to or a lack of support for such action'.

The ILO has condemned the UK for the 'unjustifiable discipline' provisions in particular. In 2005, the Committee of Experts reiterated its long-held view that:

> unions should have the right to draw up their rules without interference from public authorities and so to determine whether or not it should be possible to discipline members who refuse to comply with democratic decisions to take industrial action.[65]

In 1998, the Committee justified its view by pointing out that individuals in the UK had a free choice as to whether or not to join a union.[66] This meant that they could take into account any element of compulsion contained in union rules when making their decision about membership. Again, it could be argued that the general principle of union autonomy enunciated by the ECtHR in the *ASLEF* case is applicable here.[67]

---

64 Some claimants might still invoke the common law – for example, in the event of a breach of natural justice. But the courts might be less sympathetic now that the closed shop is no longer lawful and the consequences of expulsion are less serious.

65 ILO Committee of Experts on the Application of Conventions and Recommendations, 76th Session, 2005, Observation (on UK and Convention No. 87).

66 ILO Committee of Experts on the Application of Conventions and Recommendations, 69th Session, 1998, Observation (on UK and Convention No. 87).

67 Ewing, 'The implications of the *ASLEF* case'.

Collectivists would argue that individuals' long-term interests are best served by strong unions which can make credible strike threats to employers. But individualists would point to the unfairness of forcing the individual to choose between striking and resigning from the union, particularly when he or she might have a good reason for not wanting to strike, such as not being able to manage without pay. Neoclassicists would agree, but on different grounds: strong unions are bad for the economy, firms and individual workers, so the law should discourage them.

Further reading

For detailed textbook accounts of this topic, see S. Deakin and G. Morris, *Labour Law* (4th edn., 2005), Chapters 8 and 10, or H. Collins, K.D. Ewing and A. McColgan, *Labour Law: Text and Materials* (2nd edn., 2005), Chapters 7 and 8.

Much of the modern law was enacted during the 1980s by a government that was hostile to unions. It used both the arguments of neoclassical economics and the individualistic rights approach. For an excellent account of the development of the law, see P. Davies and M. Freedland, *Labour Legislation and Public Policy* (1993), Chapter 9. Do you think that individuals are vulnerable to oppression by unions? Was the government's concern with individual rights 'genuine', or did it serve to conceal other motives?

New institutionalist economists focus on the advantages of unions. It was suggested in this chapter that they would support some basic aspects of freedom of association, such as a duty on employers not to discriminate. But how strong do unions need to be in order to have a positive impact in the workplace? For example, would a closed shop have more impact on productivity than a mere union presence? Or would a union which could choose and discipline its members in accordance with its own rules have more influence over labour turnover than one which could not? You may find it helpful to revisit R.B. Freeman and J.L. Medoff, *What Do Unions Do?* (1984), when thinking about these questions.

For a detailed account and critique of recent developments from a (collectivist) rights perspective, see A.L. Bogg, 'Employment Relations Act 2004: another false dawn for collectivism?' (2005) 34 *ILJ* 72, pp. 72–5; and K.D. Ewing, 'The implications of *Wilson and Palmer*' (2003) 32 *ILJ* 1, and 'The implications of the *ASLEF* case' (2007) 36 *ILJ* 425. What rights should union members have against their employers? Why? Are there any costs associated with these rights? What rights, if any, should union members have against their union? Why should individuals' interests be sacrificed for the good of the group? Why should unions be given autonomy to set their own rules? When thinking about union autonomy, you may like to consider the law on union elections and political funds (discussed in the textbooks cited above, and excluded from this chapter on grounds of space), and industrial action ballots (to be considered in Chapter 12).

12

Industrial action

Strikes are not very common in the UK. The 'strike rate' is defined by statisticians as the number of working days lost through strike action per 1,000 employees. The most recent figure for the UK is for 2007, in which 38 working days per 1,000 employees were lost.[1] In general, the strike rate for the UK has been falling since the late 1980s, from a high point of 172 in 1989 to a low point of 6 in 2005, though there are occasional 'blips': two large public sector disputes in 2002 took the average up to 51. It is not yet clear whether the figure of 38 for 2007 is a similar blip, or the start of a new upward trend. Further proof that the UK's strike rate has declined to a very low level is provided by the WERS.[2] This study collects data by asking managers whether or not any industrial action has taken place in their workplace during the last year. In 1980, a quarter of workplaces reported some kind of industrial action (including non-strike action). In 1990, the figure had fallen to 13 per cent, and by 2004 it was just 3 per cent. The figures for strike action were 11 per cent in 1990, falling to 2 per cent in 2004. Nevertheless, industrial action is probably the most controversial topic in labour law. Most people have experienced the disruption industrial action can cause: perhaps your travel plans have been affected by a strike of train drivers or air traffic controllers, for example. And it provokes very different reactions from rights theorists and economists.

It is clear that industrial action does not bring any economic benefits in itself. A strike damages the employer's business and may have substantial effects on other firms, consumers and the public. However, as we shall see, industrial action plays an important role in collective bargaining. Economists' views on strikes are therefore closely linked to their views on collective bargaining. Those who see collective bargaining as damaging to firms because it enables workers to extract excessive pay rises are opposed to industrial action. Those who see collective bargaining as beneficial are more tolerant of industrial action.

Rights theorists take a very different starting point. They view industrial action either as a fundamental human right or at least as a very important labour right.

---

1 See D. Hale, 'Labour disputes in 2007' (2008) 2 *Economic and Labour Market Review* 18.
2 M. Cully *et al.*, *Britain at Work* (1999), p. 245; B. Kersley *et al.*, *Inside the Workplace* (2006), pp. 208–9.

Those who take the fundamental human rights standpoint link the right to strike to civil and political rights such as the right not to be subjected to forced labour. Those who take the labour rights standpoint focus on the role of strike action in a system of collective bargaining. They see the right to strike as an essential means of equalising the bargaining power of workers as against employers.

These competing views present legislators with a difficult set of choices. Most legal systems opt for some kind of middle position in which strikes are lawful provided that certain conditions are met. These conditions might relate to the subject matter or purpose of the strike, or to the procedure to be followed by the union before organising the strike, for example. Middle positions are easier to justify than extreme ones – they protect a version of the right to strike while minimising the disruption to the economy – but they can be quite difficult to operate in practice. Someone has to decide whether or not the conditions for the legality of the strike have been met in any particular case – a job which usually falls to the courts. And it may be difficult for the courts to perform so politically controversial a task.

Rights perspectives

The right to strike is expressly granted in many economic and social rights instruments. The ICESCR provides, in Article 8(1)(d), that states should protect 'the right to strike, provided that it is exercised in conformity with the laws of the particular country'. Some instruments link the right quite clearly with collective bargaining. Article 6 of the ESC includes an obligation on states to protect the right to strike alongside the obligation to promote collective bargaining. The EU Charter makes a similar link. Article 28 provides that:

> Workers and employers, or their respective organisations, have, in accordance with Community law and national laws and practices, the right to negotiate and conclude collective agreements at the appropriate levels and, in cases of conflicts of interest, to take collective action to defend their interests, including strike action.

Strikes play an important role in collective bargaining because they increase the bargaining power of workers as against their employer. Workers and their representatives need to have some way of persuading the employer to listen to their demands. If they have a right to strike, they are able to threaten the employer with disruption to the business. This should at least make the employer take notice, even if it does not make the employer agree to their demands: the employer might decide to take the chance that the workers will not strike or that the strike will not be very disruptive. In the absence of a right to strike, the employer can simply refuse to hear the workers without even having to make these calculations.

However, if we choose to justify the right to strike in terms of its role in collective bargaining, this has implications for the *scope* of the right. First, a legitimate strike would have to be related to the issues that were the subject of collective bargaining. Thus, if the union and the employer were bargaining about pay, a strike could take place if the workers rejected the employer's final offer in the negotiations. But a strike could not be used as a means of protesting about government policy in general. ILO jurisprudence does allow some political strikes, but only where they are about government policy on the economic and social interests of workers (the minimum wage rate, for example).[3] Second, if the right to strike is linked to collective bargaining, it should be regarded as a collective rather than an individual right. Collective bargaining by its very definition involves bargaining by a union or group of workers rather than by an individual.

Some rights theorists have sought alternative justifications for the right to strike which treat it as a civil and political right rather than a socio-economic one. Often, this is because they dislike the limitations which attach to the right to strike when it is viewed as an aspect of collective bargaining. Moreover, as we saw in Chapter 3, civil and political rights tend to attract higher levels of support and more effective legal protection than do economic and social rights. A preliminary difficulty, however, is that civil and political rights instruments simply do not mention the right to strike. Commentators have therefore tried to include the right to strike in at least three of the well-established civil and political rights: freedom of association, freedom from forced labour and freedom of expression. We will examine each in turn.

Perhaps rather surprisingly, freedom of association is the underlying basis of the right to strike in ILO jurisprudence. For political reasons, the ILO has never reached agreement on a convention containing an express right to strike.[4] However, for some years now, the right has been accepted as an essential part of the right to freedom of association protected by Conventions 87 and 98. The Freedom of Association Committee has stated that:

> Freedom of association implies not only the right of workers and employers to form freely organizations of their own choosing, but also the right for the organizations themselves to pursue lawful activities for the defence of their occupational interests.[5]

The right to strike is the main weapon in trade unions' efforts to defend their members' interests. But theorists have been more interested in including the right to strike in the freedom of association rights contained in the major civil and political rights instruments, such as the ECHR and ICCPR. Article 11 of the ECHR provides that:

> Everyone has the right ... to freedom of association with others, including the right to form and to join trade unions for the protection of his interests.

3 ILO, *Digest of Decisions and Principles of the Freedom of Association Committee* (5th edn., 2006), para. 529.
4 See T. Novitz, *International and European Protection of the Right to Strike* (2003), Chapter 5.
5 ILO, *Digest of Decisions*, para. 495.

Article 22 of the ICCPR is framed in similar terms. The argument that this right should be understood as including a right to strike relies on the phrase 'for the protection of his interests'.[6] It is argued that workers join trade unions not just because they want to be a member of an organisation, but because they want the benefit of collective bargaining by that organisation on their behalf, to protect their interests. And if a link can be made from freedom of association to collective bargaining, it is relatively easy to make the further link to a right to strike, by arguing that collective bargaining does not make sense without a right to strike. In fact, this set of arguments is very similar to the economic and social rights approach of linking the right to strike to the right to engage in collective bargaining. As a result, it suffers from the same limitations: strikes must relate to the subject matter of bargaining, and must be collective rather than individual. However, a right to strike protected through civil and political rights instruments might attain a higher level of legal protection.

Some attempts have been made to persuade the ECtHR to include a right to strike in Article 11. This jurisprudence is of particular interest because it could be relied on in the English courts under the HRA 1998. In the *National Union of Belgian Police* case, the ECtHR appeared to take the view that governments were under some obligation to provide rights for trade unions as part of their protection of freedom of association: 'what the Convention requires is that under national law trade unions should be enabled … to strive for the protection of their members' interests'.[7] However, in *Schmidt and Dahlströhm* v. *Sweden*, the Court was unenthusiastic about the right to strike.[8] It emphasised the discretion states had in promoting trade union action, and held that while the 'right to strike represents without any doubt one of the most important of these means … there are others'.[9] Similarly, in *Wilson* v. *UK*, the Court appeared to treat the right to strike and the right of a trade union to be recognised by the employer as *alternative* ways in which a state could choose to assist trade unions.[10] Thus, a state which protected the right to strike could rely on this as a partial fulfilment of its Article 11 obligations, but a state which chose not to protect the right to strike could comply with Article 11 in some other way. However, *UNISON* v. *UK* does offer some hope.[11] In this case, the union had not been able to strike, and the ECtHR held that the state had to justify this under Article 11(2), even though Article 11(1) does not require protection of the right to strike. Ewing suggests that although the right to strike remains formally unprotected, it now has a 'twilight status' under the Convention.[12]

---

6 See, for example, J. Hendy, 'The Human Rights Act, Article 11, and the right to strike' (1998) 5 *EHRLR* 582.
7 *National Union of Belgian Police* v. *Belgium* (1979–80) 1 EHRR 578, p. 591.
8 *Schmidt and Dahlströhm* v. *Sweden* (1979–80) 1 EHRR 637.
9 Ibid., p. 644.   10 *Wilson* v. *UK* (2002) 35 EHRR 20.   11 *UNISON* v. *UK* [2002] IRLR 497.
12 K.D. Ewing, 'The implications of *Wilson and Palmer*' (2003) 32 *ILJ* 1, p. 18.

Some commentators have tried to advance the right to strike using civil and political rights other than freedom of association. One possibility is the right to be free from forced labour.[13] This right has a particularly high level of support. The connection with industrial action is that if a country operates a strike ban, then it is in effect forcing workers to do their jobs. However, the argument suffers from a number of flaws. First, even if a strike ban was in operation, workers could still resign their jobs. This makes it difficult to claim that they are being forced to work. Second, workers usually expect a strike to be a temporary measure, after which they will return to work. Even if the right to be free from forced labour justifies allowing the workers to stop work, it is difficult to see how it can be used to allow them to return to work when they choose.[14]

Finally, some writers use freedom of expression as the basis of the right to strike.[15] Freedom of expression does not just protect speech. It also protects various 'acts' which are designed to express ideas, such as works of art. Strikes could be viewed as a 'speech act', in which workers are trying to convey their demands to the employer and to the wider public. This justification is particularly relevant to picketing: when striking workers stand outside the workplace in order to protest about the employer's behaviour and to make sure that others (customers, non-striking employees and so on) are aware of the strike and its aims. However, the main difficulty with this right is that – like most human rights – it is qualified. This means that the right can be limited where it causes significant harm to others. Strikes obviously cause significant harm to the employer and may have damaging effects on customers and the wider public. If a strike was seen as an aspect of freedom of expression, it would have to be justified by comparison with other modes of *expressing* workers' demands. The problem is that other types of expression – such as leaflets or public meetings – are much less harmful. This makes it difficult to justify industrial action in this way.

The discussion so far has shown that the most plausible justification for strike action is that it helps to equalise the bargaining power of workers and the employer during collective bargaining. A right to strike is usually expressly mentioned in economic and social rights instruments in the context of the state's obligation to support collective bargaining. It may also be implied into civil and political rights instruments, *if* freedom of association is interpreted so as to include rights for trade unions.

Whichever method is adopted, however, it is important to remember that the right to strike is likely to be qualified. This means that states will be able to restrict the right in order to protect other important interests. The ICESCR and the EU Charter of Fundamental Rights both provide that the right to strike is to be exercised in accordance with national laws. This gives each state a substantial

13 R. Ben-Israel, *International Labour Standards: The Case of Freedom to Strike* (1988), pp. 24–5.
14 For a counter-argument, see ibid., p. 25.
15 For example, S. Kupferberg, 'Political strikes, labor law and democratic rights' (1985) 71 *Virginia Law Review* 685.

degree of discretion to place limits on the right. The ILO's Freedom of Association Committee has held that:

> The conditions that have to be fulfilled under the law in order to render a strike lawful should be reasonable and in any event not such as to place a substantial limitation on the means of action open to trade union organizations.[16]

Article 11 of the ECHR (assuming now that it could include a right to strike) is qualified in the following terms:

> No restrictions shall be placed on the exercise of these rights other than such as are prescribed by law and are necessary in a democratic society in the interests of national security or public safety, for the prevention of disorder or crime, for the protection of health or morals or for the protection of the rights and freedoms of others. This article shall not prevent the imposition of lawful restrictions on the exercise of these rights by members of the armed forces, of the police or of the administration of the state.

Put very broadly, there are three main justifications for limiting the right to strike. First, strikes may be restricted to prevent 'disorder or crime'. Picketing and other demonstrations organised during a strike may involve the commission of criminal offences if violence or serious disruption ensues. Second, certain groups of workers may be barred from taking industrial action. The practice varies from country to country, but may include the police, army, prison officers, firefighters and so on.[17] The justification is that strikes by these workers could cause serious damage to the safety of the public or the security of the state. It is usual for the state to provide some mechanism for the arbitration of pay claims so that workers are not disadvantaged by the strike ban. Third, there is the need to protect the 'rights and freedoms of others'. Novitz identifies a number of groups who may be harmed by a strike, including employers, other workers, consumers and the public at large.[18] The protection of these groups will be explored more fully in our discussion of the economic impact of strikes, below. Any limitations on the right to strike must be carefully scrutinised in order to ascertain whether they fit within one of these justifications and whether they are proportionate to the goal being pursued.

Economics perspectives

It is virtually impossible to identify any economic benefits flowing directly from industrial action. Most obviously, strikes cause harm to the employer. Depending on the extent of the strike, the employer's ability to trade may be reduced or removed altogether. The business may be damaged over the longer term, as

16 ILO, *Digest of Decisions*, para. 547.   17 For ILO jurisprudence, see ibid., paras. 572–603.
18 Novitz, *Protection of the Right to Strike*, Chapter 4.

previously loyal customers discover other suppliers and do not return once the strike is over. Strikes may harm workers too: if the employer's business is damaged, some may have to be laid off. Jobs may also be lost in firms which supply to or buy from the affected employer. If the strike is successful, the ensuing rise in wages may lead to redundancies to enable the employer to keep costs down, and may make it more difficult for the unemployed to find work. Strikes may injure consumers where they are unable to obtain the goods or services they want. Finally, strikes may damage the economy as a whole by reducing productivity.

Rights theorists have argued that some of these claims may be exaggerated.[19] A rational trade union would not conduct a strike that would lead to substantial job losses. This would harm its members much more than missing out on a pay rise. Unions must therefore take into account the need to safeguard jobs as well as the need to improve workers' terms and conditions when formulating their demands. Similarly, while it is important to balance the right to strike against the interests of consumers, much of what consumers will suffer during a strike is inconvenience rather than harm. A one-day train strike might be a nuisance, but it is unlikely to be overwhelmingly damaging. The only strikes which have a real potential for causing harm are those in essential services, such as the police or the fire brigade. Most rights theorists would accept the need to limit strikes by these workers.

Nevertheless, the role that strikes play in collective bargaining *depends* on the fact that they cause harm to the employer. When a union bargains with an employer, it does not want to take strike action. Instead, it wants to persuade the employer to agree to its demands by threatening to take strike action. Let us imagine a simple negotiation in which the union asks for a 4 per cent pay rise and the employer responds by saying that it can only afford 2 per cent. Each side has to calculate what to do next.[20] The employer must calculate the union's bargaining power. It can do this by comparing the cost of disagreeing with the union's demands to the cost of agreeing with the union's demands. The cost of agreeing with the union's demands is relatively simple: it is the loss of profit that will occur if the firm has to give a 4 per cent pay rise to the employees. The cost of disagreeing is more complex. Management must work out how likely it is that a strike might take place, how long it might last and how much profit would be lost as a result. Similarly, the union can calculate the bargaining power of management by comparing its cost of disagreeing with its cost of agreeing. The cost of agreeing is the difference between the 2 per cent pay rise the employees will get and the 4 per cent they were hoping for. The cost of disagreeing is the loss of wages union members would suffer if they were on strike. The union will have superior bargaining power – and will get the desired pay rise – if it can make a credible threat of a strike and if the employer does not want to risk the disruption.

---

19 Ibid.
20 The model of bargaining used here is drawn from N.W. Chamberlain, *A General Theory of Economic Process* (1955), Chapters 6–8.

Inevitably, the parties do not always reach agreement. Both sides may decide that the cost of disagreeing is insufficient to outweigh the cost of agreeing. Economists have tried to identify some of the reasons why negotiations fail. One problem is incomplete or asymmetric information.[21] In other words, disagreements may arise because each party does not know what the other would be willing to agree to. Imagine, in our scenario, that the firm would in fact be willing to offer 3 per cent in order to prevent a strike. The union would be willing to accept this but believes that management can be persuaded to give 4 per cent. In theory, the parties could reach agreement on 3 per cent. But this would not happen in practice because the union would hold out for the 4 per cent it thinks it can achieve. The negotiations would end in deadlock and a strike would ensue. Once the strike is in progress, the parties may return to the negotiating table. Management's decision to tolerate the strike signals to the union that management's highest possible offer is something less than 4 per cent. Once the union has realised its 'mistake', it will lower its demand and the parties may then be able to reach agreement.

Another reason for strikes identified by some economists is the problem of 'commitments'.[22] Unions and employers may commit themselves to particular principles before the negotiations begin, making it difficult to retreat when it becomes clear that these principles will lead to conflict. In our example, perhaps managers have told the firm's shareholders that they will not agree to pay rises above 2 per cent because this is the current rate of inflation. And perhaps the union is seeking a 4 per cent pay rise because this would bring wages into line with those at other firms in the same industry. Two problems arise from these commitments. First, management and the union may 'lose face' with each other if they step back from their publicly proclaimed positions. The parties are 'repeat players' in the negotiations: they will have to go through the same process in future years. The parties will not want to sacrifice their long-term credibility in order to solve the current dispute. For example, if the union drops its 4 per cent claim, management may not believe its arguments next year. Second, the firm and the union may 'lose face' with people outside the negotiations. Management may fear the wrath of shareholders, and union leaders may fear the wrath of union members. Thus, although the parties could reach agreement at 3 per cent, they may be impeded from doing so by the commitments they have made.

Ultimately, economists' views of industrial action depend heavily on their views of collective bargaining, since the two are inextricably linked. As we saw in Chapter 10, collective bargaining is a matter of considerable controversy. Neoclassical economists focus on the ability of unions to secure pay for their

---

21 See, for example, M.J. Mauro, 'Strikes as a result of imperfect information' (1982) 35 *Industrial and Labor Relations Review* 522.
22 See, for example, C.M. Stevens, *Strategy and Collective Bargaining Negotiations* (1963), Chapter 5.

members over and above the 'market rate' for the job.[23] Although these 'rents' are beneficial for union members, they can lead to lower levels of employment and reduced productivity. Pro-union economists accept some of these arguments but believe that they are outweighed by the other benefits unions can bring, such as reduced labour turnover.[24] Of course, these economists would not advocate the widespread use of strike action, but they would be prepared to tolerate it as an essential part of collective bargaining.

In recent years, a new school of thought has emerged which emphasises the idea of 'partnership' between employers and workers, including unions. The concept of partnership is closely linked to the argument that the UK should concentrate on producing innovative goods and services which require highly skilled workers in order to compete under conditions of globalisation. Firms need:

> employees with multiple competencies, who will work diligently and thoughtfully without close supervision, use their knowledge and experience to find more efficient and effective ways of doing things, and are committed to the objectives of the firm ... Participative company cultures that incorporate high-trust and non-adversarial relationships are seen as the most appropriate to motivate people to work in these ways.[25]

Where a trade union is present in the workplace, management should build a close relationship with union leaders in order to improve communication with the workforce. Union leaders can provide managers with information about workers' ideas for improving productivity; managers can use union leaders to help explain the firm's goals and plans to the workers. Unions and employers are portrayed as having the same interest in creating a profitable firm. The idea of partnership formed an important part of the *Fairness at Work* White Paper,[26] and from 1999 to 2004 the government made funds available to support unions and employers in the development of partnership approaches.[27] The TUC has also expressed its support for partnership and has established a Partnership Institute to work with unions and employers.[28]

What are the implications of partnership for industrial action? On one interpretation, partnership implies that there are no real conflicts between the employer and the union, and therefore no place for disputes, let alone strikes. On a more moderate interpretation, there can be disputes within a partnership but these should be resolved through negotiations. This interpretation might

---

23 See F.A. Hayek, *The Constitution of Liberty* (1960), Chapter 18; R.A. Posner, *Economic Analysis of Law* (6th edn., 2003), pp. 335–42.

24 See, generally, R.B. Freeman and J.L. Medoff, *What Do Unions Do?* (1984).

25 S. Hill, 'How do you manage a flexible firm? The total quality model' (1991) 5 *Work, Employment and Society* 397, pp. 397–8, quoted in J. Knell, *Partnership at Work* (1999) (DTI URN 99/1078).

26 DTI, *Fairness at* Work (1998) (Cm 3968), especially Chapter 1.

27 Ibid., para. 2.7; and see www.berr.gov.uk/employment/trade-union-rights/partnership/index. html, and M. Terry and J. Smith, *Evaluation of the Partnership at Work Fund* (2003) (DTI URN 03/512).

28 See www.partnership-institute.co.uk/index.html for more information.

allow room for strikes, but only as a last resort when the parties' relationship has broken down. Because of this uncertainty, some rights theorists have expressed scepticism about the partnership approach, arguing that it may undermine the legitimacy of expressing opposition to management's ideas and acting on that opposition by exercising the right to strike.[29] It is easy to see how a union's attempt to represent the concerns of workers could be portrayed as 'old-fashioned adversarialism'.[30]

The law on trade unions and strike organisers

Now that we have examined the various rights and economics perspectives on industrial action, we are in a position to consider the underlying policy of English law. In this section, we will examine the law relating to trade unions and others who organise strikes. The next section will consider the position of individual workers who go on strike.

The traditional position in English law is that there is no express right to strike. This statement must now be qualified. First, there is some recognition of a right to strike within Article 11 ECHR after the *UNISON* decision, discussed above. This decision could have an impact in domestic law because, under the HRA 1998, the English courts could be called upon to scrutinise the proportionality of restrictions on the right to strike. However, it remains to be seen whether any such claims would succeed in practice. Second, the ECJ has recognised that there is a right to strike in Community law. In the *Viking* case, a union organised a strike to protest at the employer's plan to relocate from one Member State to another.[31] The ECJ held that this infringed the employer's right to freedom of establishment under Article 43 of the EC Treaty. It accepted that the union had a right to strike, but only where the strike constituted a proportionate restriction on the employer's free movement rights. This decision means that the English courts would have to recognise a right to strike in cases where Community law applies – for example, where the employer is planning to move from one Member State to another or to provide services across national borders. However, because the Court prioritised the employer's free movement rights over the union's right to strike, it seems likely that the *Viking* decision will restrict rather than facilitate industrial action in these cases.

Subject to these qualifications, it is still broadly true to say that English law does not grant an express right to strike. Those who organise a strike generally commit one or more of the economic torts. For example, by persuading an employee to go on strike, a strike organiser commits the tort of inducing

---

29 See, for example, P. Smith and G. Morton, 'Nine years of New Labour: neoliberalism and workers' rights' (2006) 44 *BJIR* 401.

30 For example, DTI, *Fairness at* Work, para. 2.2.

31 (Case C-438/05) *International Transport Workers' Federation* v. *Viking Line* [2008] All ER (EC) 127, and see A.C.L. Davies, 'One step forward, two steps back? The *Viking* and *Laval* cases in the ECJ' (2008) 37 *ILJ* 126.

breach of contract (because employees will be in breach of contract if they strike) and probably the tort of interfering with trade or business by unlawful means (because the unlawful act of inducing employees to breach their contracts of employment will prevent the employer from fulfilling its commercial contracts with customers).[32] Thus, the law's starting point is that it is unlawful to organise a strike. However, statute offers trade unions and strike organisers the possibility of an immunity against liability in tort if certain conditions are fulfilled. The immunity applies to the torts of inducing breach of contract or interfering with the performance of a contract, intimidation and simple conspiracy.[33] The immunity also applies where one of these torts is relied upon as the 'unlawful means' element of another tort, such as interfering with trade or business by unlawful means.[34] This extends the protection quite considerably.

On one view, it does not matter that English law does not grant an explicit right to strike. A legal right is no guarantee of effective protection, since it could be hedged about with exceptions and limitations (like the requirement to act proportionately in *Viking*, above). And rights can be protected by indirect means, such as a system of immunities against legal liability, provided that the immunities are strong enough. However, most rights theorists are critical of the law's approach, for two reasons. First, the common law is in a constant state of development. This means that the economic torts can be expanded by the courts to cover new situations. If the immunity is to remain effective, new torts must be added to the list in s. 219 TULRCA 1992. But many rights theorists fear that nowadays, the government would not intervene because it would not want to be seen to support industrial action. As a result, the immunity might gradually be eroded by judicial creativity. Indeed, this may already have occurred: in some public sector occupations, a strike organiser might be liable for inducing breach of statutory duty, which is not listed in s. 219.[35] Second, it is often argued that the concept of 'immunity' does not have the same rhetorical force as the term 'right', and may even have negative connotations. It is difficult to deny someone their rights without a good justification. But an immunity sounds like a privilege rather than an entitlement. Hayek describes unions as 'uniquely privileged institutions to which the general rules of law do not apply'.[36] This may have implications for the way in which the judges construe the immunities.[37] Rights would be construed generously; privileges are construed narrowly.

---

32 Space precludes a full discussion of the economic torts. For more detail, see S. Deakin and G.S. Morris, *Labour Law* (4th edn., 2005), pp. 975–89, and B. Simpson, 'Economic tort liability in labour disputes: the potential impact of the House of Lords' decision in *OBG Ltd v Allan*' (2007) 36 *ILJ* 468.

33 TULRCA 1992, s. 219(1) and (2).   34 *Hadmor Productions* v. *Hamilton* [1983] 1 AC 191.

35 See, for example, Criminal Justice and Public Order Act 1994, s. 127, concerning prison officers.

36 Hayek, *The Constitution of Liberty*, p. 267.

37 For an example, see *Express Newspapers* v. *McShane* [1980] AC 672, p. 687.

The immunity applies to acts 'done by a person in contemplation or furtherance of a trade dispute'.[38] A 'trade dispute' is defined in s. 244 TULRCA 1992, and includes the main areas that are likely to be the subject of disagreement, such as terms and conditions of employment, facilities for union officials and machinery for negotiation.[39] One matter that is not mentioned is a protest by workers against government policy. Workers cannot lawfully use a strike as an avenue of political action unrelated to their employment. This can create particular problems for workers in the public sector who must be sure to present their dispute as one about terms and conditions of employment, even though it may be closely related to their concerns about government policy.[40]

The definition of a trade dispute helps to illustrate the underlying basis of the right to strike in English law. A right to strike based on freedom of expression would probably include political strikes. Political speech is regarded as particularly deserving of protection and it would be difficult to justify restrictions on the content of the views workers could express through strike action. Instead, English law only permits strikes relating to matters in the control of the employer. The topics listed in s. 244 relate either to the process of collective bargaining or to topics about which bargaining could take place. This suggests that – to the extent that English law protects a right to strike at all – it does so on the grounds that a strike is a weapon to be used in collective bargaining.

English law also prohibits 'secondary action'.[41] This occurs where workers who are not in dispute with their own employer, B, take action to support workers who are in dispute with their employer, A. This type of action may occur for a variety of different reasons. One possibility is that B's workers simply wish to show their support for A's workers. Another, perhaps more likely, scenario occurs where employer B decides to help employer A to withstand the strike by fulfilling employer A's commercial contracts. B's workers may decide that they do not want to harm A's workers in this way. Whatever the motivation, s. 224 TULRCA 1992 ensures that secondary action does not benefit from the statutory immunity provided by s. 219.

This is a topic of considerable controversy. Rights theorists argue that secondary action is a legitimate exercise of the right to strike. English law's ban on this type of action has been condemned by the ILO:

> Workers should be able to participate in sympathy strikes provided the initial strike they are supporting is itself lawful … this principle is particularly important in the light of earlier TUC comments that employers commonly avoid the adverse effects

---

38 TULRCA 1992, s. 219(1), sometimes referred to as the 'golden formula'. See B. Simpson, 'Trade disputes and industrial action ballots in the twenty-first century' (2002) 31 *ILJ* 270.

39 The dispute must be between 'workers and their employer', thus precluding disputes about the terms and conditions of workers yet to be hired, but this was held by the ECtHR to be a proportionate restriction on the right to strike in *UNISON* v. *UK*.

40 See, for example, *Mercury Communications* v. *Scott-Garner* [1984] Ch 37.

41 TULRCA 1992, s. 224.

of disputes by transferring work to associated employers and that companies have restructured their businesses in order to make primary action secondary.[42]

This highlights one of the major arguments in favour of allowing secondary action. Employers are able to structure their businesses in any way they choose. One large firm can be broken up into a set of smaller firms which appear to be separate but in fact have close links. This makes it difficult for unions to cause disruption. If only one firm is affected by a strike, the others in the group can easily take over its work. The union is unlikely to be able to call all the workers out on strike across the enterprise as a whole, because it would be difficult to show a dispute between each of the small firms and its workers. However, from an economics perspective, the ban on secondary action can be viewed as a sensible measure to limit the disruption a strike can cause.[43] If secondary action is permitted, a strike can extend beyond the firm in dispute to associated firms or even to other firms in the same industry. These firms suffer damage to their business even though they are not responsible for the dispute and can do nothing to resolve it. The level of productivity in the economy as a whole is reduced, and multinational firms may be deterred from investing in the UK as a result.

The criteria for securing immunity from tort liability that we have considered so far apply both to trade unions and to individuals who organise strikes. But if a trade union is responsible for a strike (if the action is 'official'), there are some additional conditions that must be fulfilled if the strike is to be immune.[44] The union must ensure that the action has the support of a ballot. The balloting requirements are set out in considerable detail in TULRCA 1992 ss. 226–234A.[45] The employer must be given seven days' notice of the ballot and must be sent a sample voting paper.[46] The notice must include the total number of employees to be balloted, broken down into different categories of employee and the number of employees in each category, and different workplaces and the number in each workplace.[47] The notice need not name the employees involved.[48] The ballot must be conducted by post[49] and s. 229 TULRCA 1992 specifies exactly what must appear on the ballot paper, including a warning that a strike is a breach of the contract of employment. The union must take particular care to ensure that

---

42 Committee of Experts on the Application of Conventions and Recommendations, *Individual Observation Concerning Convention No. 87, Freedom of Association and Protection of the Right to Organise, 1948, United Kingdom* (2003), para. 2. See also ILO, *Digest of Decisions*, para. 534.

43 Department of Employment, *Removing Barriers to Employment* (1989) (Cm 655), para. 3.10.

44 Whether or not a union is responsible for the action is determined by ss. 20–21 TULRCA 1992 for the torts therein listed (and see *Gate Gourmet London Ltd* v. *TGWU* [2005] EWHC 1889; [2005] IRLR 881), and by *Heatons Transport* v. *TGWU* [1973] AC 15 for other torts.

45 For a useful account of the recent history of these provisions, see B. Simpson, 'Strike ballots and the law: round six' (2005) 34 *ILJ* 331. See also DTI, *Code of Practice on Industrial Action Ballots and Notice to Employers* (2005).

46 TULRCA 1992, s. 226A.   47 Ibid., s. 226A(2).   48 Ibid., s. 226A(2G).

49 Ibid., s. 230.

voting papers are sent 'to all the members of the trade union who it is reasonable at the time of the ballot for the union to believe will be induced by the union to take part … in the industrial action in question, and to no others'.[50] If the union fails to send someone a ballot paper who should have been sent one, and then calls on that person to participate in the strike, the ballot is invalid,[51] although accidental failures that do not affect the result may be disregarded under s. 232B. The employer must be given notice of the result[52] and at least seven days' notice of any industrial action to be taken on the basis of the ballot.[53] The ballot remains effective for four weeks (or up to eight weeks if the employer agrees).[54] If the union does not begin the industrial action during this time – for example, because it is continuing to negotiate with the employer – it must conduct the ballot again.

From an economics perspective, the ballot can be regarded as a useful tool in the negotiating process. One of the difficulties faced by employers is calculating the cost of disagreeing with the union's demands. The employer must predict the likelihood of a strike taking place and its probable duration before it can work out the loss of profits the strike would entail. Both the employer and the union are faced with the risk that the employer will underestimate the probability of a strike. This might lead the employer to think that it is not worth agreeing with the union's demands. The union will then be put to the expense of calling a strike in order to show its sincerity. This will also impose costs on the employer until a settlement is reached. The law can address this problem by providing the union with a mechanism for signalling to the employer that it is sincere about a strike threat. The balloting provisions perform this function. Once the union has conducted a strike ballot and obtained a majority in favour of the action, the employer's cost of disagreeing can be calculated with a greater degree of certainty. This might well prompt the parties to reach a settlement. Moreover, the strike ballot is only effective for a limited time. As the deadline nears, the likelihood that a strike will take place increases. This gradually raises the cost of disagreeing for both the employer and the union. At some point before the deadline, one or both parties might decide that it would be cheaper to reach an agreement.

From a rights perspective, an obligation to conduct a ballot could, in principle, be a legitimate control on industrial action.[55] It is consistent with unions' status as democratic organisations that they should consult their members before calling a strike and act on the majority view. However, the current English law on strike ballots is difficult to justify on these terms. The government which introduced the legal provisions was hostile to trade unions and had an overriding concern to discourage strike action. This motivation is reflected in various aspects of the legislation. First, the legislation seeks to discourage workers from voting in favour of a strike. For example, instead of allowing the

50 Ibid., s. 227(1).   51 Ibid., s. 232A.   52 Ibid., s. 231A.   53 Ibid., s. 234A.
54 Ibid., s. 234.
55 ILO, *Digest of Decisions*, para. 559, indicates that balloting requirements are acceptable where they are not unduly burdensome.

union to determine the content of the ballot paper, the statute prescribes the content and places particular emphasis on the fact that strikers will be in breach of their contract of employment.[56] This sounds quite frightening but does nothing to explain to workers what the practical consequences of doing so might be. Second, the legislation is highly complex. The requirement to give multiple notices to the employer – of the ballot, of the ballot result and of the industrial action – illustrates this. While notice of the industrial action helps the employer to make plans to cope with the disruption, it could be argued that the other notices simply add hoops for the union to jump through. As a result, even if a union is trying to comply, it may fail to do so.

If the conditions for obtaining the immunity are not met, and the action goes ahead, the union or strike organiser will be exposed to liability in tort. Under s. 22 TULRCA 1992, there are limits on the damages that trade unions may be required to pay, varying according to the size of the union. In practice, however, most employers prefer to stop the strike taking place instead of suffering the damage and seeking compensation afterwards. This can be done by seeking an interim injunction, so called because it stops the strike from taking place until there has been a trial to determine its legality.[57] To obtain an injunction, the employer must fulfil the *American Cyanamid* test, by showing that there is a serious issue to be tried as to the lawfulness of the strike, and that damages would not be an adequate remedy.[58] Under s. 221(2) TULRCA 1992, the court is supposed to have regard to the likelihood that the union or strike organiser could establish the immunity when considering whether or not to grant the injunction. Despite this provision, both elements of the *American Cyanamid* test are easy to satisfy. The employer can usually persuade the court that the action may not be immune, and that damages would not fully compensate for the harm that might be caused by the strike. Moreover, in urgent cases, an injunction can be granted by a court which has only heard argument from the party seeking the injunction. Under s. 221(1) TULRCA 1992, in a case involving trade dispute immunities, the court should only handle the case in this way if it is satisfied that reasonable steps have been taken to inform the union or strike organiser that an injunction is being sought. This is designed to give them a chance to put their side of the case. However, critics argue that in practice, courts are too often willing to find that this provision has been satisfied.

The employer obviously has the greatest interest in taking legal action when a strike is taking place. But the employer is not the only party with a possibility of intervening. Under s. 62 TULRCA 1992, a member of the trade union may seek an injunction to prevent the action going ahead if it does not have the

---

56 TULRCA 1992, s. 229(4), amended in 1999 to include a reference to strikers' unfair dismissal rights, discussed below.

57 See, generally, G. Gall, 'Research note: injunctions as a legal weapon in industrial disputes in Britain, 1995–2005' (2006) 44 *BJIR* 327.

58 *American Cyanamid* v. *Ethicon* [1975] AC 396.

support of a validly conducted ballot. This allows union members to force the union to comply with internal democracy provisions. A broader right to seek an injunction is granted to individual members of the public who can show that the strike is unlawful (in any respect) and that it will 'prevent or delay the supply of goods or services' to them.[59] So far, there have been no successful actions under this provision.[60] However, it raises the possibility that even if the employer chose not to use litigation to tackle the dispute, a member of the public could intervene.

Strikes can and do take place in the UK. But trade unions and strike organisers must comply with substantive limitations (on the types of strike that are allowed) and procedural controls (on the procedures they must follow before calling a strike). These restrictions can be viewed in different ways: as the inevitable result of the link between strikes and collective bargaining; as legitimate attempts to limit the economic damage caused by strikes; or as illegitimate attempts to undermine workers' rights. But before you draw your conclusions, we need to examine the position of individual workers who go on strike.

The law on individual strikers

Individual strikers are almost always in breach of their contract, whether it is a contract of employment or a worker's contract. This is because they are refusing to perform some or all of their contractual obligations. So the law on individual strikers starts from the same premise as the law on strike organisers: a strike is in principle unlawful, but those involved may receive some degree of statutory protection. From a rights perspective, the difficulty with this is that strike action may be viewed by commentators and judges as a privilege rather than an entitlement. Moreover, workers may feel deterred from participating because they do not want to act unlawfully. Some countries treat a strike as a suspension of the contract of employment in order to avoid this problem.[61]

The main consequence to follow from the fact that a strike is a breach of the contract of employment is that the employer is under no obligation to pay strikers' wages. This is uncontroversial: it is accepted by the ILO[62] and it is the position adopted by many other countries.[63] If strikers were paid, there would be very little incentive on their part to end the dispute, while the pressure on the employer would be overwhelming. For the same reason, most countries (including the UK) do not give social security payments to strikers.[64] Some rights commentators

---

59 TULRCA 1992, s. 235A.
60 Though it has been invoked: *P* v. *NASUWT* [2003] UKHL 8; [2003] 2 AC 663.
61 A.T.J.M. Jacobs, 'The law of strikes and lockouts', in R. Blanpain (ed.), *Comparative Labour Law and Industrial Relations in Industrialized Market Economies* (9th edn., 2007).
62 ILO, *Digest of Decisions*, para. 654.   63 Jacobs, 'The law of strikes and lockouts'.
64 N. Wikeley, A.I. Ogus and E.M. Barendt, *The Law of Social Security* (5th edn., 2002), pp. 379–81 and 505–14.

have argued that this amounts to the state intervening to help the employer break the strike.[65] But if the state did support strikers financially, it is easy to see how this could be characterised as state intervention to help the union. Traditionally, unions help their members who are on strike by giving them 'strike pay', but this tends to be a relatively small sum of money.

Although the 'no work, no pay' principle is uncontroversial, its application in practice can be difficult. If the worker takes part in a one-day strike, how much pay should be deducted from his or her wages? Should it be one day's pay, or should it be the loss to the employer of not having the individual in work for that day (which might be more than a day's pay when other benefits, such as holiday pay, are taken into account)? In the recent *Cooper* case, it was held that the maximum that could be deducted for a one-day strike was one day's pay: damages should be measured by what the individual could have claimed if the employer had refused to pay him or her.[66]

The position is even more complicated where workers take action short of a strike – for example, by performing most but not all of their duties. Again, it is clear that the employer can make a deduction from wages in respect of the duties not performed. But in *Wiluszynski* v. *Tower Hamlets LBC*, the employer was allowed to withhold pay completely.[67] The council's employees took industrial action by refusing to answer queries from elected councillors while continuing to perform their other duties as normal. Over a five-week period this amounted to some three hours of missed work. However, the employer told the employees in advance that if they refused to perform part of their duties, they would not be paid at all, and any work they did would be regarded as voluntary. The court accepted that because the employer had made its position clear, it was entitled to withhold the employees' pay in full for the period of the industrial action.

From an economics perspective, this decision is a curious one. It gives employees no incentive to use less disruptive forms of action. If they are not going to be paid at all, they might as well cause maximum disruption by going on strike. Of course, there are still reasons why union members might vote for action short of a strike. Strikers generally want to secure the support of the public, and in sectors such as transport or education, continuous action would quickly become unpopular. And there might be some justification for the *Wiluszynski* decision. If Mr Wiluszynski had won his case, he would have been able to continue his industrial action for a considerable period of time because he would only have lost a small proportion of his salary. The employer would suffer disruption, but perhaps not enough to outweigh its perceived cost of agreeing with the union's demands. Thus, the dispute could have rumbled on for years without reaching a satisfactory resolution.

---

65 K.D. Ewing, *The Right to Strike* (1991), Chapters 5 and 6.
66 *Cooper* v. *Isle of Wight College* [2007] EWHC 2831, interpreting *Miles* v. *Wakefield MDC* [1987] AC 539.
67 *Wiluszynski* v. *Tower Hamlets LBC* [1989] ICR 493.

Strikers are also vulnerable to being dismissed. Workers do not receive the protection of unfair dismissal law (as Chapter 9 explained) so their dismissal is governed by the ordinary principles of contract law. Since taking strike action is likely to amount to a repudiatory breach of contract, the employer will usually be entitled to terminate a worker's contract without notice. Employees fare rather better because they may be able to secure some unfair dismissal protection. However, this depends on a set of complex criteria, most of which are outside the control of the employees themselves.

If the industrial action is unofficial, it is automatically *fair* for the employer to dismiss the strikers.[68] Industrial action is unofficial where some or all of the strikers are trade union members and the trade union has not authorised or endorsed the action in accordance with ss. 20–21 TULRCA 1992.

Some dismissal protection is available if the action is 'not unofficial'. This occurs either where some or all of the strikers are trade union members and the trade union has authorised or endorsed the action, or where none of the strikers is a trade union member. Thus, it applies both to trade union action and to action where there is no trade union involvement at all. In this situation, the employer cannot be liable for unfair dismissal provided that it dismisses all the strikers and does not re-engage any of them within three months of the dismissals.[69] If the employer only dismisses the employees it thinks were responsible for organising the strike, for example, the employment tribunal would have jurisdiction to hear their claims for unfair dismissal. The level of protection afforded by this provision depends on what proportion of the employer's workers are on strike and how easily new recruits could be trained. If a large proportion of a highly skilled workforce is on strike, they are relatively well-protected.

If the industrial action has been organised by a trade union and is lawful, in the sense that all the requirements for immunity from tort liability (discussed above) have been met by the trade union, the action counts as 'protected' and much better unfair dismissal protection is available to the employees taking part. It is automatically *unfair* for the employer to dismiss the employees within twelve weeks of the start of the action for taking part in the strike.[70] After the end of the twelve weeks, it may still be automatically unfair to dismiss the strikers in certain circumstances – for example, if the employer has not taken reasonable procedural steps to resolve the dispute or if the employer has reacted to the strike by locking the workers out (which might prevent them coming back to work before the twelve weeks expires). Once the twelve-week period and any extension to that period have expired, the action ceases to be protected and the employees move into the category of 'not unofficial' strikers, with protection against selective dismissal only.

The dismissal provisions offer another insight into the underlying basis of the right to strike in English law. Although some protection is afforded to non-union

---

68 TULRCA 1992, s. 237.   69 Ibid., s. 238.   70 Ibid., s. 238A.

strikers through the provisions on 'not unofficial' action, the main focus of the legislation is on protecting those who take part in lawful action organised by a trade union. The link with trade union activities suggests that, once again, the right to engage in collective bargaining is the basis for the right to strike.[71]

Perhaps the most controversial aspect of the dismissal provisions is the fact that protection is generally limited to twelve weeks. From an economics perspective, this can be justified as a means of controlling the disruption caused by strikes by limiting their likely duration. Once a strike starts, the union's cost of disagreeing gradually increases as the workers lose more and more money in wages. Towards the end of the twelve weeks, the union's cost of disagreeing may increase substantially if it believes that the employer is likely to dismiss the striking workers. This may be enough to outweigh the union's cost of agreeing and may therefore lead to a settlement. From the employer's perspective, the cost of disagreeing also increases as the strike goes on because it loses more and more in profits. But the employer knows that the expiry of twelve weeks (coupled with a plausible threat to dismiss all the strikers) is likely to alter the union's calculations. If the employer thinks that the cost of a twelve-week strike is greater than the cost of agreeing with the union, it is likely to try to settle the dispute at an early stage. If the employer thinks that the cost of a twelve-week strike is less than the cost of agreeing with the union, it is likely to hold out for twelve weeks in the hope that the union will be more willing to make concessions at the end of that period. The government argues that the limit helps to promote the settlement of disputes.[72]

However, many rights theorists regard the twelve-week limit as an illegitimate restriction on the right to strike. According to the ILO's Freedom of Association Committee, allowing employers to dismiss workers for taking part in a strike (however long it lasts) is a serious form of discrimination against trade unionists and a breach of Convention 98.[73] The government's counter-argument is that few strikes last for more than twelve weeks, so strikers are well-protected. However, there may be occasional instances in which the employer waits until the limit has elapsed and then dismisses all the strikers.

Further reading

For a detailed textbook account of the law, see S. Deakin and G. Morris, *Labour Law* (4th edn., 2005), Chapter 11, or H. Collins, K.D. Ewing and A. McColgan, *Labour Law: Text and Materials* (2nd edn., 2005), Chapter 9. For a comparative perspective, see A.T.J.M. Jacobs, 'The law of strikes and lockouts', in R. Blanpain (ed.), *Comparative Labour Law and Industrial Relations in Industrialized Market*

71 This approach is accepted by the ILO, *Digest of Decisions*, para. 524.
72 DTI, *Review of the Employment Relations Act 1999* (2003), para. 3.37.
73 ILO, *Digest of Decisions*, para. 661.

Economies (9th edn., 2007). Statistical data on strikes in the UK is available from the UK Statistics Authority (www.statistics.gov.uk).

For an excellent general account of the reasons for protecting and for restricting the right to strike, see T. Novitz, *International and European Protection of the Right to Strike* (2003), Chapters 2–4. The book is a comprehensive study of ILO, ECHR and ESC standards, so it is a valuable source of further information on these topics too. For critiques of English law from a rights perspective, see K. Ewing, 'Laws against strikes revisited', in C. Barnard *et al.* (eds.), *The Future of Labour Law* (2004); J. Hendy and G. Gall, 'British trade union rights today and the Trade Union Freedom Bill', in K.D. Ewing (ed.), *The Right to Strike* (2006); and T. Novitz and P. Skidmore, *Fairness at Work: A Critical Analysis of the Employment Relations Act 1999 and its Treatment of Collective Rights* (2001), Chapter 5. What is the best justification for the right to strike? Is it linked to the right to engage in collective bargaining or to some other right? What restrictions can legitimately be imposed on the right in order to protect other people? How can we distinguish between a legitimate restriction on and an interference with the right?

The real question from an economics perspective is whether or not the benefits of collective bargaining are sufficient to outweigh the damage done by the occasional strike, so you should revisit the literature on the economic impact of collective bargaining listed in the further reading section in Chapter 10. The role of strike action in a 'partnership' model of industrial relations is particularly controversial. Does partnership make strikes illegitimate? Or just unnecessary? Could a strike serve a useful purpose within a partnership model?

The incidence of industrial action depends not just on the laws about strikes, but also on the laws regulating trade union activities more generally. What is the relationship between the recognition procedure discussed in Chapter 10 and strike action? Is the possibility of legally enforced collective bargaining likely to increase or reduce the incidence of strikes? And what about the relationship between strike action and the controls on the closed shop and union discipline explored in Chapter 11?

What next?

This postscript is not intended to draw any conclusions from our discussions. The purpose of this book has been to present you with a variety of, often conflicting, perspectives on labour law, and to leave you to draw your own conclusions about which arguments you find most persuasive. Instead, this postscript looks towards the future. Labour law is in a constant state of flux. Sometimes policy-makers may be more heavily influenced by rights arguments; sometimes they may act on economic imperatives. And as we saw in Chapter 4, labour law is regulated in many different layers: international, regional and domestic. So the competing arguments may carry different weight at these various levels, leading to conflicts between them. How is labour law likely to develop in the next few years?

The economic and social context

At many points in this book, we have referred to the process of globalisation. Multinational enterprises are able to locate their management, research and production activities virtually anywhere in the world. Cost is a major factor in their decisions. The fear is that a country like the UK will seem unattractive because of its high labour costs, and that this will lead to substantial job losses. National governments will lose control over labour law because they are beholden to the multinationals. Many fear that this will lead to a 'race to the bottom', as governments seek to reduce their labour standards to the lowest possible level.

Those who are strongly opposed to multinational enterprises and their activities argue that globalisation can, and should, be stopped. The job losses would end and governments would get control over labour law again. But there are at least two reasons for thinking that this view is too simplistic. First, in our capacity as consumers rather than workers, we usually welcome globalisation. It means that we can buy products such as clothing or electrical goods at a much lower cost. Some consumers might be prepared to pay extra in order to get a guarantee that the workers who made the goods were well-paid, but not all consumers are concerned about these issues. Second, although jobs might be lost in developed countries as a result of globalisation, new jobs are being created in developing countries. Globalisation produces winners as well as losers. And these winners are often countries which have high levels of poverty and unemployment. They are in desperate need of foreign investment so that they can improve their health-care and education systems, transport infrastructure and so on. Of course, the benefits of globalisation might not be distributed fairly in some countries. Perhaps the ruling elite might take a big chunk of the profits, leaving ordinary workers with very low wages. But this is not a reason to stop the process of globalisation altogether.

Most economists believe that globalisation is an inevitable process that could not be stopped even if this was what we wanted to do. This suggests that the debates we have been having in this book will remain highly relevant in the future. It will still be necessary to ask whether developed countries should adopt the neoclassical or new institutional prescriptions for survival. And rights theorists will still need to be able to defend their claims against arguments that rights are too costly and create too much of a burden on businesses in the globalising world economy.

The international dimension

One way to deal with some of the problems of globalisation might be to address them at the international level. Globalisation forces governments to compete with each other in order to attract multinational corporations to their countries. But there would no longer be competition on labour standards if they could be agreed by all states. The ILO is the obvious forum in which this could take place. However, although globalisation makes international agreements seem more necessary, it also makes them more difficult to achieve. Developing countries suspect that developed countries are trying to take away their competitive advantage by imposing impossibly high labour standards on them. And developed countries suspect developing countries of exploiting their own workers in order to maintain that advantage.

In 1998, the ILO gave a renewed impetus to its activities through the Declaration on Fundamental Principles and Rights at Work. This document was intended to do two main things. One was to require all ILO member states to respect a set of very basic and (relatively) uncontroversial labour rights. The other was to address developing countries' economic concerns by making it clear that labour standards would not be used to protect developed countries from competitive pressures.[1] More recently, the ILO has developed the Decent Work Agenda.[2] This focuses on the traditional ILO concerns about rights at work (both individual and collective), but also on the broader issue of job creation. The ILO regards productive employment in decent jobs as a key method of reducing poverty and improving living standards worldwide. These developments highlight

1 ILO Declaration on Fundamental Principles and Rights at Work 1998, para. 5.
2 www.ilo.org/global/Themes/Decentwork/index.htm

the importance of the rights and economics perspectives at the international level. The ILO has repositioned itself as an organisation with a human rights agenda; but, at the same time, it is concerned with economic issues such as employment levels in national economies. However, relevance remains a key issue for the ILO: how can it ensure that states take notice of its activities? This is particularly important in relation to the UK. Successive governments have been happy to disregard the ILO's criticisms of our labour law.

Another area of interest is the role of the World Trade Organization (WTO). The WTO is responsible for managing and enforcing the General Agreement on Tariffs and Trade (GATT), which governs the conditions for trade between different countries. This body sounds as if it has nothing to do with labour law. But it may have a role to play, at least indirectly. Some countries, in despair at the ILO's failure to enforce labour standards worldwide, have sought to impose them themselves through trade incentives (such as reduced tariff barriers for countries with good labour standards) or trade sanctions (such as refusing to trade with a particular country with poor labour standards). The USA and the EU have pioneered these (admittedly controversial) approaches. However, the rules of the GATT may limit states' ability to use trade incentives or sanctions in this way.[3] What is interesting is that the WTO – a trade body – may end up dealing with disputes about labour standards, even though it may not be well-qualified to do so, because it is difficult to keep the issues separate.[4]

Although labour law can seem to be a very 'domestic' subject, it is important not to ignore the international dimension. However, as some of the world's larger economies (including that of the UK) head into recession, it may be more difficult to get countries to agree on issues like labour rights. Competition between countries to attract investment from multinational enterprises and to preserve jobs may become more fierce.

The EU

The UK might also look to the EU for some protection against globalisation. Not all firms will want to consider locating their factories anywhere in the world. If they face significant transport costs, for example, they might want to produce goods nearer to their main markets. In these cases, the UK is competing not with the rest of the world, but with the rest of the EU. Much of the EU's social and labour legislation, particularly in the early years, was motivated by a desire to prevent Member States from undercutting each other by lowering standards. So what does the future hold for the EU? It will be suggested here that although

---

3 See WTO DS 242 (Thailand) and DS 246 (India), both challenges to aspects of the EU's Generalised System of Preferences which grants preferential trade treatment to developing countries. The EU revised the scheme in the light of the Appellate Body's judgment in the India case.

4 See, generally, C. McCrudden and A.C.L. Davies, 'A perspective on trade and labor rights' (2000) 3 *JIEL* 43.

the EU has an important rights agenda, it faces significant deregulatory pressures from a variety of sources.

Perhaps the strongest deregulatory pressure facing the EU is globalisation itself. Although the EU can prevent damaging competition between the Member States, it must still compete with the rest of the world. Jobs in manufacturing are under threat from countries with lower labour costs. Technology makes it possible for jobs in service industries, such as call centres, to be located outside the EU. And developing countries are keen to export to the EU, particularly in the agricultural sector. The EU may also face deregulatory pressures internally. As the EU has expanded eastwards, it has become a much bigger organisation. This makes it more difficult to reach agreement on new policy areas, particularly since the EU's decision-making processes have not been modernised due to the failure to agree the EU Constitution and now the Lisbon Treaty. More generally, the newer Member States may be reluctant to accept additional obligations in the field of labour law, given how much catching up they have had to do in order to join the EU. And, inevitably, much depends on the political composition of the EU at any given time: some national governments may wish to pursue a deregulatory agenda.

Interestingly, further deregulatory pressure has recently come from the ECJ. Although the ECJ has done much to contribute to the development of Community labour law, particularly in the field of equal pay and discrimination, it is strongly committed to the core Community aim of market integration. Labour law and other social policies can sometimes clash with this aim. In the *Laval* case, for example, a Latvian firm wanted to post some Latvian workers to work on a building site in Sweden.[5] The relevant Swedish trade union tried to negotiate a minimum wage for the workers. Agreement could not be reached and ultimately the Latvian firm gave up trying to operate in Sweden. The ECJ held that the actions of the trade union (and the Swedish government in allowing the union's actions) constituted an infringement of the Latvian firm's ability to provide services across national borders in accordance with Article 49 EC. There is a directive which covers these situations, the Posted Workers Directive,[6] and the ECJ held that this set the limits to what Member States could do in terms of regulating the terms and conditions of posted workers. What is significant about *Laval* is the idea that labour law – the regulation of terms and conditions of employment – is regarded by the ECJ as a potential hindrance to free trade within the EC which Member States must be able to explain and justify when they apply it to firms from other Member States. And if Member States are limited in the labour laws they can impose on workers who are posted to their state, they are likely to come under pressure to reduce labour laws for domestic firms to enable them to compete. At the time of writing (2008), it is unclear how far the

5 (Case C-341/05) *Laval v. Svenska Byggnadsarbetareförbundet* [2008] All ER (EC) 166.
6 Directive 96/71/EC.

ECJ will take this, arguably very radical, idea, and how (if at all) the Community's political institutions will react.

Not all the policy pressures within the EU are deregulatory, however. As we saw in Chapter 4, considerable emphasis has been placed at the political level on new institutionalist defences of labour law. For example, a number of recent policy documents from the Commission have focused on the concept of 'flexicurity'.[7] The idea is that workers in the EU should be flexible, in the sense that they are highly skilled and adaptable, so that they can move between workplaces (and countries) in response to demand. But they should also enjoy some security in the labour market. This may not be in the traditional sense of security of tenure of a particular job. Instead, they should derive a sense of security from being highly employable in the labour market generally and from the knowledge that there are social security protections to back them up if things go wrong. The Commission is keen to avoid creating the impression that flexicurity will involve the removal of labour law protections for workers, though it does suggest that in some Member States, overly 'rigid' labour laws may need to be reconsidered. An interesting issue for the future is how the concept of flexicurity will translate into specific policy initiatives. Although there are some legislative proposals at present – for example, in relation to working time – they are relatively modest. Will flexicurity protect labour law against deregulatory pressures, or is it potentially deregulatory itself, at least in some Member States?

The Community also has a more explicitly rights-focused dimension. We have seen that the EU Charter provides an up-to-date statement of human rights with a strong focus on labour and other social rights. Two attempts have been made to give legal effect to the Charter – in the EU Constitution and in the Lisbon Treaty – and both have failed. However, giving legal effect to the Charter is still on the EU's agenda and may yet occur at some point in the future. The EU's possible accession to the ECHR remains a live issue too. Normally, we would expect to see the argument that an emphasis on workers' rights would protect them against deregulatory pressures and would do so more powerfully than new institutionalist arguments, which are subject to debate in the light of empirical evidence. But the EU may be an example of a context in which this is not the case. In the *Viking* and *Laval* cases, the ECJ recognised – for the first time – the right to strike as a fundamental principle of Community law.[8] But for many rights theorists, the Court undermined this by going on to hold that the right to strike had to be exercised in a way that was proportionate to employers' free movement rights under Community law. The concern is that the Community's economic focus may serve to undermine its ability to protect rights. However, as noted above, these decisions are recent and the Court's interpretation may evolve

---

7 European Commission, *Towards Common Principles of Flexicurity: More and Better Jobs through Flexibility and Security* (2007).

8 (Case C-438/05) *International Transport Workers' Federation* v. *Viking Line* [2008] All ER (EC) 127; *Laval* v. *Svenska Byggnadsarbetareförbundet*.

over time, particularly if the Charter comes to occupy a stronger position in the Treaty architecture.

The EU's complexity as an institution makes it difficult to pin down its policy on labour law. There are tensions between competing economics perspectives on labour law, and further tensions between these perspectives and a rights approach. The ECJ's recent decisions have brought these tensions to the fore, and it will be interesting to see what impact this has in the next few years.

The UK

The issues we have considered so far – globalisation itself, and the role of international and regional organisations – are bound to influence what occurs in domestic law. But their influence is by no means straightforward. The domestic response to the pressures they create depends on a range of factors. One is the policy of the government of the day: whether it is pursuing a deregulatory strategy, or a high-productivity or pro-rights approach. Another factor is the attitude of the various key actors in labour law, notably the trade unions and employers' organisations. Yet another is the role of the courts: for example, the HRA 1998 may affect labour law in unpredictable ways. These factors interact with the economic context and external pressures in the process of creating the labour law of the future.

The current Labour government remains broadly committed to a 'third way' approach to labour law, in which workers' rights are regarded as having a positive contribution to make to the competitiveness of UK firms and the economy as a whole. After an initial flurry of legislative activity, the government has been making a series of more modest changes to the law. In general terms, it seems that the government has broadly put in place the legislative framework it envisaged when it came into office in 1997, and is now adjusting it in the light of experience. For example, the right to request flexible working was introduced initially for parents of young children, and has now been extended to those with responsibility for caring for elderly relatives.[9] The government was able to argue that the initial policy had worked well – it was popular with parents and had not caused major disruption to employers – so it could be extended to another group of carers with similar needs. Importantly, the government is not just using the incremental approach to extend the law: it is also willing to repeal policies that have not worked as intended. The recent repeal of the dispute resolution procedures in the Employment Act 2002, which were unpopular with employers and employees alike, is an example of this.

This incremental approach to policy-making can be viewed as a smart regulatory strategy in that it allows the government to experiment and to learn from experience. It fits well with 'third way' thinking because the argument that labour laws can benefit the economy is one which can (to some extent at least) be tested empirically. We can explore whether managers and workers feel that

9 ERA 1996, s. 80F, as amended, Work and Families Act 2006.

information and consultation rights have improved communications within the firm through surveys and interviews, for example. So it makes sense to introduce changes gradually and to research their impact.

More generally, after more than ten years of the new institutionalist approach, it should be possible to start considering whether or not it is succeeding as a strategy for dealing with globalisation. Have multinational firms continued to invest in the UK? Have low-skilled jobs lost in manufacturing been replaced by high-skilled jobs in information technology? The new institutionalists assume that countries with lower wages cannot offer the same benefits in terms of worker attitudes and qualifications. But this might be regarded as a rather patronising assumption. India is a good example of a relatively low-wage country with a good education system whose workers can compete not only on cost but also on quality. Indeed, many firms have outsourced IT and call-centre operations to India for this reason. So there are some important research questions for economists at both the macro and micro levels. And if new institutionalism is not working, what (if anything) is the alternative?

Leaving aside these broader questions of effectiveness, there are also some important challenges to the third way and to the incremental approach, from both the neoclassical economics and the rights perspectives. Perhaps most obviously, the global financial crisis and the prospect of recession is likely to increase calls for deregulation – or at least for a pause in the creation of new regulation – from firms struggling to cope in a difficult economic climate. If unemployment starts to rise, workers themselves may feel less inclined to press for change, because they will be grateful to have a job at all. Neoclassical economics arguments seem likely to grow in popularity as the economic climate worsens.

The government's preferred strategy is also challenged by rights-based, hard law regulatory developments from the EU and the ECtHR. As we have seen, the EU has also adopted new institutionalist arguments in its policy pronouncements, and has placed less emphasis on the enactment of new labour legislation in recent years. However, it does still have a legislative agenda – for example, it wants to reform the Working Time Directive to tighten up the practice of opting out of the forty-eight-hour week – and in pursuing this agenda it may come into conflict with the UK government, which regards a degree of flexibility in this area as desirable. The ECtHR has also been a significant source of decisions on workers' rights in recent years, and this has given rise to conflict with the UK government. For example, we saw in Chapter 11 that commentators have criticised the amendments to TULRCA 1992 after the *Wilson* case, for failing to give full effect to the Court's judgment on the requirements of Article 11.[10] However, the government has argued that employers should still be able to derecognise unions if they want to, and has tried to retain this flexibility in the legislation.

---

10 *Wilson* v. *UK* (2002) 35 EHRR 20; and for discussion, see A.L. Bogg, 'Employment Relations Act 2004: another false dawn for collectivism?' (2005) 34 *ILJ* 72.

It remains to be seen whether and to what extent the EU and the ECtHR will act as drivers of a rights agenda in UK labour law in future years.

Finally, it is important to note that the Labour Party may not survive in government at the next general election, which must be held by 2010. At the time of writing (2008), it is not clear what policies the other major parties, particularly the Conservatives, would adopt in relation to labour law. Thus, there is a possibility of a significant change of direction – perhaps towards neoclassical economics and deregulation – in the medium term.

Whatever the policy of the government of the day, the courts will still play a key role in shaping the labour law of the future through their role in developing the common law and interpreting legislation. We saw in Chapter 4 that the courts have long been regarded with suspicion by trade unions and by many labour lawyers. Their use of contract doctrine (and their emphasis on the ideology of freedom of contract) often leads to a perception that they are favouring employers over workers. And their emphasis on the individual makes it difficult for them to deal with collective interests such as the claims of trade unions. Are there signs of change? Judicial decisions continue to present a mixed picture. In the area of atypical work, for example, the Court of Appeal adopted a creative interpretation of s. 212 ERA 1996 in order to provide additional protection to casual employees in the *Prater* case,[11] but refused to use the common law device of the implied contract to provide protection to agency workers in *James* v. *Greenwich LBC*.[12] The courts clearly regard Parliament as having the primary responsibility for labour law, and, on the whole, judicial creativity in this area is unusual.

Perhaps surprisingly, the HRA 1998 has not yet had much impact on the decisions of the English courts. *ASLEF* v. *Lee* is a striking example of this.[13] The EAT held that Article 11 ECHR was not relevant to a dispute about an individual's expulsion from a union for his membership of the BNP. However, litigation before the ECtHR – in *Wilson* and *ASLEF* in particular – has had positive results for trade unions and has led to changes in legislation.[14] The domestic courts are obliged under s. 2 HRA 1998 to take account of the Strasbourg jurisprudence, so these cases may have an ongoing impact on English law if there is litigation in these areas in the future. Interestingly, there has been some recent debate at the political level about the development of a UK Bill of Rights that would build on the rights in the HRA 1998. This would provide an opportunity to include economic and social rights, and thus to develop a Bill of Rights with greater relevance to labour law which the courts could enforce. However, it seems unlikely – given the controversial nature of labour rights – that

---

11 *Cornwall CC* v. *Prater* [2006] EWCA Civ 102; [2006] 2 All ER 1013.
12 *James* v. *Greenwich LBC* [2008] EWCA Civ 35; [2008] ICR 545.
13 *ASLEF* v. *Lee* UKEAT/0625/03/RN, 24 February 2004.
14 *Wilson* v. *UK*; *ASLEF* v. *UK* (2007) 45 EHRR 34; and see Chapter 11.

agreement could be reached on a Bill of Rights that would make a significant impact in the labour law field.[15]

The perspectives revisited

Predicting the future is, of course, a dangerous game. This is particularly true at a time when there are significant economic difficulties worldwide and a real possibility of a change of government in the UK. Perhaps all that can be said with certainty is that labour law will continue to reflect compromises between the advocates of regulation (whether they are using rights or economics arguments) and the advocates of deregulation. Which camp will be able to claim victory on any particular issue will depend on a whole host of factors: political, legal, economic and social. The purpose of this postscript has been to show that the perspectives used throughout this book will help you not only to analyse today's labour law, but also to analyse the labour law of the future, whatever shape it may take.

15 See Joint Committee on Human Rights, *A Bill of Rights for the UK?* (2008) (HL 165; HC 150, 29th Report of Session 2007–8), Chapter 5.

Index